POSITIONS AND PRESUPPOSITIONS IN SCIENCE FICTION

Positions and Presuppositions in Science Fiction

Darko Suvin

Professor of English and Comparative Literature
McGill University, Montreal, Canada

The Kent State University Press

© Darko R. Suvin 1988

Published in the United States by
THE KENT STATE UNIVERSITY PRESS
Kent, Ohio 44242

Printed in Hong Kong

Library of Congress Card No. 87–18352
ISBN 0–87338–356–7

Library of Congress Cataloging-in-Publication Data
Suvin, Darko, 1930–
Positions and presuppositions in science fiction / Darko Suvin.
p. cm.
Bibliography: p.
Includes index.
ISBN 0–87338–356–7
1. Science fiction—History and criticism.   I. Title.
PN3433.8.S88 1987
809.3'876—dc19   87–18352
                                                                    CIP

To Ivan V. Lalić and the memory of Vojo Kuzmanović – friends and SF swappers from the archaic torso of Zagreb in the 1950s, our socialist youth

Contents

Preface

All one can do, without too many illusions about success, is to speak what has been cognized, and for the rest to work in the professional musical domain toward the instauration of a proper and cognitive relationship to its object instead of an ideological consumption. The latter can be countered only by fragmented models of a relation to music, and of a music itself, that would be different.

(Adorno, *Einleitung*, p. 81)

0. As usual, the Preface is written last. Furthermore, it is being composed in an economic situation where I have about two days' time and 2000 words for it. In such straits, I must content myself with briefly asking and articulating a few questions. Two to begin with: Where does this book come from? How does it hang together?
1. Its title was chosen to suggest that this book is unified by an endeavour to both clarify and develop the theoretical and historical conclusions reached in my first two books on SF, *Metamorphoses of Science Fiction: On the Poetics and History of a Literary Genre* (1979) and *Victorian Science Fiction in the UK: The Discourses of Knowledge and of Power* (1983), as well as to record an implicit dialogue I carried on about their achievements and lacunae with the collaborators and readers of the journal I co-edited from 1973 to 1981, *Science-Fiction Studies*.[1] The positions indicated in the above subtitles, advancing from a stress on genre poetics as developing in history to one on discourses of identifiable social groups about their disputed values, are presuppositions for this book. They are developed in a double set of further presuppositions isolated as Part I of this book, and answering the questions (1) 'Why discuss paraliterature?' and (2) 'Why SF?'

Indeed, why? Isn't the study of great world fiction, from the *Book of the Odes* to today's Latin Americans, not only too immense for however busy a lifetime but also chock-full of the sublime emotional cognitions that ought to satisfy anybody with such interests? Yes, it is; and I suspect fans who never read anything but SF are poor people and poor appreciators of SF to boot. Yet Eliot's or Lukács's classicist idea of a great tradition of masterpieces calls to my mind the historical semantics of 'classic' – that pertaining to the highest class of value as defined by the highest class of master-people (itself first defined by King Servius Tullius's division of the Roman population into military-cum-economic social classes). Not that I dispute the existence of value-classes; on the contrary, this book is a sustained wrestle with defining and redefining them. But I find the historical practice of masterpieces limited by individualism and elitism. Should cultural investigation accept as defining category *and value* the market fact of publishing stories in book-volumes? I doubt this: the basic slicing up of the world of culture is some complex grouping of books into macro-texts. Obversely, the historical choice among book-titles is challenged by democracy: all the individual texts are, so to speak, God's chillun and got wings; they have an at least potential dignity of their own (and if they squander it they are answerable for it); and they ought to be considered (as somebody said of ascending Mt Everest) because they are there. Paraliterature, too, exists – indeed it is the new majority. Once upon a time the *Book of Odes* songs were peasant ditties, Shakespeare performed for groundlings, and Brecht played in cabaret. But more important, the basic materialist curiosity is also oriented toward values. My central argument has always been that SF is defined by its estranged techniques of presenting a cognitive novum. Surely we badly need all orts and scraps of true novelty to be found in our terrible and fertile times? Shouldn't we carefully look them up, examine and circulate them?

The second question 'Why SF?', then, means for me primarily 'How do I think one should approach SF?' Let me answer this by transcribing in the next three paragraphs the speech I sent to the SF Research Association when it gave me its annual Pilgrim Award:

From my earliest reading of Verne, Wells, Thomas More and the Groff Conklin anthologies which circulated from hand to hand in postwar Yugoslavia, I have, as a socialist, been fascinated by the 'it ain't necessarily so' aspect of SF – which, for me, does not start with Gernsback, Verne or even Shelley, but with the universal legends of Earthly Paradise and the Promethean impulse toward a knowledge to be wedded to self-governing happiness on this Earth. Of course, this embraces also all the narrations which deal with analogues to such radically new relationships among people – however narratively estranged into other worlds and other figures such relationships might be, for the good and sufficient reason that one needs a complex optical system in order to see oneself. Bearing in mind that every SF narration is a dialogue with the reader here and now, this also embraces all the stories that deal with radically worse relationships than the reader knows, since his/her reaction to such stories – by the rule of minus times minus makes plus or of negating the negation – recuperates these new maps of hell for the positive vision.

Looking back upon my criticism of SF, it seems to me that I have tried to mimic in it this stubbornly contrary and contesting backbone of the narrations I was writing about. I have contested Henry Ford's saying 'History is bunk', and tried to persuade my readers that an understanding of the living, even if subterranean, traditions of the past is the only way to give the present a chance of evolving into a tolerable future. I have contested the saying, whose equally immortalizable author I forget at the moment, 'SF is what I mean when I point at some books', and tried to persuade my readers that any general statements about SF have to be a negotiation between empirical evidence and logically as well as socio-historically defensible notions and systems of notions. I have contested the twin orthodoxies that SF is either the singer of technological progress/breakdown (as the case may be) or a thin disguise for the expression of eternal and mythical human-cum-cosmic verities. Instead, I have tried to at least approach a systematic argument on how history and society are not simply the contexts of fiction but its inly interfused factors, shaping it at least as intimately as shores shape a river or blanks shape a letter. Finally – and possibly as a premise to all the other stances – I have contested on the one hand the academic elitism wrinkling its none too perfect nose at the sight of popular literature and art, and, on the other hand, the fannish shoreless ocean of indiscriminately happy passages to continents full of masterpieces miraculously emerging year upon year.

And yet, SF is not only 'it ain't necessarily so' but also 'things could be otherwise'; not only militant but also (at least in approximation) triumphant. Taking my cue from the matter at hand (as any materialist should), I too have tried to be positive about it and about its criticism, and to say something about those writings which help us to illuminate our interrelated existences: of More, Cyrano, Morris, Wells or Zamyatin, but also of Čapek, Dick, Le Guin, the Strugatskys or Lem. How much I may have succeeded in that in my own writings, or in editing (with Dale Mullen, Robert Philmus, Marc Angenot and Charles Elkins) some books, but above all the journal *Science-Fiction Studies*, is for you to say.

2. How is one, further, to revise essays first published between 1973 and 1984?[2] I shall paraphrase a quite non-Marxist source here, Husserl, who had to face (*si licet*) similar problems in a new edition of *Logical Investigations*. He adopted as a guideline the practice of not letting anything be reprinted which he didn't believe useful as basis for further analyses, while bettering all that could be bettered without changing the original style – primarily, by clarifying and foregrounding what was earlier implied or uncertain. I have, however, made quantitatively major changes only to the essays 'For a "Social" Theory', originally written for other purposes, and 'The SF Novel as Epic Narration', originally written for a 20-minute presentation. Husserl may also serve as an ally to meet a frequent criticism of *MOSF*: that it was prescriptive rather than descriptive. Never mind that *MOSF* spent 200 large pages on describing four centuries of a genre's history, let me just address the logical confusion underlying such apparently libertarian complaints. True, *MOSF* (as any other study) was normative in the sense of possessing norms of value induced from both the critic's presuppositions and the texts (see Mukařovský, *Aesthetic Function*) and reapplied to texts. Furthermore (as different from some studies) my book foregrounded such norms in order to leave its readers the true freedom of knowing what they were reading and being able to thoughtfully agree or disagree. Yet norms only have sense if they can exist outside of the critic's head. My treatment (in *MOSF* and this book) of the writers mentioned in the foregoing paragraph may be sufficient to prove that they do so. Further, if I say 'a teacher should be learned', I should be credited with knowing there are stupid teachers (after all, I have been both a pupil and a teacher for decades). What my sentence then means is that only a learned teacher is a *good* teacher, that this is what a teacher according to his ends and her potentialities *could be* (in given favourable circumstances). This is *a value-judgement*, as is 'SF should be pleasurably cognitive' (by means of estrangement etc.). 'A teacher should not be dumb' means 'a dumb teacher is a bad teacher' and further, 'the less dumb a teacher, the better he is'. The normative maxim ('Love thy neighbour' or 'Don't exploit other people') posits a basic value for its domain. 'SF should be cognitive' (in the way – discussed in my writings at length – a particular genre of fiction can be such) means that an SF text is good in proportion to, among other factors, its cognitiveness. Technically, this position is not prescriptive, but of course it *is* judgemental. However, the judgement is mediated by falsifiable compositional (syntactic) and meaning-bearing (semantic) elements. Thus, there is a traffic not only between norm and practice (which can change the norm) but also, and primarily, norm and its inner articulation (which can clarify what the norm meant, and whether the reader should agree with it).

This and all such (presup)positions are developed in the present book rather as a dog worries a bone or an old slipper: by picking it up at different points, shaking it, getting at it in all ways to be thought of. It carries over into Part Two which deals with five theoretical problems that reared up as central in the 1970s: a reaffirmation of the *MOSF* position of close kinship between SF and utopia (which I hope to tighten with further tools soon, but could not do in the spacetime at my disposal); an examination of the relation between SF and SF criticism; and two centripetal circlings around the proposition that ideological alienation or success in SF must be proved by means of a text's narrative logic. The essay on teaching is, finally, a transition to applied positions on SF practice, which constitutes Part Three (itself shot through with the preceding presuppositions). I wish to stress that all of these essays were written in consultation with many colleagues from the *SFS* board, but that two of them were co-authored with its co-editors, respectively my friends Marc Angenot and Charles Elkins. Their generous intellectual friendship has prompted them to give me the final pleasure of including the two essays into this book, whose demerits must be mine but whose merits must be shared by them.

As to the essays in Part Three, the problem in them is finding the right link in the unbroken chain that an opus presents. This is an intuitive and not theoretical problem, and it can be mainly judged from its yields. Are Asimov, Yefremov and Lem representative for large cultural areas (the three that matter most to me personally), and if yes are they representative of those dominant horizons I have identified in those areas? Are their and the following writers' opuses sufficient to suggest a certain spread of modern SF? Is de-alienation the strategic position for understanding Le Guin, or artifice and artificiality for Dick? Can the utopia (Harmonyville) of classless relationships, starting out bright and remaining as the background to increasing sombreness, have that function for the Strugatskys respectively the Brauns? Indeed, should one continue to slice the SF continuum according to authors, an ideologically disputed matter? Go thou, reader, and decide by the taste of the pudding. I want to stress, however, that the collocation of 'SF as Metaphor, Parable . . .' as conclusion is a bid at unifying the theoretical interests from Part Two in narratology as overcoming the pernicious 'formal *vs.* sociological' split of cultural studies – and particularly in the parable as a specific form both of narration and of reference beyond the narrative surface – with the practical but already theoretically informed analyses from Part Three. It is therefore deliberately constructed as the major (and the furthest advanced beyond *MOSF* and *VSF*) piece of theoretical argumentation in this book, flowing into the analysis of a puzzling and (I think) cryptic but ideologically very important SF story which should provide the proof of this pudding, and retroactively of the whole book's symposium.

3. In conclusion, I still remain impenitently committed to seeing SF as a potentially cognitive genre, often hindered from realizing its potentialities by analysable forces in a complex but manmade history. I do not believe that critics can remain bound by the consciousness of the author at hand, nor that they can fetishize 'the text' at the expense of the crucial interface between the text and our common world of ideologies and bodies. In fact, I see the focus of paraliterary criticism in the confrontation of aesthetic and/or political value-judgements with the present situation of the book market, the film, TV and video industry. In the US, all these are almost exclusively profit-oriented, with alienating narrative recipes which make for the overwhelming success of ideological constructs of the Three Laws of Robotics, *Star Trek* and *Star Wars* type. (The situation is somewhat different in the USSR and some other Warsaw Pact countries, but it is after all not fundamentally different. Only the kind of alienation has changed from profit pressures to direct bureaucratic pressures. This still left me with the necessity of exploring in some ways different but also comparable contradictions.) In particular, it would today be necessary to analyse the present shape of the US book and film market. The best-seller mentality invading it from Hollywood is a clear example of how the potentialities of SF are co-opted and sterilized by the economic and ideological forces of the New Right. This has already resulted in vastly overblown novels, poorly organized, often chauvinistic, and reducing the level of SF to that of the best-seller (for example, Pournelle-Niven or the later Herbert). It has also resulted in a startling change of guard among new SF writers: where we had a number of overambitious writers in the 1960s whose reach exceeded their grasp, now we have a number of underambitious writers who do not reach as far as they could grasp (or so I hope). Of course, some masters of the postwar decades are still with us, and some interesting new voices have come up. But I think there is a preponderance of encroaching flippancy, cynicism, ritual cruelty, and power-worship. This includes the return of crude sexism (for example, Norman's *Gor* series) as counterbalance to the most significant SF development of the last dozen years, some women writers following on Russ, Le Guin and Piercy (Tiptree, Butler, Charnas, Cherryh, Elgin, Holland, Lynn, McIntyre, Sargent, etc.). Thus, the outlook is on the whole disquieting.

I realize full well that – to apply the following essays' analyses to myself – within a 'social theory' of SF criticism between cognition and ideology I stand on antinomic ground. I shall paraphrase Adorno's analysis of musical life (I hope without his – or Lem's – European elitism): 'Because of the coincidence between the established SF writing and criticism and the power of dominant social tendencies, all those that productively and legitimately dissent are being pushed toward sectarianism and marginality, which weakens their legitimacy. Such persons and groups swimming against the main current often suffer a sea change into powerless and heretically charged minorities: they are theoretically "right" but practice gives them the lie.' I hope to have avoided such sectarianism hoarsening my voice and embittering its tone, thus keeping it efficient. But I fully agree with Adorno's Marxian conclusion: 'Nonetheless, the intransigent critique of established cultural processes is to be kept up' (*Einleitung*, p. 152). Facing the Leviathans, we still have our typewriters.

Montreal 1986   D.R.S.

NOTES

1. These three presupposed sources are unavoidably so ubiquitous in this book that I have abbreviated them in the text as *MOSF*, *VSF* and *SFS*. Beyond these three abbreviations, I have to mention three further technical conventions: I write 'utopia' in lower case except when referring to More's country and book (a disambiguating convention I would dearly like to see generally used); some people argue that the indispensable acronym 'SF' for 'science fiction' should be hyphenated

when indicating adjectival use, but this has seemed pedantic and I trust the reader to interpret it correctly; all essays have been supplied with the original publication date(s) to clarify the context sometimes alluded to.

2. For the record, this volume is a rather strict selection from my writings on SF in periodicals and books by various hands. I have in them published (beside entries in the encyclopaedias edited by Peter Nicholls in 1979, Frank N. Magill in 1979, and C. C. Smith in 1981 and 1985) four bibliographical surveys in *SFS* (1976 and 1978) and *Canadian–American Slavic Studies* (1980 and 1981), two theoretical articles on utopianism and science in *The Minnesota Review* (1976) and *Brave New Universe* (ed. Tom Henighan, 1980), as well as a dozen miscellaneous items – articles, reviews, notes and panel discussions – in *Extrapolation, College English, SFS, The Magazine of Fantasy and Science Fiction, Quarber Merkur, Canadian–American Slavic Studies, SFWA Bulletin*, and *imagine* . . . . Beyond these, I would have particularly liked, had there been space, to include into this volume: 'The Science Fiction Novel in 1969', in James Blish (ed.), *Nebula Award Stories Five* (New York and London, 1970 and 1972); 'Significant Themes in Soviet Criticism of Science Fiction', *Extrapolation* (1970); 'Criticism of the Strugatskii Brothers' Work', *Canadian–American Slavic Studies* (1972); 'The State of the Art in Science Fiction Theory', *Science-Fiction Studies* (1979); 'Counter-projects: William Morris and the Science Fiction of the 1880s' (forthcoming).

Acknowledgements

Chapters 1 (in part), 2, 4, 5, 7, 9, 10 and 12 were originally published in the periodical *Science-Fiction Studies*, and I thank my co-editors, and in particular R. Dale Mullen and Robert M. Philmus, not only for allowing me to reprint them but also for allowing me to write them by creating and morally and materially supporting *SFS*. A number of these chapters were circulated in first draft to them and the *SFS* editorial board members and redrafted after intense discussions; only in the case of Chapter 4 has an adequate record survived (see note there) but I wish to stress this for all these essays. A more developed but still rather different from the present form of Chapter 1 was first published in *Culture & Context*, edited by my colleague and friend George Szanto, who also read and commented on many of the other chapters as well as on this book project as a whole. My warmest thanks go to all who have helped in this way.

Chapter 3 was first published in *The Minnesota Review*, no. 2/3 (1974); Chapter 5 was incorporated into my *Victorian SF in the UK* (1983), and it is reprinted by permission of G. K. Hall & Co., Boston, Mass. Chapter 6 first appeared in a much smaller form in Zoran Konstantinović *et al.* (eds), *Proceedings of the IX Congress of ICLA* (Innsbruck, 1982); Chapter 8 appeared in Thomas J. Remington (ed.), *Selected Proceedings SFRA 1978 Conference* (Cedar Falls, IA, 1979); Chapter 11 appeared partly in *Canadian–American Slavic Studies*, no. 3 (1974) and more fully both in *Foundation*, no. 17 (1979) and as 'Introduction' to the Gollancz and Bantam 1980 translations of the Strugatskys' *The Snail on the Slope*. My 'Conclusion' first appeared in Jean Emelina and Denise Terrel (eds), *Actes du 1er Colloque de s-f de Nice, Métaphores*, no. 9–10 (1984). Though a number of editors properly return the copyright to the author, my thanks go to all involved. I am further beholden to the SSHRC of Canada for a Leave Fellowship in 1980/81 during which Chapter 5 was written, and for travel grants to conferences at Innsbruck in 1979 and Nice in 1983 at which papers were presented that evolved into Chapter 6 and the 'Conclusion'. Work on the first chapter also benefited from the kind help of the British Museum and Library and the University of London Library, as well as of Professor Randolph Quirk and Dr John Sutherland of the English Department, University College, London. Patrick Parrinder's comments (and of course his writing) xviii *Acknowledgements*

were particularly helpful for Chapters 5 and 6. Other debts are recorded in notes to some essays. Charles Elkins was one of the 'circulated' people for many essays, and he has co-authored with me Chapter 7 'On Teaching SF Critically': I still remember with awe and pleasure the telexes and couriers which went between Montreal and Miami on that memorable occasion. As to Marc Angenot, my thanks to him in book after book would perhaps begin sounding stale if they were not constantly renewed by my constantly new learning from him: he was the prime begetter of my fastening on to presuppositions, my guide in the labyrinths of literary sociology and metaphorology, the co-author of the essay 'Not Only But Also' where I truly cannot distinguish what was 'originally' mine and what his, and a constant inspiration through stimulative discussions on almost all matters in this book, from recondite matters of historical detail to narrative semiotics, but especially on those pertaining to Chapters 1, 4, 5 and 6, and the 'Conclusion'. Nena not only read all but provided terrestrial and celestial nourishment for the writer.

At the end I wish to thank Ms Robin Pollock and Ms Holly Potter for word-processor typing and Mme Hectorine Léger for pre-word-processor preparation, and Frances A. Arnold for much editorial patience.

Part One
Some Presuppositions

1

For a 'Social' Theory of Literature and Paraliterature: Some Programmatic Reflections

1.   TOWARD A 'SOCIAL' THEORY OF FICTION

1.1.   Against the 'Sociology of Literature' Ghetto

I would impenitently maintain the strong scepticism toward 'sociology of literature' formulated in several previous articles – one of which was commenting on a bibliographic survey of about 70 books of sociology of 'high' literature (see Suvin, 1980; Angenot and Suvin, 1981). This is based both on the state of the art (I do not believe we have today more than a few cornerstones for a properly critical sociology or anthropology – cf. Shaw) and on the refusal of politico-philosophical presuppositions which split culture into individual *vs.* collective, also low *vs.* high. If literature is to be approached as *either* collective *or* individual, and its system as *either* 'popular lit.' *or* 'high lit', we are on the horns of a dilemma. No doubt such a system has been brought about by the bourgeois market, but I refuse to accept it as a 'natural' basis for permanent judgements (though as a practising critic I may at times have to prefer being impaled on one rather than the other horn). It is that split basis itself, the existence of the horns, that I wish to question, following Benjamin's great maxim that every monument of civilization is simultaneously a monument of barbarism. In the articles mentioned, I stressed further that literary texts have a very tricky and delicate relationship to what is usually called the social and historical context. If it is said that a text 'expresses' the context, the insoluble question remains: how is it that literary texts from a more or less identical context – say two succeeding tales or poems by the same author – are so different as not to be reducible to each other,

3

that is, more or less unique? The fact is, sociologists are not radical enough for me. *History and society are not an external yardstick to be applied to the literary work: on the contrary they constitute its very structure and texture.* Even if one started from the building bricks of literature, from language, any sophisticated school of linguistics today will acknowledge this. Jakobson's language model, for example (to my mind less encompassing than Rossi-Landi's or Bakhtin/Vološinov's), presents us with six principal factors or relationships, each of which may become the dominant function. They are, as is known: (1) the addressor, the emotive function; (2) the addressee, the conative function; (3) the context, the referential function; (4) the code, the metalingual function; (5) the contact, the phatic function; and (6) the message, the poetic function. Now if one combines the 'appellative' or conative relationship of the literary work to the *addressee*, the representative or referential relationship of the work to its *context*, and the metalingual relationship to what Jakobson – I think misleadingly – called its *code* (which in verbal art is not confined to vocabulary plus operational rules but has an eminently socio-historical character): clearly, a combination of at least these three functions marks the ineluctably socio-historical character of every literary work.

In particular, I paid homage to the pioneering gathering of data about either the addressee or the context of literary texts by old-fashioned 'sociology of literature', say Auerbach's *Publikum* (1933), Escarpit's *Sociology* (1971) and Nye (1970); I wish we had much more of it (for example, there is a bad dearth of encompassing and non-trivial studies of readers, i.e. as they incide on forms of writing – cf. the discussion and references in *VSF*). However, I conclude (in Suvin, 1980) that whenever empirical studies are not blended into an approach foregrounding systematic value-judgements and thus consciously correcting for its bias, the text itself will be left to an unholy alliance of technical description and ideologizing impressionism (such as forms the bulk of both the Rosenberg–White anthologies). Even the potential corrective of communication studies – focussing on the relationships between the work's *emission* from the writer, its important *transmissions* such as editors, publishers, financiers, distributors, censors, etc., and its *reception* by various types of reading publics – began with crass versions of the same split. However, communication studies are well suited to socio-psychological and political discussion of who has the power to evaluate and transmit which information, and who is supposed to be at the receiving end of such evaluation and transmission – a discussion particularly pertinent to para-aesthetical media such as TV and paraliterary genres such as SF. Strivings toward such a horizon are visible in communication studies which have broken both with the stimulating but finally unsubstantial dazzlements of McLuhan and with the earlier empiricism (cf. Williams, 1970; Dröge, 1972).

Whatever refinements have in the last 15 years or so been added to a sociology of the literary audience by new schools such as that of 'reception aesthetics' in Germany, there seem to be two crucial conditions for making such pursuits into anything more than a sociology and/or a history extrinsic to literary studies: first, an encompassing model of relationships between literary production and consumption (with all the mediations sketched above), and second, a historically and sociologically precise identification of the particular socio-ideological sodality or community of interests which in fact has a given attitude to given aspects of word-art or social discourse, beginning with given literary works. These are horizons opened up by Marxism, though, of course, not all scholars within them have necessarily a Marxist ideological commitment (some of the pioneers clearly do not, e.g. Auerbach, Mukařovský, Watt and Hoggart). Yet the insistence that social classes have not only a *different position* in society but *different interests and strivings* – a quite basic realization without which there can to my mind be only market research, not scholarship – is clearly a Marxist one, and most of the leading researchers have, in spite of exceptions such as some articles by Lenin and Trotsky's book, been somewhat unorthodox Marxists or 'fellow-travellers' (Bakhtin, Burke, Goldmann, Hauser, Lowenthal, Lukács, Sartre, Williams, Žmegač).

1.2. 'Democratic' Novelty, Commodified Alienation

Perhaps in the long run at least as important as the identification of a class interest having produced and remaining embedded in a fictional text, however, is the specifically Marxist anthropological diagnosis of the relationships between work and creativity, production and consumption, alienation and society. These are themes started by Marx and Engels in their early works (e.g. *The German Ideology*), and they provide the ground bass of the whole opus culminating in *Capital*. Out of a number of very promising leads, each of which would properly require a book-length discussion, I shall focus briefly on two: Marx's approach to these themes in his *Grundrisse*,[1] the first rich if inconclusive sketch for *Capital*, and their being taken a stage further by the 'commodification' theory of modern texts adumbrated in Benjamin's unfinished work of the 1930s.

Marx wrestles among other things with the extremely complex relationships of production and consumption, for which – significantly – art is a privileged extreme case:

> The object of art – like every other product – creates a public which is sensitive to art and enjoys beauty. Production thus not only creates an object for the subject, but also a subject for the object. . . . It thus produces the object of consumption and the motive of consumption [in the form of a need felt by the consumer]. Consumption likewise produces the producer's *inclination* by beckoning to him as an aim-determining need. (*Grundrisse*, p. 92)

However, as the sensual or qualitative *use-value* of any product is in circulation within class society transformed into quantitative *exchange-value*, which depends more on the conditions of exchange (market, money, etc.) than on its intrinsic properties, so

> the exchange relation establishes itself as a power external to and independent of the producers. . . . The product becomes a commodity; the commodity becomes exchange-value; the exchange-value of the commodity is its immanent money-property; this, its money-property, separates itself from it in the form of money, and achieves a general social existence separated from all particular commodities and their natural mode of existence . . . . (ibid., pp. 146–7)

Thus, production of commodities becomes crucially determined by circulation – in modern times by capital which is '*direct unity* . . . of production and circulation' (ibid., p. 332). Since circulation is subsumed under accumulation of capital, and radically warped by the profit principle, a basic opposition arises between the product as use-value and as object of such capitalist circulation. As Marx himself suggests (e.g., ibid., p. 587), this contradiction is clearest in artistic production (say in the production, consumption and circulation of a book manuscript): the product as 'a specific quality, as a specific thing, as a product of specific natural properties, as a substance of need [is] in contradiction with its substance as [exchange] value' (ibid., p. 406). Thus, the transformation of products into money, which originally rendered large-scale production possible (and Marx unambiguously admires all such achievement of capitalism, as opposed to all Romantic cries of 'back to Arcadia'), grows in developed capitalism into both the barrier to further production and the agency deforming all use-values (for example, texts exploring the intrinsic possibilities of their thematic nuclei) into exchange-values (for example, texts tailored primarily toward selling well, regardless of all else). As a consequence:

> while capital thus appears as the product of labour, so does the product of labour likewise appear as capital – no longer as a simple product, nor as an exchangeable commodity, but as . . . *alien property*, . . . and establishes itself opposite living labour as an *alien power*. . . . Living labour therefore now appears . . . as mere penurious labour-capacity in face of this reality alienated from it, belonging not to it but to others . . . (ibid., pp. 453-4)

While it is impossible to go here into ramifications of such basic insights (but see Suvin, 'Discours' (1985) and 'Commodities' (1985)), it is clear that Marx started with the realization which Joyce expressed as 'my producers they are also my consumers' (*Finnegans Wake*), but proceeded from there into a rich sequence of theories which could provide the much needed basis for adequate analysis of social alienations in cultural production of fiction or fictionality – in literature, movies, comics or TV. Its value lies in its blend of scholarly sophistication and fierce ethico-political value-judgements, which brands capitalist production as hostile to art and poetry, and yet does not condone the artist-producer's cynically giving in to this hostility:

> A writer must naturally earn money in order to be able to live and write, but under no circumstances must he live and write in order to earn money. . . . The writer in no wise considers his work as *means*. It is an *end in itself*; so little is it a means for him and for others that he sacrifices *his* existence to *its* existence, when necessary; and like a religious preacher, in another sense, he applies the principle: 'Obey God rather than men' to the men among whom he is himself confined with his human needs and desires.[2]

Admittedly, such horizons receive only a stimulating first sketch in Marx, and subsequent official socialist thinkers – both social-democratic and Leninist – have shied away from them. The fate of Lukács's early and (alas) sole philosophically significant development of such notions, in *History and Class Consciousness*, which he was forced to recant, has led to their being developed by Marxist 'guerillas', on the margins of political orthodoxy, with all the strengths and weaknesses arising from this position. They are mainly Germans – Adorno, Benjamin, Bloch, Brecht, Enzensberger, Holz, Marcuse, Sohn-Rethel, Winkler, but also Bakhtin (under his name and the pseudonym of Medvedev), Sartre, Rossi-Landi and Macherey. A first stock-taking in English can be found in Fredric Jameson's *Marxism and Form*, Raymond Williams's *Marxism and Literature* and Terry Eagleton's *Literary Theory*, while the influence of Bakhtin reaches into the newest 'sociocriticism' (cf. Cros, 1983).

I would now like to get closer to modern literature by briefly summarizing and attempting to develop Benjamin's hypothesis of a homology between its central characteristics and commodity production in general – because, and in so far as, literature is produced and consumed as a commodity. Both are forms of social relations; both – most importantly for the matter at hand – depend on *novelty* or newness. It is, however, a paradoxical and deeply contradictory novelty because commodity has, as noted above, two types of value: its intrinsic sensual qualities issue in the use-value, while production for the market issues in quantitative exchange-value. Building on the arguments in Marx that the devaluation of the sensual world of things alienates the producers/consumers, Benjamin turns his attention to the fact that people's experiences are daily inexorably moulded by a network of inescapable rules based on exchange-value, by the type of societal relations signified in the price of commodities and of labour-power. In commodity production, the product's newness is indispensable for stimulating sales, but the newness is at the same time necessarily subordinated to the permanent principle of and commitment to circulation as such rather than to what is circulating (a Ford '86 is a private car, etc., just as a Ford '85) – to an 'infinite repetition' (Benjamin, 1980–2, i/2: 660, 673, and 680). From the nineteenth-century rise of commodity mass-production and circulation on, the apparently new is intrinsically also the permanently same: 'Novelty is a quality which does not depend on the use-value of the commodity. . . . [The] illusion of novelty is reflected, like one mirror in another, in the illusion of infinite sameness' (Benjamin, 1973, p. 172). In Goethe's terms, 'the strange' is substituted for 'the significant' (cited in Benjamin, 1980–2, ɪ/1: 152).

This type of approach can also subsume the striking insights from the first great work of philosophical historiography on the politics and psychology of a fully bourgeois society – Tocqueville's *Democracy in America*. He noted how bourgeois society is based on a perpetual fostering of people's desires for possessions. These desires are greater and more widespread but more often disappointed than in earlier, less materially ambitious societies. Their goal of prompt and easy consummation means that most citizens would rather satisfy them incompletely but immediately rather than not at all. As distinct from feudal times, enrichment is now based on selling cheaply to all rather than dearly to a few. The general rule of workmanship for commodities is therefore 'to manufacture a larger quantity of goods, nearly similar, but of less value'. However, this is necessarily accompanied by efforts to give such mass-produced commodities an appearance of possessing the 'attractive qualities' they do not possess: the particular 'democratic' variant of hypocrisy is – to adapt Tocqueville – the 'hypocrisy of quality' (Tocqueville, 1900, ɪ:50–5).

Thus, in a literature adjusted to the exchange-value and the market, novelty grows recurrent in both senses of this word: it becomes necessarily *frequent*, a conscious goal of literary production, but also necessarily divorced from a radical – that is, a consistent – novum. Instead of cumulative cognition, the pursuit of inner aesthetic *truth* (determined both by the fictional narrative's inner logic and by its referential richness), what Baudelaire called 'the venal muse' is wedded to quantic shocks of seasonal *fashion*: 'Fashion is the eternal return of the new' (Benjamin, 1980–2, ɪ/2:677). Or: 'The fashions of meaning changed almost as fast as the price of commodities. In fact, the meaning of commodity is called "price"; it has no other meaning, as commodity.'[3] What will in our days come to be called the 'culture industry' concerns itself mainly with the maximal diffusion of the texts' mechanical reproductions. To that end, it needs quickly revolving, paradoxically transitory novelties that catch the eye but do not threaten the framework of revolving, the politico-economic presuppositions of market circulation. Change for its own sake grows into an article of ideological faith. It is because of its abstractness and self-referentiality, because of its monomaniac reproduction of itself in variations that amount to an infinite repetition, that the production of commodities is homologous to fashion, which is equally indifferent toward use-value (for example, fashions in cars are not based on but at best superadded to and at worst substituted for the pertinent norms of saving time, saving fuel, etc.). Another aspect of that homology is the reifying denial of personality, especially associated with masses and large cities: in proportion to its novelty, a dress, for example, dominates fashionable people to the point of making an assembly of them appear, strangely enough, dressed in uniforms (not in unique but in unified forms, as Zamyatin was to punningly remark of the frozen fashion in *We*). Thus, the intrinsically utopian, liberating aspects of any significant work of art – its fullness of meaning, its necessary and sufficient structuring of parts into a whole without power-hierarchies, its denial that what exists in the writer's here and now is the sole possibility, its uniqueness, its historical depth and vitality – are attacked at their very root. The inalienable utopianism of fiction will increasingly be inscribed into it as concave into convex – that is, inscribed by the even formally noticeable, narratively illogical absence of the utopian aspects or spread of dystopia. Finally, fashion is exasperated into *sensationalism* – a series of greater and greater 'effects' or shocks. In another momentous paradox, very significant for a general sense of history or time, *progress becomes indissoluble from catastrophe*: 'For men as they are today, there exists only one radical novelty – one that is always the same: death' (ibid., I/2:668). In the sensitive seismic apparatus of SF, the greatest progress (creation of life) threatens, ever since Shelley's emblematic *Frankenstein*, to result in the most wholesale catastrophe (destruction of life, later isolated in her *Last Man*).

Exemplary for and intimately involved with this whole process is the rise of that specifically bourgeois and capitalist addition to social discourse – the *press*. The mass-circulation newspapers were financially based on the innovation of carrying advertisements, which allowed them to keep a relatively low price and attract a large readership. In them, the 'brief and abrupt information began to compete with the staid report', leading to the day-by-day changing look of the journal (ibid., I/2:528–9). Since the ads were to be read by the largest possible number of people, 'a "hook" or bait became necessary which was addressed to all regardless of their private opinion, and whose value lay in its putting curiosity in place of politics' (Nettement, cited ibid., I/2:531). Thus was born the serialized novel in the *feuilleton*, and that is why astronomical prices began to be paid for such *roman-feuilletons* to Dumas the Elder or Sue. Both by formal example and by direct ordering, the newspaper came to occupy the power position of the trend-setting literary commodity, the one that shapes the structure of feeling for all other written discourse. As to the formal example, 'The principles of journalistic information [are] novelty, brevity, intelligibility, and, above all, lack of coherence [*Zusammenhangslosigkeit* – non-consistency, disjointedness] between the individual news-items' (ibid., 1/2:610). Welcoming 'the journalism of the age', Poe saw in it 'a sign of the times – an indication of an era in which men are forced upon the curt, the condensed, the well-digested . . .'. In somewhat different but complementary (less commercial and more conceptually ideological) ways, this applied also to the growing importance of the new periodicals. Poe expressly noted also that they, especially the faster monthlies, were in keeping 'with the rush of the age. We now demand the light artillery of the intellect; we need the curt, the condensed, the pointed, the readily diffused – in place of the verbose, the detailed, the voluminous, the inaccessible . . .' (Poe, 1906, vi:218 and 98–9).

In fact, while in despotic societies ignorance resulted from too little information, Tocqueville perspicaciously noted that in citizens of democratic ones ignorance results from too much information: 'The chief features of each picture are lost to them in a bewilderment of details'; and these consumers of information acquire the habit of not paying attention (Tocqueville, 1900, ii:233–4). This is most intimately connected with the very nature of information in capitalism. An information which would be both universally accessible and durably valid would have the greatest use-value but no exchange-value at all. It is only by rapid obsolescence that information can become a quantified, marketable commodity; obversely, investors are interested only in this rapidly obsolescent information (cf. Ciccotti *et al.*, 1979, pp. 112–14). In Tocqueville's terms, democratic equality produces equally strong tendencies toward thinking new thoughts and toward ceasing to think, and a curiosity that is 'at once insatiable and cheaply satisfied', eager 'to know many things quickly rather than to know anything well' (Tocqueville, 1900, ii:12 and 334). All durable or significant literature is in that sense intrinsically non-capitalist, if not anti-capitalist. There is little doubt that such new democratic-cum-capitalist structurings of literature had a strong bearing on the pointed non-coherence or inconsistency of the SF pessimums discussed below (see Chapter 5 on 'Narrative Logic' but also Chapter 6 on 'Epic Narration' and Chapter 9 on Dick).

However, beside such very important formal exemplarity, the market factors – here the press owners and publishers – also intervene directly, from Sue and Dickens to the present, in the conception of the best paid fiction, the serialized novel. The pulp and pocketbook publishing practice is – as in SF – to have the texts either signed by a 'house' name or to commission ongoing rehashings of a package that sells well (from *Superman* comics to Herbert's *Dune*). Shrewd writer-entrepreneurs, beginning with Dumas the Elder in the novel and Scribe in drama, integrated into this system by keeping poor hacks or 'niggers' (wage slaves) at work on their scenarios, behaving like industrialists who supply raw materials turned into finished commodities by hired 'hands' (here pens or brains).

Already in the eighteenth century Kant had written bitterly: 'An experienced . . . publisher will not wait for scribbling and ever-ready writers to offer him their own commodities for sale; like a factory manager, he will concoct the matter as well as the form which will, supposedly, meet with the greatest demand or at any rate the greatest sales . . .' (quoted in Widmann, 1952, p. 246; cf. also Winkler, 1973). But it was only in the nineteenth century that such economic relationships took their place in the best paid and most famous literature, began to attain hegemony, and added the overwhelmingly intense pressure of direct financial carrot-and-stick to the extensive, diffuse exemplarity of press-style writing. As of then, writers divided not only along economic but also along ideological lines, into the integrated and the disaffected. Many among the most significant writers retreated into a profound hatred of the bourgeoisie: Baudelaire began referring to literature as 'column-fodder' and to writers as prostitutes. Tocqueville formulated this with urbane lapidarity: 'Democratic literatures are always infested by those writers who look upon letters as a mere trade (*une industrie*): and, for some few great authors you may see there, you may count thousands of idea sellers' (Tocqueville, 1900, II:64). Baudelaire's very similar line, 'Moi qui vends ma pensée et qui veux être auteur' ('I, who sell my thought and who want to be an author'), palpably modulates from the theological connotations of 'author' to the dominant market connotations – a process shown in reverse to produce the peculiar dystopian effect alluded to earlier.

There is even less doubt than in the case of press style that these new power-relationships were destined to have a lasting and revolutionary influence on fiction and narrativity, and on SF narrations in particular.

Another key homology to fiction as commodity – and in fact the model attitude for the new type of experience not immersed into use-value continuities (*Erfahrungen*) but composed of point-like occurrences (*Erlebnise*) based on empathizing into or feeling with the exchange-value or money-price of the sensually devalued things – is in Benjamin's view gambling. It is an activity that also begins each time anew, from zero, yet remains a permanent variation of the same (both on the gaming table and on the stock market). To live off writing becomes a permanent gamble with the writer's existence. From Verne on, both the SF writers and their protagonists are overwhelmingly engaged in a breathless race with and endeavour to neutralize time, to circulate with increasing acceleration in an excited and exciting parallel to commodity circulation. Fashion, gambling, quick turnover of money and commodities, time-anxiety, newspapers dominated by advertisements, and, finally, written discourse as a commodity submitting to all their laws – all of them have a psychic common denominator in the new type of human experience. It is a *customer experience* of repeated shocks wedded to a sense of *excitement*. Tocqueville expatiated on how, in consequence of the all-pervasive domination of money (the universal equivalent of commodities) and the pursuit of riches, all passions are channelled toward the same goal, giving them a 'family likeness' and making people's lives – in a further paradox – simultaneously much more agitated and much more monotonous: '[As] the same successes and the same failures are continually recurring, the name of the actors only is changed, the play is the same' (Tocqueville, 1900, ɪɪ:238–9). In this situation, only permanently renewed excitement guarantees the restless audience's interest. '[Sue's] first, and in fact his sole object, is to make an exciting, and therefore saleable book', remarked Poe acutely, because enviously, of the supposedly radical *Mysteries of Paris*, the first and foremost example of the newspaper serial-novel or column-fodder, whose immense influence will be felt in SF too (Poe, 1906, ᴠɪ:145; cf. also Eco, 1978, p. 43). In short, the art 'of the present-day bourgeoisie is economically determined by profit, sociologically . . . above all as an instrument of sensation' (Benjamin, 1980–2, ɪɪ/2:764).

Therefore, in the final analysis, the fashionable and fashion-like type of fiction novelty is oriented 'rather [toward] its themes' saleability than [toward] their cognition' (ibid., II/1:383). In literature, use-value is *significant aesthetic cognition*, while exchange-value is to be understood as *the narrative domination of infinitely recurring superficial strangeness*, a 'hypocrisy of quality'. In fully developed commodity economies, bourgeois ideology is not only indifferent toward a cognition of overall relationships between people, it grows increasingly inimical to such understanding: it 'shackles the production of intelligence' (ibid., II/2:693, *die Produktion der Intelligenz* – a splendid pun englobing also the shackling of 'the productive capacity of the intelligentsia'). From Balzac, Poe and George Eliot, the best writers from the bourgeoisie oscillate therefore between constant revulsion from its world and the frequent impossibility to imagine a better alternative. Hating the present, they turn to the past or the catastrophe. This holds also in paraliterature, for example, in SF: besides Mary Shelley and Poe, for Villiers, Twain, Jefferies and Wells in the nineteenth century, *e tutti quanti* in the twentieth. Much more rarely, the prefiguration of a fundamental, cognitive novum manages to survive this obstacle course. The resulting tension between novum and pseudo-novum will be taken up as the ground bass of all the following essays, and explicitly discussed both in terms of general narrative theory and of particular narrative practices in SF.

These are the approaches to be developed if a 'social' theory of literature is to be articulated: in particular, if its key question of the intimate permeation of 'text' and 'context' is to be developed as a basic determination of all 'printed matter'. Without such development and articulation, the theory of literature will remain limited by an arbitrary (or, worse, still, parochially class-bound) pre-selection of 'great texts' which are Literature with a capital 'L', as opposed to all other existing fictional texts which are literature with a lower-case 'l' or paraliterature. In other words, all the conclusions of such a theory of literature will have been (are) preempted by an unargued and all the more potent cluster of ideological presuppositions and maxims about its 'proper', 'tasteful', 'significant', etc., field or domain. That domain in practice boils down to a (relatively) extremely small number of texts from half a dozen present or past world super-powers, which have been erected into a canon of 'world literature' by the bourgeois critics and academics in the past hundred years. Thus, all the present histories and discussions of fiction are 'histories of the generals'. General historiography oriented itself toward the 'foot-soldiers' with, say, Ranke and Michelet. It seems high time that literary and cultural historiography – while holding fast to some indispensable criteria of value, which I suspect would have to be significantly different from the currently dominant criteria – take a plunge into such dangerously democratic waters.

2.   ON PARALITERATURE

2.1. Briefly on Conventions, Social Addressees, Middlemen, etc.

How does one apply the various 'sociologies' of literature so far to the study of paraliterature? Again, I can only draw attention to one basic problem-expanse: the need for a general hypothesis about paraliterature and its rapid expansion in this age. However, before that I wish to at least mention approaches based on the fact that paraliterature is composed of clearly and even strictly observed genres, which I have discussed in 'Reflections' (Suvin, 1980). I noted there how fruitful might be a specification of genre-expectations by imaginary or implied readers who are identifiable as programmed into the very texture and structure of texts and entire generic forms. The resulting genre conventions are, no doubt, partly transgressed (as a rule, by contamination with other genres and forms) in significant texts, but these conventions remain the common ground between the writer's production, the readers' interest, and the economically and ideologically crucial, channelling middlemen (such as the famous magazine editors of SF). Of course, the implicit reader, or better the *social addressee*, is not the same as the real readership. It is an heuristic construct highlighting how expectations clash and change when sufficiently specific clusters of social groups and classes clash in the societal dialogue represented by a literary genre (cf. my long discussion in *VSF*, Part II, section B).

I concluded by noting that these horizons offer prospects for a great deal of work in paraliterary criticism, on the relation of various audiences to various genres, authors and devices within it. A few of them have been explored, but as a rule either without sufficient socio-economic differentiation of the readers involved or without sufficient differentiation of the text-aspects involved. It is by now rather banal to investigate the relationship of, say, 'X in SF' (whatever X may be) to, say, the US audience. Even assuming we know the US audience is male and in roughly the 15–30 age group (which is by no means sure), fundamental questions remain to be asked: X in *which type* of SF? (author, sub-genre, ideological horizon, etc.); in the opinion of *which part* of the US audience? (male/female, middle/working/capitalist class, urban/rural, high/middle/low education, WASP/ethnic, and so on). Only then can one get beyond bourgeois mystification of 'the' reader responding to 'the' work of so-and-so (cf. Barthes, 1970); only then can value-judgements go beyond impressionistic ideologies and noises of approval or disapproval. Only then could critics proceed to large-scale overviews. One could, for example, compare various national situations, which at a given time will be found not always synchronic: thus, reader expectations in French SF in the 1950s and 1960s was largely a sub-set of US reader expectation 10 years earlier, while Russian expectations of SF diverged from the common European norm in the 1920s, setting up a new normative system which opened up to international stimuli only after 1956.

Perhaps most illuminating could prove comparisons of various ideological positions in SF correlative to different readerships: 'hard science' devotees *vs.* 'soft science' devotees, readers of Heinlein and Niven *vs.* readers of Le Guin and Disch, etc. Such comparisons would, I believe, indicate that the major sociological and ideological problem – not only in contemporary SF but possibly in paraliterature as a whole – is the indiscriminate consumption of quite disparate sub-sets of works with incompatible ideal readers, by what seems (but perhaps wrongly?) the same real readership. This problem is intimately bound up with and part of the degradation of paraliterature as a phenomenon to pure consumption dominated by capitalist circulation and by the intermediaries of transmission (editors, publishers, distributors, financiers – in the final analysis, though all of this is largely secret, large multi-media corporations). Should this be true, it would confirm the strictures which say that paraliterature has by now become a medium which is its own message rather than the bearer of any particular poetico-cognitive messages – strictures which I am still reluctant to accept fully. In order to decide about this, we would need an inventory of motifs, topoi and attitudes in different genres and sub-sets of paraliterature, and of the relations of such sub-sets to other genres both of the older 'high lit.' (for example, the nineteenth-century psychological tale) and of contemporary 'low literature' or paraliterature.

2.2 Whence the Triumph of Mass Literature? Hints for a Hypothesis

How can a 'social theory' approach, then, help us toward a general hypothesis on paraliterature?

Paraliterary studies (see Angenot, 1975; Bürger, 1973; Cawelti, 1976; James, 1963; Langenbucher, 1964; Nagl, 1981; Neuburg, 1977; Nutz, 1962; Orwell, 1957; Schenda, 1970; Schulte-Sasse, 1971; and Ziermann, 1969) have been wittily classified by Umberto Eco, himself one of the most prominent practitioners in the field, into 'the apocalyptics' who reject mass culture wholly and 'the integrated' who accept it fully (the familiar 'highbrow/lowbrow' dilemma, so fruitless in approaches to SF). Eco himself pleads – with pioneering examples – for a third way, without automatic acceptance or rejection, but with formal and ideological discrimination. This is difficult but possible (cf. Frye, 1978; Seesslen and Kling, 1973).

Beyond this, what makes modern paraliterature so complicated is the sea-change it suffered in the last two or three generations. In almost all epochs before the nineteenth and twentieth centuries, there existed a profound difference between the popular or plebeian (largely oral) culture and the official ruling or upper-class (usually written) culture – and, of course, between them and the culture of the intermediate classes. Since the rulers have always written history, including the history of culture, it is the upper-class writings which have been, abusively, called Literature in the official, consecrated or canonic sense. Such Literature with a capital 'L' is composed of officially 'higher' genres (tragedy, ode or psychological novel). But Literature in this sense has always – as suggested in 1.2. – a twin in its complementary, plebeian or vulgar narrative discourse, which one would then have to call Paraliterature. This literature (lower-case 'l') is an ensemble of non-canonic or 'lower' genres, such as proverbs, humour, fables, sagas, detective tales, SF. The deep paraliterary tradition, old as class society, penetrates into official Culture and Literature only occasionally, during those favourable socio-political periods when its bearers – the lower, plebeian classes – rise to at least a partial participation in the canonic culture. It is also only at such periods that historians of culture are politically and epistemologically able to turn some attention to those forms.

The 'iceberg' character of the paraliterary tradition(s), where historically only a small fraction survived to be recorded above the surface of neglect, persecution and oblivion, is thus the result of

deep tensions which have split every nation's culture into at least
'two nations', as Disraeli formulated it. The cultures of these 'two
nations' have been connected by various antagonistic relationships,
from suppression to partial permeation. As a rule (except for special
historical moments of cohesion, say, in the face of common outside
catastrophe threatening all classes in a society, as in the Elizabethan
Age of England), the 'patrician' and 'plebeian' – literary and
paraliterary – cultures, consciousnesses, conventions or structures
of feeling have in the past, in spite of all their interesting and
important dialogues, preserved their separate identities. The
plebeian literature appeared often (this may be a rule springing out
of the basic class splits in society) as a stylistic, thematic, etc.,
reversal and subversion of the dominant, officially recognized
literature. When that dominant or 'first' literature is measured and
solemn as in French classicism, its reversal is manneristically
burlesque (for example, in Cyrano); when it has a sober middle-class
self-confidence, then the reversal is romantically enthusiastic (cf.
Blake, the Satanic school, or the *Sturm und Drang*); when upper-class
culture is sentimental, the reversal is apt to be ascetically severe (cf.
Büchner). If the dominant literature is calculated to encourage their
consumers to plunge headlong into the depicted characters and
involve themselves in a world that pretends to a substitute actuality,
as happened in Individualistic high lit. from *Madame Bovary* on, then
the reversal stresses critical distance (cf. Brecht). Such paraliterature
then develops in and out of subliterary forms, nearest to lower
classes and under relatively less effective censorship (up to the
eighteenth century, mostly within oral literature). It is well known
that renewals of culture come about by the rise of earlier non-
canonic forms to canonic status together with the rise of the social
group that was the ideal and real reader of those forms (for example,
the psychological novel and the bourgeoisie).

However, the situation grows much more complex in the last 100
years. Who is now the ideal reader or bearer of the new 'structures of
feeling' for paraliterature, whose group-consciousness does it
correspond to? I would very briefly and without the necessary
mediations venture the hypothesis that the central complication
determining modern paraliterature is the fact that of all the
democratic revolutions only the most bourgeois one (the American
1776 secession from the motherland) fully succeeded, while the
Jacobin and all subsequent European radical revolutions failed; and
that, very similarly, of all the socialist revolutions only the one

taking place in the most despotic environment (the Russian Bolshevik one) for a time succeeded. The logical developments of both these great subversive traditions were violently cut short. Such a course had been known to happen before, always with a high political and cultural price being paid: for example, the suppression of all popular autonomy in seventeenth-century France and England, or of the bourgeois revolution in nineteenth-century Germany – events culturally symbolized by the murder of Cyrano and the exiles of Shelley and Marx. In our time, the coming about of almost universal literacy, a much better economic standard and a certain political influence for the plebeian classes of the metropolitan one-fifth of the globe have paradoxically been the obverse of the rise of imperialism and the welfare/warfare state (getting ever more warfare and less welfare-like in these last years). Very approximately, this has happened in France from the beginning of the nineteenth century, in USA, Britain and Germany from the 1870s, and in most other countries of the globe's 'North' somewhere between 1880 and 1960. In culture, there ensued a very specific and complex amalgam of suppression and permeation of plebeian and bourgeois horizons which has still been barely identified, much less properly studied (for first approximations see Williams, 1971; Hall, 1981 and 1978). But it could be assumed – at least as working theses – that a number of themes, concepts and devices from the plebeian or 'low' culture have in our epoch permeated 'high' culture and literature, contributing decisively to its change. However, usually – with exceptions such as the stormy golden age of Europe c.1910–30 and analogous movements elsewhere, say in post-revolutionary Mexico – this was achieved at the expense of the plebeian horizons, lost to the bourgeois cultural domination.

Such dialectics of defeat would account for the genesis of a number of major 'contained' cultural phenomena, for example, jazz or popular movies. It is to my mind the key to paraliterature. In Gramsci's terms, the hegemony of the bourgeois ideology and consciousness has been strongly challenged but not overthrown; new forms and genres rose into official culture (for example, the mass media) at the expense of their original plebeian horizons, at the price of ideological sterilization, containment or co-option (see Marcuse, 1966 and 1972). This rise means a temporary – usually on the whole spurious or fake but to a certain, larger or smaller, degree also necessarily genuine – renewal of official culture, now 'democratized' in a Tocquevillean sense – in exact parallel to the politico-economic power of the lower classes – into 'mass' or 'popular' culture and literature:

> 'popular culture', in these later periods, is a very complex combination of residual, self-made, and externally produced elements, with important internal conflicts between these. At another level, and increasingly, this 'popular' culture is the major area of bourgeois and ruling-class cultural production, moving towards an offered 'universality' in the modern communications institutions, with a 'minority' sector increasingly seen as residual and to be formally 'preserved' in those terms. (Williams, 1981, p. 228)

However, this also means that the new forms and genres pay the price of co-optation by failing to live up to their potentialities, to their own cognitive nature and end. This is clearly the case with SF and its novum, as analyzed in the succeeding essays of this book. Indeed, the new literary system leads even, in extreme cases, to the creation of cognitively spurious but commercially promising addictive genres – an opium for the masses much cruder than good old religion – such as pornography (not the same as erotic fiction) and 'science fantasy' (not the same as SF – see Lem (1984) and *MOSF*).

It would be useful to approach some carefully chosen subsets of paraliterature and see whether a full investigation would confirm or invalidate this hypothesis.[4] To my mind, such endeavours would be very important. For a new, valid literature – a necessary part of that political and intellectual renewal which this planet must go through unless we are to render it uninhabitable – can, as Gramsci well intuited, only come from readers of paraliterature, from movie, TV and video-watchers; and this can only happen if new writers would subsume and transcend its popular tradition – as Dostoevsky did with the *roman-feuilleton* and criminal stories *à la* Sue. And of course, if power over circulation will reside in hands and brains sympathetic to genuine and probably startling newness. The stakes, thus, are the highest imaginable. To put it perhaps pathetically, but I believe precisely: the education of *Homo sapiens* for earthly salvation is finally at stake.

(Original version 1980)

NOTES

1. Karl Marx, *Grundrisse der Kritik der politischen Oekonomie*, written 1857–8, published in entirety only 1939; cf. the first 'complete' (in fact still incomplete) edition of Karl Marx and Friedrich Engels, *Werke* (Berlin DDR: Dietz, 1956–68) vol. 13. In English, the best instrument for study is today the Pelican Marx Library (London: Penguin, and New York: Vintage, in progress), in which the *Grundrisse* are available as a separate volume (1973). For briefer introductions to Marx in English, see Karl Marx and Friedrich Engels, *Selected Works in One Volume* (New York, 1968), or Robert C. Tucker (ed.), *The Marx–Engels Reader* (New York, 1972). Of my other main authorities, Walter Benjamin, *Gesammelte Schriften* I–V (Frankfurt, 1980–2), will be quoted by volume/sub-volume:page numbers, in my translation; and Alexis de Tocqueville, *Democracy in America*, vol. 2 (New York & London, 1900), by page number, with the above translation in places revised by me.
2. Quoted from Marx's article 'Wages', in Lifshitz (1977), the best comment on this subject, which should be read together with Meszaros (1970), Sánchez Vázquez (1973) and Birchall (1972).
3. Walter Benjamin, quoted by Rolf Tiedemann in his 'Nachwort' to Benjamin, *Charles Baudelaire* (Frankfurt, 1973) p. 204; see also Holz (1972) and Sánchez Vázquez (1973).
4. Sociological investigations of SF in particular reached adolescence with the special *SFS* issue no. 13 (1977), 'The Sociology of SF', which was introduced by an embryonic form of this essay. In it I gave a thumbnail sketch which concluded that we were then at the very beginning even of empirical investigations, much less of intelligent overviews. I mentioned two first bids at an overview, Leon Stover's 'Science Fiction, the Research Revolution, and John Campbell', *Extrapolation*, 14 (1972–3) 129–48, and *La Science-fiction américaine* (Paris, 1972), which treated SF as a response to the Research-and-Development 'revolution', and Gérard Klein's much more encompassing and sophisticated 'Discontent in American SF', *SFS*, no. 11 (1977) 3–13, which identified US SF as being based in the 'scientifically and technically oriented' petty bourgeoisie or middle class, with the basic horizons of SF changing parallel to the massive ideological realignments in that class. A number of useful discussions followed (e.g., in *SFS* after 1977 or in Nagl (1981), but we are still in the teens).

2

The Significant Context of SF: A Dialogue of Comfort against Tribulation

A [*A is an SF fan trying to become an SF writer: he has a BA*]: I have just been asked to teach, in a nearby community college, a course in SF, in the 'Science and Literature' slot, entitled 'SF and Future Shock'. So I'm thinking of subscribing to *SFS*, just as I'll subscribe to *Extrapolation* or a number of fanzines, because I hope to find in it articles about people like Clarke, Heinlein, Asimov or Ballard, which I can use in my course.

B [*B is a graduate student of literature*]: I have lately become somewhat interested in SF because it seems to me some nuggets of social criticism can be found in it, though it feels entirely too comfortable in the Amerikan Empire for my taste. If *SFS* will – as opposed to the mutual back-scratching and, as far as I can understand, meaningless little feuds in the fanzines – bring out the ideological function of SF as a branch of mass literature to keep the masses quiet and diverted, I might read it in the university library and use it in my freshman course 'Literature and Changing the World'.

C [*C is a university professor in an English department*]: I am fascinated by SF as an example of modern urbanized folklore, which is of greatest theoretical significance for anybody interested in poetics and its paradigms. I do not mean that we have to stick to structuralist orthodoxy – indeed, what is so fascinating about SF is how its paradigms evolved out of the oral legend, the *voyage extraordinaire*, the utopia, the Swiftian satire, etc., under the impulse of scientific popularization, socio-political changes, etc. I will subscribe to *SFS* on a trial basis hoping it will not be either pragmatic and positivistic, as *A* would like, nor forget that it deals with a genre of literature out of which you cannot pick ideas – critical or otherwise – like raisins out of a cake, as *B* would seem to want.

B: Whatever I seem to you to want, I hope you will agree we do not need one more among the unconscionable overpopulation of academic or quasi-academic journals. If SF is worthy of sustained critical attention . . .

A: Hm. I fear that too much of that will kill it off cleanly.

C: Scholarly and critical attention, I would say.

B: If you wish – I don't see the difference between them. Anyway, we must first of all ask 'What are the uses of SF?'

C: Better, 'What are and what could be the uses?', and furthermore, 'What can criticism tell us about them, and which type of criticism can tell us anything significant about them?'

A: SF is the literature of change, more realistic than realism.

B: Ah, but is it? I spent some time yesterday with the *UN Statistical Yearbook 1971*, a pastime I recommend to you two gentlemen as quite eye-opening, and culled some figures out of it which I wish to enter into the record of this discussion. I have divided them into two columns, 'DC' for 'Dominant Countries' (Europe with USSR, North America, South Africa, Australia, and New Zealand), and 'RW' for 'Rest of the World', and rounded all figures off. So here goes.

	DC	RW
Population	1070 millions	2560 millions
Energy production (in coal equivalent)	4500 million tons 4.3 tons per head	2500 million tons 1.0 ton per head
Newsprint consumption	16,900 million kg 15.8 kg per head	4500 million kg 1.8 kg per head
Income*	1900 US$ per head	200 US$ per head
Book production†	370,000 titles 344 titles per million heads	90,000 titles 35 titles per million heads

* The ways of UN statistics being inscrutable, the 'DC' statistic here includes Japan but not the USSR and is thus valid for 925 million people; the RW statistic includes only Africa and Asia without the 'socialist' countries and thus is valid for 1600 million people.

† Without – again the mysterious omission! – the People's Republic of China.

To point out the moral: not only each country, but also our old Terra, as *A* might say, is divided – despite our unprecedented technical capacities for making it finally inhabitable in a fashion befitting human potentialities – between the haves and the have-nots. The haves are concentrated in the nations comprising about 30 per cent of mankind, which – as it happens – are also almost exclusively White. The economy and therefore the communication system (including book and periodical dissemination) of the haves differs radically from that of the have-nots. More than 80 per cent of all book titles are written by and published in the have, and therefore politically dominant, countries.

C: This is a fascinating exercise in literary sociology, to which one should, however, add that, as we know, the number of copies per title is disproportionately higher in North America and Europe than anywhere else, so it's only fair to assume that *over 90 per cent of all books produced and consumed in the world circulate in a closed circuit, in what you called the politically (and should have added economically) dominant countries.*

B: And, of course, if we added Japan to those countries, and since the rest of the world quite rightly concentrates on textbooks and similar immediate necessities, we will see that *'literature' or 'fiction' in the sense developed by the European civilization with the rise of mass printing and a bourgeois world view, is in 70 per cent of the world totally unknown.* Or if it is known, it is confined to an extremely thin stratum of intellectuals, and it functions as very effective shop-window dressing for the imperialist ideology that more and bigger means better – that, say, the paramilitary NASA Moon program is the realization of SF dreams. Thus, it conditions and channels in that direction the expectations of people.

C: For better or for worse, it does seem inescapable to conclude that our normative circle of teaching, reading and criticizing 'literature' (a term I'm increasingly dubious about, anyway), with all our supporting institutions such as foundations or ministries for culture, prizes and clubs, editors and publishers, kudos and heartbreaks, bestsellers and near-starvations, is a charmed closed circle.

B: Irrelevant to the majority of mankind. And if you see, from some other statistics I will spare you, that even within the 30 per cent of the White bourgeois civilization there are entire social groups that do not consume literature but newspapers, comics, movies or TV, if anything – then that majority becomes quite overwhelming. Then we have to conclude that SF is written for a petty-bourgeois reader, who is indoctrinated by some variant of a late-capitalist, often wildly Individualistic ethos.

C: Well, I would make all kinds of reservations to this big leap of yours, such as saying SF is here and now written for such a reader, and that of course there are exceptions, as we know that corporation executives and air-force generals, who are certainly not petty-bourgeois, also read it. And anyway, what do you mean by petty-bourgeois – shopkeeper?

B: No, obviously I mean anybody who is not a worker or farmer working with his hands, not a capitalist employing people to work for him, but in between. The three of us discussing SF are all petty-bourgeois.

A: Now that you have again noticed me, let me ask you one little common-sense question: if SF is all that irrelevant to anybody, except perhaps in the past and to the virtuous socialist society in Russia and China, why bother with it? And with a magazine devoted exclusively to it? Why don't you just go away (*to B*) into the streets or jungles, or (*to C*) into your well-upholstered ivory tower study, and leave us who love SF in peace?

B: First of all, I never said anything about 'socialist' societies. In Cuba and China there is, as far as I know, and I tried hard to know, practically no SF; in the Warsaw Pact countries, it has its own troubles which we can save for another discussion but which have prevented its bulk and average from being more significant than the SF from NATO countries. Second, even if the circuit within which SF happens comprises only, say, 10 per cent of the world population, it is an extremely important 10 per cent, and quite worthy of investigation.

A: But you would investigate them only as petty-bourgeois worms wriggling under your microscope?

C: Well, I don't know what *B* would do, but I would plead for the introduction of another factor into our equation. We have so far talked about the present, or better, synchronic, and thus necessarily socio-political context of SF. But it also has a temporal, diachronic context as a genre. Now if you'll allow me to go on about this a bit, I have just been going through E. D. Hirsch's *Validity in Interpretation* (1971) for a graduate seminar, and Hirsch – however one may disagree with him on other issues – argues persuasively (as do other people such as R. S. Crane, Claudio Guillén, etc.) that for any utterance, an essential part of its context – by which I mean 'the traditions and conventions that the speaker relies on, his attitudes, purposes, kind of vocabulary, relation to his audience,' etc. (Hirsch, 1971, pp. 86–7) – is represented by its genre. A literary genre is a collective system of expectations in the readers' minds, stemming from their past experience with a certain type of writing, so that even its violations – the innovations by which every genre evolves –

can be understood only against the backdrop of such a system. The properties of a genre enforce meanings for any given readership. I would add to Hirsch & Co. that the basic property of all present literary genres is that they are a mode of 'leisure activity', made possible by certain existential situations – by normative economic possibilities and political decisions, such as limiting the working time to so many hours per week, putting a certain price upon the reading, etc. As other genres, SF is integrated into the normative system of 'literature' – first by opposition to it, then as marginal, now sometimes aspiring to the status of socially approved 'high' literature, etc.

A: If I translate what you have been saying into plain English, it says that SF is a recognizable group of works distinct from other groups, which we knew anyway. So why all this fuss?

C: Ah well, the good old Anglo-Saxon empirical common-sense! But unfortunately, following your logic we would need no science at all, because we all know that a rocket can go to the Moon anyway. Well, perhaps we do, but did we until somebody studied it with a lot of equations and technical jargon? You mean that gravity is self-evident? Or that social gravity – the power-relationships in society, which enmesh culture too – is self-evident? No, what you nicely call 'the fuss' is just the sound of specialized science at work. Yes, so far I have used a certain specialized discourse to say that SF is distinct from, but also linked with, other literary genres, which are distinct from, but also linked with, other forms of human behaviour within certain normative social expectations. But only such a specialized discourse can eventually provide us with a way of using the socio-political insights of friend *B*, without forgetting that we are – as you will agree – dealing with literature. For the most important principle in any genre, as Aristotle suggested some time ago, it is *purpose*, which is to be inferred from the way the genre functions. That purpose channels the genre into determined social forms; it unifies the writers and readers by means of 'a notion of the type of meaning to be communicated' (ibid., p. 101). Thus, genres are strictly culture-bound, historical and not metaphysical, they are 'guiding conceptions that have actually been used by writers' (ibid., p. 109); and no criticism of SF has a chance of being relevant if it does not first identify the purposes of the chunk of SF it is considering – a story, the opus of a writer, the works of a period, etc.

A: Why not simply ask the writer?

C: Ah, but common sense is a very limited instrument in

scholarship. The writer may be dead, or she may have forgotten, or – most importantly – she may not be right about the purpose of her tale: the creature has a life of its own if it is more than a plug or ad. It communicates something to the readers even if the author is unknown.

A: OK, why not ask the readers? Here this sociology stuff could finally be of some use: just send them forms with questions.

C: Of course, the critical community should try to assemble as much information as possible about the author's overt purpose and about the ways her work was accepted by different categories of readers. But again, what readers – those of the publication date or of today? Opinions about Shakespeare, say, have shifted radically through time, and just imagine how radically they will shift about Arthur Clarke. And why should not all readers of a given time be collectively on the wrong track? The history of Athenian first prizes for tragedy is almost as sad as that of the Hugo Awards for SF. No, I'm afraid that the critic's final evidence is the interaction of his own knowledge and sensibility with the words on the page. In that respect, the formalists were right and we all have to start by applying their insight: when judging literature, one begins by a close reading of it and a discussion of its compositional, agential, spatial, ideational, rhetorical and other inner relationships.

B *makes a grimace and a sceptical sound.*

A: Well, such things may after all be useful in my teaching, and I hope *SFS* will concentrate on them, and never mind the sweeping theories.

C: No doubt, both *B*'s sociological context and your 'pragmatic formalism' should have a place under the sun – if done really well. There are too few good SF critiques around for a good periodical to be able to stick to any scholarly 'line'. But now we come to my main conclusion which, I think, transcends both your positions. For I maintain that there is no way to understand what one is reading unless one has an approximately full knowledge of the range of the words and the meanings of their juxtapositions. This knowledge forms part of *historical semantics*, that is, it pertains to ever changing social tastes, which differ from period to period, from social class to social class, from language to language. And so, *consistently intelligent 'formalist' criticism leads to consistently intelligent 'sociological' criticism, and vice versa; or better, both must fuse for a criticism that will be able to render justice to any literary genre, and in particular to SF.*

B: This may all be very interesting, but don't you think that we live in a catastrophic world, with genocidal warfare, starvation in half of the world, rising tensions within Amerika itself, ecological collapse, very possibly an economic crisis, and so on, all looming threateningly ahead? And is not therefore the usual SF-as-escape ludicrously irrelevant to us too, not only to the other 90 per cent of the world? And shouldn't it therefore be judged by how much it serves the cause of a liberated mankind?

A: There you go again! Can't you liberate mankind without SF?

C: Precisely, I think if you want to liberate mankind – which I am much in favour of – you cannot start by asking for servitude. I think SF cannot be your handmaid, but it could be your ally – and an ally is to be treated with consideration and met half-way. For SF, as all literature, has always (and I think this is the answer to A's objection about why bother) existed in a tension between the sociologically dominant tastes of its readership and its own bent toward the truly, the radically new. This has always been an ideologically subversive genre, and most of its very visible weaknesses today can be traced back to strong existential pressures on its writers and readers.

A: Well, I would admit some of that exists, even in the USA – just think about the troubles Tom Disch had with *Camp Concentration* and Norman Spinrad with *The Iron Dream*. But this was finally rectified . . .

B: That's not the most important category. A more sophisticated weapon is financial: hunger has the power to kill, and enforce obedience, more surely than bullets. That is called repressive tolerance, I believe. And I would like to see in *SFS* critics with enough information and guts to take a long, cool look at the powerful shapers of taste and enforcers of orthodoxies in SF, such as magazine editors and publishing houses.

C: Serious structural investigations could, and I hope will be undertaken of phenomena such as Campbell's enforcing of his various orthodoxies, or the normative publishing format of 60–80 thousand words for SF novels from 1940 to 1965, and the deep consequences such taboos have had on US SF. And similarly crass taboos should be shown up from other countries and ideological climates. However, the most insidious pressures on SF are neither administrative nor commercial, but psychological. Most of us, readers and writers, have been to some extent brainwashed . . .

A and B [*in chorus*]: Speak for yourself!

C: . . . brainwashed, even if with wailing and gnashing of teeth, into the broad individualistic consensus. Many SF writers probably do not feel too unhappy in their little niche within the one-dimensional vision of the world; after all, they have invested great pains into the carving out of that niche. Yet the temptation of being creative somehow, wondrously, pops up here and there even against such terrible pressures – a 'mission of gravity', indeed. But creativity has then to pay a high price for emerging: instead of the straight vertical of creative liberation, we get a bent ballistic curve, or, in some exceptionally powerful take-offs, at best a tangent. Yet a tension persists between social institutions – the centres of political, financial and ideological power – and the writer struggling to cut a path through their jungles armed only with a typewriter and some paper. That tension between entropy and energy, between the existential powers-that-be and the creative reaching out toward a vision of the new, is always rekindled and always revolutionary. And it would seem to me the goddam duty of the critic to be always on the side of the writer in his subversions of what exists.

B: Marx called that 'a pitiless criticism of all that exists.'

C: Quite. Including official Marxist orthodoxies. For the demand that we go into the streets or jungles or the rice fields of Honan is, here and now at least (and that might change), impractical for most of us, and therefore sectarian. It would, I think, create that very state of emergency, when all specifically humanized pursuits are abolished in favour of direct measures for collective survival, which we are – or at least I am – trying to avoid.

B *makes another grimace.*

C [*somewhat hastily*]: This is, of course, not a sneer at working, or if need be, fighting, in the streets, jungles or rice fields: it simply acknowledges that the pursuit of life, liberty and happiness-through-reading-SF, or in other words, that the autonomous criteria of all art, including very much SF, will (if we are only consistent enough to hold fast to them without deviating under the pressure of irrational, exploitative and class-bound prejudices) lead us toward a classless humanism. [*Pontificating*] Thus, all art works against dehumanization in direct proportion to its significance established according to its own autonomous criteria.

A: You mean according to whether there is a poetic theme, a clear plot, consistent characterization, effective composition, and so on?

C: Yes, I mean that too. But beyond those aspects common to all art, I mean that SF has a particular historically determined, scholarly recreatable and critically evaluatable purpose. And I contend that the minimal common denominator of that purpose, the source of its creative pathos and the reason for its existence, is something that I like to call *cognition* – a central and informing concern for conceiving and discussing radically new views and understandings of human relationships and potentialities (even when they are masked as Nautiloids or what not). That is the specific poetry of SF. Therefore, SF which is significant by the most immanent, inner or formalist criteria imaginable, will necessarily clarify hitherto mystified and obscured relationships. It will permit us a better orientation in our common world; it will militate against class, nationalist, sexist or racist obscurantism which prettify the exploitation of people (and nature) by people. I may be too optimistic, but I truly believe that SF at its best does its bit of such a 'production of man by man', and does it in a powerful and inimitable way. This is to my mind the answer to 'Why SF?', or what are and could be its uses. And if *SFS* can contribute to the understanding of both how and also how come SF does that, then the question of 'Why *SFS*?' will also have been answered.

B [*not quite persuaded*]: Well, let's hope so, but . . .
A [*not quite persuaded*]: Well, let's wait and see, but . . .

The discussion went on for quite some time, but lack of space in SFS forces us to cut it short here.

(Transcribed and edited on the occasion of the first appearance of *Science-Fiction Studies*, 1973)

Part Two
From Presuppositions to Positions: On SF Theory

3

Science Fiction and Utopian Fiction: Degrees of Kinship

1. What is utopia? A literary genre defined, first of all, by the setting up of a radically different location for the relationships of its figures. Similarly SF.

How does utopia operate? By an explicit or implicit comparison of its imagined community with the author's environment, by example or demonstration. At the basis of all utopias is an open or hidden dialogue, a gesture of pointing, a wide-eyed glance from here to there, a 'travelling' shot moving from the author's everyday lookout to the wondrous panorama of a far-off land in space or time:

> it was winter when I went to bed last night, and now, by witness of the river-side trees, it was summer, a beautiful bright morning seemingly of early June.   (W. Morris, *News from Nowhere*, ch. II)

Morris's abruptly beautiful trees should be taken, as they were meant to, for an emblem of this place and state: utopia is a vivid witness to desperately needed alternative possibilities of the world of people (H. G. Wells, *A Modern Utopia*, ch. 1), of human life. Similarly SF.

Perhaps the *first* question about utopias is why and how do they arise, what collective psychological needs do they fulfil? Similarly for SF. Perhaps the final question about them pertains less to socio-psychology than to the politics and even cosmology of the human species: how is *Homo sapiens* to survive and harmonize with its segment of the universe? Similarly for SF.

As different from such first and last questions, perhaps the central question about utopia today is just in which ways does it operate as a verbal artefact. Before being anything else, such as prophecy or guide to action, utopia is a metaphorical image, a verbal gesture, and a literary genre with procedures and parameters proper to it as

33

such. One cannot properly explore its signification by considering its texts simply as a transparency transmitting ideas: what it says (how it signifies) has to be understood as well as what it signifies. Similarly for SF.

As different from religious ideas about other worlds such as Paradise or Hell, utopia is an *historically alternative* wishful construct. Its islands, valleys, communities or worlds are constructed by natural intelligent beings – human or humanoid – *by their own forces*, without transcendental support or intervention. Utopia is an Other World immanent to the world of human or at least psychozoic endeavour, dominion and hypothetic possibility – and not transcendental in a religious sense. This differentiates it from myth, horror-fantasy and fairy-tale, which happen outside history – even an alternative or hypothetical history; it similarly differentiates SF from kindred yet opposed genres.

As different from general and abstract utopian projects and programmes, literary utopias construct a particular and unique community. Similarly SF, as different from futurology.

As I have argued at length earlier,[1] we can divide prose literature into naturalistic and estranged genres, according to whether they endeavour to faithfully reproduce textures, surfaces and relationships vouched for by human senses and common sense, or turn their attention to empirically unknown locations for the new relationships shown in the narration. In that division, utopia and SF, having an alternative formal framework, are both *estranged* literary genres, 'providing a shocking and distancing mirror above the all too familiar reality' (Bloch, 1972, p. 10).

It follows, as has been increasingly recognized by critics, that utopia and satire are really two sides of the same coin. Satire is directed against a corrupt empirical environment, using criteria of the good and beautiful, the true and the just, which are alien to such an environment. Such criteria have only to be explicated and the alienness systematically incarnated into a community in order to arrive at utopia. And vice versa; every utopia is an implicit satire of the author's empirical environment. More, Morris or Wells are always aiming at England and the European civilization. Similarly, much SF – though not all, because as we shall see SF is not tied to the concept of a more perfect community in the same way as utopia – falls into the category usually called 'new maps of hell', or satirical socio-critical SF, from Wells to Pohl, Vonnegut, Sheckley or Brunner. In fact, utopia, SF and satire seem all to have originated in tales and legends connected with the folk-inversions of the Saturnalia – that extraordinary time of the year when sexual, political and ideological roles were all reversed, when glimpses of new and radically different existential possibilities were allowed to appear as a vent in the surcharged atmosphere of rigid class society.

2. It should be clear already from this incomplete survey that utopia and SF are kindred estranged genres. It remains to try and focus on their differences, thereby establishing the degree of kinship. In order to do that, it is useful to proceed more systematically, by delimiting precisely both genres and comparing these delimitations. I shall start by giving a definition of utopia which I have discussed at length in another essay,[1] and commenting on one after the other of its elements. Utopia is, then, a literary genre or verbal construction whose necessary and sufficient conditions are *the presence of a particular quasi-human community where socio-political institutions, norms and individual relationships are organized on a more perfect principle than in the author's community, this construction being based on estrangement arising out of an alternative historical hypothesis.*

'Particular community' emphasizes the need for a vivid description, as different from projects of an abstract and general nature, not concretized into an exemplary presence. 'Quasi-human' is shorthand for saying that utopia, just as SF, always functions by reference to and comparison with the human relationships, but that, as different from SF, its figures are either human or explicitly compared and closely related to humans, such as Wells's Morlocks and Eloi, Stapledon's Venusian and Neptunian Men, or Swift's Yahoos and Hoyhnhnms. In Wells and Stapledon, we are – because of the biological and other strangeness of the creatures – already on or beyond the limits where utopia merges into SF: on the other hand, Swift's clear moral and political intents keep Book IV of *Gulliver's Travels* clearly within the utopian-antiutopian tradition.

Further, talking about a 'community where socio-political institutions, norms and individual relationships are organized on a more perfect principle' makes, I believe, a number of significant points. First of all, it indicates that the field of utopia is socio-politics understood as human destiny: people's destiny is not – as in mythology, fantasy or fairy-tale – outside them, but is incarnated in manmade, changeable institutions, norms and relationships.

Secondly, mentioning in one breath institutions, norms and relationships enables us to discuss all utopias, regardless of whether they are 'warm', decentralized and anarchistic, such as Morris's, or 'cold', centralized and 'archistic', such as Campanella's (More would be somewhere in between). Thirdly, the point about organization seems to me crucial. An unorganized ideal place may be Terrestrial Paradise or the Land of Cockayne, but it is not utopia in any precise sense of the word. All utopias are counter-projects to the bad organization, the moral and often material chaos around the author; the essence of a counter-project, which has to go in for detailed surveys of an alternative country, is necessarily a clearly spelled-out alternative order. That order may be libertarian, communal and federative, or it may be, as is often the case with utopias, disgustingly over-centralized, but it is never going to make for a lawless place, a place without at least some social forms, norms and institutions guaranteeing and indeed symbolizing the new relationships between individuals.

Finally, 'more perfect' in my definition refers to a delusion which ought to have been laid to rest as soon as anybody had read Plato's *Laws* or Bacon's *New Atlantis*, or at least any utopia of the industrial age, say after Saint-Simon – the delusion that utopia has to depict an absolutely perfect place. This has been the tendency of a number of earlier writers, but it just does not exist as a requirement of the genre. Even in More there is slavery, strict control of movement, death penalty for atheism, etc. What is necessary is a *'more perfect'* society, in the sense of a basically more perfect principle for the life and type of horizons involved. A more perfect principle would, for example, involve a community organized without the need for warfare or with safeguards against chemical or ethical pollution – and not just a small alteration in the rate of pollution, frequency of wars, etc. A radical change from the author's situation is clearly implicit in utopias, but it is not necessarily a final one that cannot be improved upon. In fact, I cannot think of any significant utopia after about 1800 which is static – that characteristic is from that time on understood as diametrically opposed to utopias, and reserved for anti-utopias. Anti-utopias can, of course, be obtained from the above definition of utopia simply by changing 'a more perfect principle' into 'a less perfect principle' – and making a community claim to have reached perfection is in the industrial and post-industrial dynamics of society the surefire way to present us a radically less perfect state.

In the first chapter of *MOSF*, I defined SF as a literary genre or verbal construct whose necessary and sufficient conditions are *the presence and interaction of estrangement and cognition, and whose main device is an imaginative framework alternative to the author's empirical environment.* Let me recall once more the above definition of utopia: utopia is, then, a literary genre or verbal construction whose necessary and sufficient conditions are the *presence of a particular quasi-human community where socio-political institutions, norms and individual relationships are organized on a more perfect principle than in the author's community, this construction being based on estrangement arising out of an alternative historical hypothesis.* If we compare these two delimitations, we shall see that both these genres – besides being based on or rooted in estrangement which is not supernatural or metaphysical but an alternative historical hypothesis – relate to each other as the general and the particular. 'A particular quasi-human community' in the sense I have explained above is a special case of 'an imaginative framework alternative to the author's empirical environment'. Equally, a 'community where socio-political institutions, norms and individual relationships are organized on a more perfect principle than in the author's environment' is a particular form and example of cognition about the imaginative framework.

I have further argued in *MOSF* that SF is narratively dominated by a fictional novum (novelty, innovation) validated by cognitive logic, and that this means a feedback oscillation between two realities. The SF narrative actualizes a different – though historical and not transcendental – world corresponding to different human relationships and cultural norms. However, in SF the 'possible world' induced by the narrative is imaginable only as an interaction between two factors: the conception which the collective social addressee of a text has of empirical reality, and the narratively explicit modifications a given SF text supplies to that initial conception. The resulting alternate reality or possible world is, in turn, not a prophecy or even extrapolation but an *analogy* to unrealized possibilities in the addressee's or implied reader's empirical world: however empirically unverifiable the narrative agents, objects or events of SF may be, their constellation in all still (literally) significant cases shapes a parable about ourselves. It also means that the dominant novum determining narrations in this genre is itself an ineluctably historical category, brought about by identifiable forces in societal pragmatics (actions) and semantics (language), and necessarily explained in terms of concrete, if imaginary, spacetimes (chronotopes), agents and events in each tale. I then go on to argue that the novum can be differentiated, first, by degree of magnitude (from single event or gadget to a cosmic-cum-societal totality); second, by kind of cognitive validation; and third, by degree of relevance (fake *vs.* superficial *vs.* deep and/or lasting). Finally, since freedom is (in Ernst Bloch's formulation) the possibility of making it different, this last differentiation by relevance is the nodal point where aesthetical and ethico-political qualities meet. The transposition and condensation of history into an analogical historicity is the epistemological key logically necessary for interpreting or allotting meaning to any SF tale.

If this is accepted, then utopian fiction is not only, historically, one of the roots of SF, it is also – as argued in chapter 3 of *MOSF* – logically, if retroactively, one of its forms, that validated by and only by socio-politics. Utopian fiction is the socio-political subgenre of SF, it is social-science-fiction or SF restricted to the field of socio-political relationships or to socio-political constructs understood as crucial for the destiny of people. Perhaps this is a good place to explain that I have no particular imperialist ambitions toward utopology or 'utopian studies'. It is clear that – as the *Dao de jing* pregnantly remarks – when the formless is formalized, terms appear; so that different formalizations, made for different purposes and interests, will use different ways of kneading the formless into form. For given purposes, if and in so far as these are deemed pertinent, it might therefore (or might not) be quite possible to speak about utopia without invoking SF. What I *am* claiming is, first, that the historically very intimate connection of utopian fiction with other forms of SF (extraordinary voyage, technological anticipation, anti-utopia and dystopia, etc.) is surely neither accidental nor insignificant. It reposes, in fact, on the cultural interpenetration of the validating intertextual category of utopian fiction (socio-politics) with the validating categories of the mentioned cognate forms (foreign otherness, technocracy or wrong politics).

3. Further, and possibly more immediately illuminating, some important consequences pertaining to the even more intimate connection of the narrative logics at hand flow out of these resemblances and differences between utopias and SF. Utopian fiction is, narratologically speaking, SF in which the always necessary element of explicating the novum (the 'lecture'), which is usually both masked and distributed into various narrative segments, has remained systematically discursive; that is, the conceptual explanation constitutes almost the whole plot. As Barthes has indicated in *Sade, Fourier, Loyola*, the plot of utopian fiction is a panoramic sweep conducted along the well-known, culturally current socio-political categories (geography, demography, religion, constitution, economics, warfare, etc.). In other words, the proportion of 'showing *vs.* telling' is in utopian fiction different from the norm of the Individualist novel. (But let me sceptically add that should somebody do a good statistical comparison of Balzac's famous descriptions of entire economic branches with some of the more agitated utopian fictions, we might be in for a surprise. The resulting possibly not too dissimilar proportions of telling to showing might necessitate the realization that our understanding of the novel norms has been etiolated since the heyday of Balzac or Tolstoy, so that we ought to put the adjective 'late' or some such pejorative synonym in front of 'Individualist norm'.) It is true that Henry James and Georg Lukács would, unfortunately, agree to consider this different proportion as an adverse judgement on utopian fiction, and that even some considerations of utopia (such as Gerber's) have introjected this criterion, but the limitation of aesthetic cognition to sensual surfaces remains a quaint bourgeois-romantic prejudice.

In the terms of Northrop Frye (which are useful even outside his system), the concentration of utopian fiction on and its exclusive interest in socio-political constructs on the basis of a postulated (more or less stable) human nature make it naturally fall within the form and tradition of 'anatomy', rather than within the form and the tradition of the Defoe-to-Henry-James novel of individualist psychology. The anatomy 'deals less with people as such than with mental attitudes', and at its most concentrated 'presents us with a vision of the world in terms of a single intellectual pattern' (Frye, 1966, pp. 309–11). Our critical expectations and judgements should take this into account. In particular, there is no point in expecting from utopia's characterization and plotting the qualities and criteria established in the psychological novel. Most modern SF, on the other hand, stemming as it does from a union of adventure-tale and such anatomy, belongs to the intermediary form and tradition of prose fiction between the anatomy and the novel, which Frye calls the romance. Its plots and agential characterizations will be what Frye calls stylized, and what I would call semi-allegorical or halfway between the naturalistic literary norm of the average reader and the allegorical tradition of the writer's form. This is an uneasy compromise, which demands a particularly favourable sociological conjunction and/or particularly talented writers to carry off so as to compare with either the best utopias or the best novels. The halfway house between King Utopus and Madame Bovary is difficult to locate.

Further, some basic structural characteristics of utopian fiction seem to flow logically from its status as a discourse about a particular historically alternative and better community. Since such a discourse will necessarily present an opposition which is a formal analogy to the author's delimited environment and its way of life, any utopia must be (1) a rounded, *isolated* place (valley, island, planet – later, temporal epoch). Since it has to show more perfectly organized relationships, the categories under which the author and her age subsume these relationships (government, economics, religion, warfare, etc.) must be in some way or other (2) *articulated* in a panoramic sweep whose sum is the inner organization of the isolated place: as Barthes remarks, the syntax or composition of elements is identified with creation in such works. Since not only the elements but also their articulation and coordination have to be more perfect than the categorization in the author's civilization (for example the federalist pyramid from bottom up of More's Utopia as opposed to the centralist pyramid from top down of More's England and Europe), (3) a formal *hierarchic system* becomes the supreme order and thus the supreme value in utopia: there are authoritarian and libertarian, class and classless utopias, but no unorganized ones. (Morris's reticence about organization and hierarchy in *News from Nowhere* places that work halfway between utopia and pastoral.) Usually, the installation of the new order must be explained – a contract theory, as Frye observes, is implied in each utopia (King Utopus, socialist revolution, gas from a comet, etc. being the arbiters or contract-makers). The utopian contract is necessarily opposed to the dominant contract-myth in the author's society as the more reverent 'contract behind the contract', human potential which existing society has alienated and failed to realize. Lastly, utopia is bound to have (4) an implicit or explicit *dramatic strategy* in its panoramic review conflicting with the 'normal' expectations of the reader. Though formally closed, significant utopia is thematically open: its pointings reflect back upon the readers 'topia'. Critics have even conveniently found a three-act dramatic structure in More's *Utopia*; whether this is exact or not, there is no doubt that an analysis of protagonists and settings in Kenneth Burke's 'dramatistic' terms is here appropriate. For example, utopia is invariably a frame-within-a-frame, because it is a specific wondrous stage, set within the world stage; techniques of analyzing the play-within-the-play could be gainfully employed when dealing with it. The varieties of the outer frame – usually some variant of the imaginary voyage – have been readily noticeable and as such have been the object of critical attention; less so the correlation of, say, the humanistic symposium of More or the socialist dream-which-might-be-a-vision of Morris with the experience in the inner frame.

SF shares the first and last but not the middle two elements in this characteristic utopian structure. It employs local isolation and a dramatic strategy. It has the alternative place, 'the world beyond the hill' as Alexei Panshin calls it. But since it can be based on any kind of cognitive estrangement and not just on more perfectly organized communal relationships, it does not have to be articulated in an even disguised panoramic sweep whose sum is the plot of the book. True, SF also has to find a way to present its alternative world, but this is usually done through a skeleton of epical adventure hurried along at a fairly brisk pace in which panoramic and close-up shots alternate. Further, since its subject matter will invariably deal with power relationships – not necessarily in clearly socio-political but perhaps in biological, cosmological or other terms – SF is not committed to a formal hierarchical system: nihilist SF is quite possible and indeed one of the main horizons of this genre. But, finally, like utopia, SF is in a constant implicit dialogue with the 'normal' expectations of its reader, only partly – and only in the many second-rate works – overlaid by his familiarity with the conventions of SF.

The fact, duly noted in the above definitions, that utopia and SF are first of all, whatever other uses they may be put to, verbal constructs is extremely pertinent. It allows such an approach to bypass the old theologizing quarrel whether a utopia can be realized. There are two opposed but equally dogmatic schools of thought about this. For the first or Mannheimian one, only that which is realizable should properly be called utopia (the opposite is called ideology); for the second one, which strangely fuses liberal pragmatism and nineteenth-century Marxism (for example Engels) only that which is unrealizable should be called utopia (the opposite is called reality or science). However, if utopia is neither prophecy nor escapism, it should – as some critics have remarked – be treated as an 'as if', an imaginative experiment or 'a methodical organ for the New' (Bloch, 1959, 1:180). Utopia is an heuristic or educational device for perfectibility, an epistemological model and not an ontologically real country. Equally, I hope my definition of SF can enable us to bypass the new theologizing quarrel about whether SF is more real than realism. Neither prophetic futurology nor an empty game like chess, SF is also an 'as if', an imaginative experiment, a methodical organ for the New in the history of human relationships toward society and nature, a cognitive model.

The verbal mode appropriate to an 'as if' stance is the subjunctive. Just as utopia, SF is an exploratory organ based on the 'lateral possibilities' of history-making, analogous to the hypothetico-deductive method in experimental sciences and mathematics – for example, to non-Euclidean geometries which start by saying 'what if such-and-such an axiom of Euclid's did not apply?', and deduce from it a universe of possibilities. It is a possible strangeness, a cognition, understanding or sensibility which does not pretend to hold up a mirror to either present or future nature but to the possibilities inherent in nature – human, social or cosmic. Just as utopia, SF is a 'serious game', a play with realities which teaches us to understand and, if need be, to modify our empirical reality.

So, to conclude, what is the degree of kinship between utopia and SF? As was said, strictly and precisely speaking, utopia is a sub-genre of SF. But it is also more than that – it is also one of the formal and the foremost among the ideological ancestors of SF. All SF is, if not a daughter, then at least a niece of utopia – a niece usually ashamed of the family inheritance but unable to escape her genetic destiny. For all its adventure, romance, science popularization or wish-fulfilment, SF can finally be written only between the utopian and the anti-utopian horizon. All imaginable intelligent life, including ours, can in the final instance only be organized more perfectly or less perfectly: there is no value-free wonder or knowledge. In that sense, utopia and anti-utopia are not only literary genres, but also horizons within which humanity and all its endeavours, including SF, is irrevocably collocated. As in *News from Nowhere*, the river-side trees of SF and utopia, finally, bear witness to the chances of our awakening again into the bleak winter of our discontent, or of our awakening, together with William

Morris, poet and socialist, as Guest in 'a beautiful bright morning seemingly of early June'.

(Original version 1974)

NOTE

1. See two earlier books of mine, *MOSF* and *VSF*. Bibliographies on the theory of utopia and history of utopian fiction will be found in *MOSF*, and all references in this essay are keyed to it.

4

Not Only But Also: On Cognition and Ideology in SF and SF Criticism*

Each of us is all the sums he has not counted . . .
(Thomas Wolfe, *Look Homeward, Angel*)

We must be systematic, but we should keep our systems open.
(A. N. Whitehead, *Modes of Thought*)

Thus art is a peculiar and fundamental human capacity: not a disguise for morality or a prettification of knowledge but an independent discipline that represents the various other disciplines [such as ethics or cognition] in a contradictory manner.
(B. Brecht, *The Messingkauf Dialogues*)

No, don't attack us, gentlemen, we're our own opponents anyway and we can hit ourselves better than you can.
(R. Hausmann, 'The German Philistine is Angry')

The present (1979) moment of SF, SF criticism and of our own views on both prompts us to try going back to basics – to reflect on where we are now and what ways may be open or closed to us. Since we do not believe in the independence of subject from object, of heuristic method from social practice, we shall often have to shuttle back and forth between SF and SF criticism in our argumentation. These are not quite systematic reflections, and we hope they will be

* Co-author: M. Angenot

44

understood as being provisional. As Brecht, one of our own models, used to say, 'progressing is more important than being progressive'.[1]

1. IDEOLOGICAL AND COGNITIVE CRITICISM

1.1. What might be the basic criterion by which criticism worthy of its humanistic calling should finally judge SF (as all other art)? Our first proposition is that all literature occupies a continuum whose poles *are illuminating human relationships, thus making for a more manageable and pleasurable life in common, and obscuring or occulting them, thus making for a more difficult life.* SF situates itself within this general alternative of liberation *vs.* bondage, self-management *vs.* class alienation, by organizing its narrations around the exploration of *possible new relationships*, where the novelty is *historically* determined and critically evaluatable. Thus, the understanding of SF – constituted by history and evaluated in history – is doubly impossible without a sense of history and its possibilities, a sense that this genre is a system which changes in the process of social history.

All this means that *criticism (and in particular SF criticism) is centrally dealing with the interaction between text and context, the unique literary work and our common social world.* In other words, an adequate critical approach will *at the end of its exploration* relate literary production to its social meanings, since it will not find it possible to divorce literary from socio-political judgements. The SF critic should, no doubt, begin by knowing the 'first principles' of his trade or craft – internal coherence, clarity, resolving power, distinction of levels of relevance, economy of proceedings, informativeness, etc. A first step in literary analysis is to identify the actual development of significant features in the narration (though even this beginning is only possible because there are some basic or 'zero' assumptions about people and the world with which we approach literary analysis itself). But all this is merely basic critical 'literacy': after the ABC, other steps follow in a critical reading. This indispensable first step will remain useless if it is not integrated with identifying those narrative bonds that can be defined as the relation between the set of elements in the text and the larger set of elements from which the textual ones have been selected (for example, the relation of a blue sun to all other stars). In other words, the world that is excluded from the text cannot fail to be tacitly reinscribed into it by the ideal reader cognizant of that world: she will notice that the sun is not simply blue but blue-and-not-yellow. (It is of course possible and not infrequent for readers to have a distorted perception of our common world, through ignorance, misinformation, mystification or class interest: for them literature will not be properly 'readable' until their interests change. None the less, a text contributes to the education of its readers more than is usually assumed.)

Such a *'not only but also' procedure*, though not taught when most of us were students, should be a central tool of every literary critic, and quite obviously of every SF critic. Against all 'positive' common sense, *a text is constituted and marked as much by what it excludes as by what it includes* – and it excludes much more than it includes. Therefore the critic cannot simply judge 'what the author says' – a fetishized 'text as thing' – without smuggling even into a first description some presuppositions he/she should therefore openly acknowledge. When we read a text we should understand *not only* its internal narrative articulation *but also* its relation to wider paradigms. The result is that the text inescapably amounts to a given *interpretation* or model of the extra-textual universe. To put it in spatial terms, any literary text exists on two levels of similarity: it is in some ways 'like' that set of elements which it actually presents – effects of a blue sun – but it is in other ways also 'like' the whole of the universe from which that set of elements is taken, a universe in which there are blue and non-blue suns, with certain possibilities of planets and life on them, distances to each other, etc. To put it in temporal terms, each literary text contains its historical epoch as a hierarchy of significations *within* the text, just as the epoch contains the text both as product and factor.

1.2. Our second proposition is that the SF critic can in his approach mimic mature art, which is many-sided and cognitive, or primitive art, which is one-sided and hence ideological.

Like any other *artistic modelling*, literature can fuse the strengths of a game model and a scientific model. A game model (a card game, say) can only refer to vague, quite abstract relationships, without any precise reference, direct or indirect, to reality outside the game: the game model is *semantically empty*. A scientific model, on the contrary, has a precise referent in reality, it is semantically full, but it is at the same time *one-sided* (univalent): only one semantic system is true in any scientific model, all others are false. Now an artistic model – if properly used, that is, if its potentialities are fully realized – can be both semantically *full and many-sided*. Full, since it always refers to an extra-literary reality (Stapledon's *Sirius*, say, refers to possible new relations among people, perhaps centred on an intellectual like the author?); many-sided (plurivalent), since several semantic systems, played off against each other, coexist in mature artistic cognition (not only Sirius's but also Plaxy's, her father's, the narrator's, all interactive within a continuum between the poles of the animal and the spiritual). All literature that attempts to be either an empty game or a 'science' is *ideological* in direct proportion to such confusion. In the latter case it confuses fact with fiction and analogy with prediction. A limit-case of quite some interest as an awful warning is constituted by all the Velikovskys, Hubbards, von Dänikens and ufologists who erect standard SF topics – which are within fiction neutral or indeed meaningful – into 'true' revelations, thereby instantly converting them into virulent ideologies of political obscurantism.

The term 'ideology' can in such a context be used in two mutually exclusive ways. It can mean any system of ideas, any structure of socio-political sensibility; or it can mean those systems of ideas and structures of socio-political sensibility which obscure the real foundations of human relationships and thus impede easier living. In the first, wider sense, all art and literature inescapably participates of ideology and 'is ideological'. In the second, narrower sense, only systems of meaning and sensibility which make people's economic and psychological existence in common more difficult and less pleasurable are to be considered ideological. Both meanings of 'ideological' have impressive authorities to recommend them, inside as well as outside of Marxism, but only the second, narrower, meaning will be used in this chapter. The argument for this choice would necessarily be longer than the rest of the chapter, so that we can only hope it will be justified by its fruits.

However, there are not only important parallels but also important differences between 'ideological SF' and 'ideological SF criticism'. A work of fiction written within the same ideological horizon as a work of literary criticism has some inbuilt saving graces *in proportion* to the aesthetic or formal qualities which it may possess, for they will endow it with the contradictoriness inherent in all meaningful artistic endeavours. In the perhaps slightly emphatic terms of D. H. Lawrence's 'Study of Thomas Hardy': 'Every work of art adheres to some system of morality. But if it be really a work of art, it must contain the essential criticism of the morality to which it adheres. . . . The degree to which the system or morality, or the metaphysic of any work of art is submitted to criticism within the work of art makes the lasting value and satisfaction of that work.'

Therefore, though fictional systems can contribute to systematically notional cognition – as witness Marx's or Freud's use of Shakespeare or Sophocles – yet critical cognition cannot simply transpose elements or aspects of the fictional insights into its own discourse. When Dick satirically dramatizes a world of ubiquitous simulacra in *Ubik*, he is identifying some new experiences of the 'little man' in mass-consumption capitalism. But when some French critics (and lately, alas, Dick himself) use some novels of his as a proof that life in capitalism abolishes all difference between the real and the imaginary, then they are making a systematic theory out of a dramatized presentation: they are engaging in ideology, and thus betraying the very function of critical thinking.

1.3. We believe all criticism to be ideological and mystifying which tacitly and surreptitiously transforms its particular, operatively necessary approach or point of view into a universal, eternal axiom. True, all knowledge is inescapably codetermined by its subject's point of view as well as by its object. The mystification comes about when this historically located construct and heuristic choice, which is basically an 'as if' ('if we agree for the duration of this critique to look at that text under this point of view, then so-and-so necessarily follows'), grows, like a djinn from the bottle, into a transcendental entity and metaphysical essence. Such mystifying criticism installs a blind spot, a *conceptual fetish* degrading it into ideology instead of cognition, at the centre of its vision. This fetish has its variants; it can be signified by the terms Myth, Author's Intention, Theme, Ethics, Scientific Extrapolation, Economic Determination or the Unconscious (Freudian or post-Freudian). In all cases, however, the fetishizing operation *eliminates the interaction between the text and the history in which it was written and is being read*, so that the contradictions and mediations of a history-as-process are passed over in silence. This fetishized criticism is, when all is said and done, in a position not too different from that of the often invoked SF ghetto, which is why it feels so comfortable within it, as a subsidiary epicycle – the ghetto of SF criticism.

Of course, the commonsensical – supposedly 'empirical' or 'positive' – approach is just a shamefaced variant of such fetishism. Its slogan, 'let us look at things as they are and never mind the theories', is a mystification by omission, as the variants mentioned above are by commission. It assumes it has got hold of an Adamic language which can proceed straight to the non-contradictory essence of a text or social experience. This constitutive assumption is simply wrong, another bit of theologizing ideology disguised as bluff realism. It conceals a tacit denial of anything beyond the surface appearances, of any depths beneath or alternatives to the holy Experiences-That-Be and Powers-That-Be. No doubt, when anyone is *truly* the first to survey and name a socio-cultural phenomenon – such as the opus of an SF writer, the run of a magazine, or the SF production of a brief period – she/he is in fact in the Adamic position of first namer. In that case it is often – for the nonce – tolerable to establish more or less commonsensical categories, describe the subject at hand with their help, and suspend further discussion. But empiricism and positivism erected into a permanent principle, as so often happens in studies of 'popular culture', makes one suspect that a great deal of libido has been diverted into a perverse enjoyment of impotence. A truly critical attitude will necessarily take into account both the text and its gaps, the choices made by the author and the set chosen from; and for this it will need categories more useful than those of common sense.

1.4. But then, what is a truly critical attitude? One that would eschew as many ideological traps as is humanly possible in this inhuman, antagonistic world of ours? We have no dogmatic recipe to offer. But we would like to try and define a horizon within which the no doubt numerous variants of such an attitude become possible. It is, unashamedly, the horizon of a modern, epistemologically self-conscious and self-critical *science or cognition*. This is the only horizon that incorporates the viewer (experimenter, critic) into the structure of what is being beheld (experiment, text). It is therefore the only horizon which permits the provisional method situated within it to be integrated into social practice and to become self-corrective on the basis of social practice, and which has a chance

– if used intelligently – to show realistically the relationships of people in the material world. The apparent paradox of cognitive or non-ideological criticism is that it does not try to eliminate the historical – historically limited but not arbitrary – choice on which it is based. Rather, it explicitly recognizes this choice as the basis of its whole enterprise. It is thus enabled to eliminate the bias introduced by its own presuppositions. It should be clear that such a scientific horizon is quite different from and indeed incompatible with that of the 'objective' nineteenth-century scientism. On the contrary, such realistic and materialistic cognition implies that people's consciousness, arising out of and feeding back into a complex network of social practice, is the indispensable mediation and component of that practice.

Ideology claims today to be 'scientific', just as in the Middle Ages it claimed to be religious (or indeed to be the science of religion, theology). But scientific is exactly what ideological propositions are not: at this point, ideology becomes analytically vulnerable. What science *is* in historico-cultural disciplines, such as literary and cultural criticism, is a subject much too vast for these reflections. But perhaps one could set up two provisional first criteria which criticism would have to satisfy in order to begin being scientific:

(1) A scientific approach begins with the distinction between (though also continues with the interaction of) processes in existential economic reality and processes of thought; it begins with *the distinction between being and cognition* and continues with *the intervention of cognition into being;*

(2) A scientific approach takes *our social existence as both source and goal of human thoughts and emotions, of art and science.* This does not mean that art is a 'superstructure' erected on a material 'basis'. On the contrary, literature and other arts are – in their own, autonomous though not independent, way – material products of human creative potentialities, and one of the best means for clarifying human relationships and values. *Literature, film and so on, can provide sets of manageable and explorable models of social existence.*

2. CHARACTERISTICS OF IDEOLOGY IN CRITICISM AND FICTION

2.0. Thus a critical approach can be either cognitive or ideological – to take theoretically pure extremes again. Ideally, of course, criticism (which we here do not distinguish from scholarship) is conducted by elaborating a logical conceptual system, and it should therefore always be a cognitive pursuit. Ideology, though it constructs pseudo-systems, is strictly speaking not a conceptual system but a transposition of incompatible propositions into a mythical pretence at a logical system. Ideological criticism is therefore always half-baked: it may be useful in some ways but it does not go far enough. If its system seems to work while confined to paraphrasing a fictional text (in which, as we argue, incompatibles can coexist when organized in aesthetically convincing even if conceptually unclarified and indeed contradictory ways), it will become clearly untenable as soon as the critique is exposed to everyday existential criteria. The critic's task is, thus, not merely to clarify the textual propositions but also to ask whether – beyond the author's craftsmanship – such propositions can be translated into a tenable conceptual system. To take the text at face value, to erect the necessary preliminary homework of understanding what Asimov or Zelazny is saying into an uncritical conclusion (usually a tacit one, by omission) that whatever he may be saying should also be the reader's cognitive horizon – this is the mark of an ideological critic. And yes: SF criticism today is chock-full of ideological critics . . . .

Here we cannot but indicate at least briefly that such an overriding ideology is not only a matter of theoretical consciousness operating in a pure realm of ideas, but also a material force and power based on given interests. Positivist scholarship in literature has its own long history and function in the educational system. It first made possible the academic system under which we are living today, the system of 'publish or perish' (or should one call it 'scholars for dollars'?) which supposedly yields quantifiable results. A great number of academic careers have been and are being built within such an ideology, which has fairly substantial prizes and penalties to offer at this time of threatening economic and psychological insecurity: jobs, promotions, publication opportunities, research funds and so forth. We cannot analyse here this complex and mostly hidden network by which an ideology becomes material power, but we should at least state that such a network largely explains the hold of this ideology even in such a relatively new and fresh field as SF criticism.

2.1. If we want to avoid such one-dimensionality and fetishism, and do justice to the richness of possible human relationships in history, then we have to begin compiling a brief inventory of current ideological fetishes that dominate first, SF texts, and second, SF criticism. The first such ideological pseudo-system has been given a handy name by Marcuse: it is a sub-species of the general ideology of *repressive tolerance* (a fake tolerance, of course).

A first mark by which such ideological criticism can be caught *in flagrante*, is precisely its reduction of the self-contradictory aesthetic unity into a consensual system – it is its *hatred of contradiction*. For example, it is ideological to say Heinlein is a Calvinist, unless one in the next breath adds that Heinlein is *also* a Calvinist without Calvinism. Heinlein's opus is (to a degree still to be determined) built around the *contradiction* of a class of Democratic Elect, who exist without a complete value-system that would logically validate their Electedness. For, instead of believing that only an elite will find grace in God's eyes, a pseudo-Jeffersonian democrat must believe that all men can learn how to handle technology (usually in Heinlein some form of military technology, from arms and rockets to psychological warfare). The resulting pragmatist ideology of the Elect who are recognized by their performance is logically or scientifically untenable within Heinlein's sincerely democratic framework, and leads him to construct strange 'two-tier' democracies in Orwellian states where some are more equal than others. These incompatibilities make possible interesting tales of how to recognize such an Electedness, as well as boring tales about the exploits of the Elect (like the aptly named Lazarus Long). The reasons for such simultaneously rich and logically untenable contradictions are, of course, to be sought in Heinlein's personal variant of the historical antinomies underlying the social existence in the United States of the 1920s, 1930s, etc., more than in any 'history-of-ideas' preoccupation of this or that author with Calvinism, Jeffersonian ideas, or anything of the sort. If such historical antinomies are not merely taken up but – necessarily – strongly reinterpreted by the writer, as here by Heinlein, then the readers (including the critics) cannot but be faced with the choice of whether or not to accept the text's version and interpretation of a common social reality and its conflicts.

This means that the critic cannot simply be the writer's advocate. No doubt, he/she has to be able also to function on the writer's wavelength in order to understand and explain what the text is conveying. But the critic should, we believe, overridingly be the advocate of an ideal non-alienated and libertarian reader who has the right to receive all the evidence of how, why, and in whose interests the writer has interpreted our common universe – of where is the text situated within the inescapable polarity of illuminating or occulting human relationships. To put it in different terms, the critic cannot choose not to be the advocate of some values: all presentations of human relationships (however disguised these might be in SF) are heavily value-fraught. Indeed, the values transmitted, denied or yearned for are the main significance of such presentations. The critic can only choose *which* values to advocate, and how to go about it – to begin with, covertly or overtly. Thus, a critic trying to construct a conceptual system by refusing to see the paradox which is at the core of Heinlein's narration is wrong – even when a clever arguer – because she/he has succumbed to an unexamined ideology. It is precisely the author's self-contradictions which should be explored. Equally, the significant SF writers in our time – say Delany, Dick, Le Guin, Lem, Piercy, Spinrad, the Strugatskys, Tiptree – all deal in quite painful contradictions, often within their protagonist(s). To remain bound by the author's consciousness means for the critic to abdicate his/her cognitive task in favour of ideology.

2.2. A second mark by which ideology in SF and SF criticism can be known is *crass individualism*. This category reflects and reinforces the separation of public and private, characteristic of bourgeois life. All of SF's conflicts between 'man' (our hero – necessarily a super-hero and therefore not man but superman!) and 'society' (a totally anachronistic feudal dictatorship as in *Dune*, or in the best case a faceless 'them' – if not 'us' – as in the later Delany) develop within the unstated and therefore textually unshakable ideology which denies the existence of meaningful groupings between THE individual and THE society. In other words, there are no social classes with collective and diverging economic interests, and therefore there are no unsurmountable class conflicts. In wishdream SF (for example, space operas) the individual will win out, in more mature cases he will be defeated. (He, not she: for a long time, the mere presence of a heroine – necessarily the representative of an oppressed group – was subversive, since it involved at least a perverted image of class conflict in the gender/sex conflict; but we have now begun getting heroines – say in Janet T. Morris – as mystifying as the heroes.) In both cases, however – in all individualistic SF – the game is played according to the just described ground-rule of *THE INDIVIDUAL* (me) excluding *THE SOCIETY* (us), and vice versa, and of everybody being no more and no less than an individual. The trouble with this ground-rule is that it is reductionist and false, taken over wholesale from the dominant bourgeois ideology. Since any upper class in a 'democratic' state has to claim that it is simply composed of the 'natural' leaders, that it is not a special-interest class, its ideology will stress the struggle of the fittest *individuals* as 'natural' (that is, as validated by natural sciences, no less). Just as the bourgeois upper class remains in power by claiming that there are no social classes, so its ideology remains dominant by claiming that there are no ideologies (and especially no existentially and logically irreconcilable ideologies): that there are only individual opinions, which have to be tolerated, as well as 'natural', 'simply human', attitudes – the behavioural equivalent of the existing consensus in politics within which every isolated individual can safely have her/his own 'opinion'. Such a ground-rule is then particularized in SF as 'natural' reactions for or against technology, for inner *vs.* outer space, and so forth.

Yet the originality of SF as a genre is that its characters are used in attempts at systematic analyses of a *collective* destiny involving a whole community – a people, a race, a world, etc. Therefore the final horizon of individualistic – psychological and/or ethical – criticism is simply inadequate and (if used as the dominant critical approach and not as an initial tool) ideological.

2.3. A further and closely related mark of occulting ideology, we believe, is that it *displaces and isolates* (or fragments) the semantic space of cognition, that it deforms and distorts the very field to be understood, isolating it from other social spaces and categories of cognition and practice. Most strictly, this is the case of such key cognitive spaces as *political economy* (who works at what for whom for how much and in whose interest), conspicuous by its absence even in the seemingly most progressive SF such as that of Le Guin (except for a first approach to it in *The Dispossessed*, the crowning novel of the US 'leftist' trend). If anybody ever works at anything among the significant characters in SF except at war, crime, and adventures, it is at travelling, cerebrating or at saving the galaxy. Live? – our servants will do it for us, said the French aristocrats. Produce? – our robots will do it for us, imply the strictly consuming or at best redistributing SF protagonists. One never has any inkling who builds all those spaceships, who feeds and clothes our hero and heroine. They certainly don't do it themselves. As for the fetish of Technology, we can fortunately refer the reader to the incisive analysis by Joanna Russ (1978) of how in SF – and elsewhere – this is divorced from economics.

2.4. Thus, we see SF as a genre in an unstable equilibrium or compromise between two factors. The first is its cognitive – philosophical and incidentally political – potentiality as a genre that grows out of the subversive, lower-class form of 'inverted world'. The second is a powerful upper and middle-class ideology that has, in the great majority of texts, sterilized such potential horizons by contaminating them with mystifications about the eternally 'human' and 'individual', which preclude significant presentations of truly *other* relationships. If the above holds for literature in general, it is particularly blatant in the case of SF, which as a genre deals centrally not only with collective destiny but also – and more particularly – with *power relationships*. Power might be defined (following Nikos Poulantzas) as the ability of a given class to put into effect its specific interest by endowing it with the social force of a general constraint. The power struggles in SF, however, are usually displaced in one of two ways. First, from society into biology (Social-Darwinism, up to racist and sexist chauvinism) or even cosmology (natural catastrophies, from Jefferies and Wells to Ballard and the Strugatskys, to mention only the best). Second – when they do remain a human affair – the power struggles are displaced into uncouth mixtures of politics and individualistic psychology, often parapsychology (from Van Vogt and Asimov to Herbert and even some Dick or Le Guin); or they are displaced into cyclical theories of history where the future is just a weird repetition of the past, or into its obverse ideology of pseudoscientific and technological extrapolation, where the future is just a weird repetition of the present in a state of grossly inflamed and irritated distension (as Wells self-critically said of his prototypical *When the Sleeper Wakes*).

We must be careful to note that, while in principle all such displacements could serve as vehicles of a parable on existential economic power relationships, and have sometimes done so (in the best Dick or Simak and in most of Wells or Le Guin, say), usually they do not. Instead of being a vehicle, the displacements are presented as literal, 'thought-experiment' propositions, so to speak. From Mary Shelley and Wells on, the bane of SF has been such confusion of ends and means. It issues either in sensationalism – the superficially acute but meaningless conflicts of galactic empires or strange menaces from inner space – or in fantasy – the supposedly suggestive but unverifiable and non-cognitive wonders used for purposes of psychic purgation and titillation.

Leaving aside in this essay the genre of fantasy – that dark twin of SF in which the sense of 'it ain't necessarily so' breaks away from the sense of what is even potentially a material possibility, and with which SF criticism should urgently come to grips – we should like to pursue a little further the illuminating instance of *sensationalism*. It is not defined simply by the presence of an adventure-laden plot – in itself a possible analogue of the science-fictional adventure of cognition and therefore often great fun – but by the anxious, eunuch-like way such a plot avoids exploring the otherness of the novum which made those adventures possible: the new locus, people, scientific element, society, etc. Potentially (as any SF reader knows), a dynamic plot subverts the initial situation; actually (as too many SF critics do not see), this potential remains unfulfilled in sensationalist SF, whose surface dynamics present no meaningful Other at all (for example, the *Star Wars* white-clad goodies *vs.* black-clad baddies). A classical case, trend-setting for SF, was the turn-of-the-century reduction of Wells's *War of the Worlds* to sensationalism in the US yellow press by the simple expedient of leaving in all the 'action' (Martian death-rays, crowd fights) and deleting all the discussions in which Wells's narrator tries to make sense of the action, to reflect on its causes, effects and possible meanings. Such a 'cut the guff' he-man reductionism amounts, of course, to a terroristic suppression of cognition, now happily internalized in much SF as a one-dimensional tradition and market constraint (the market having been shaped by such censorship in the first place). Curiosity, the interest in causes and effects, is thus degraded to suspense, the interest in effects sundered from causes. Criticism that would simply 'explicate the text' would in all such cases clearly be a victim of a massive censorship disguised as 'entertainment', 'we are all competing for the idiot multitude's beer money', 'the great Gernsback tradition' (or, complementarily, 'the great New Wave tradition', where sensationalism turns introvert), etc., *ad nauseam*.

It becomes clear that to give anything like a full account of SF, textual analysis has to be integrated with a highly critical account of all traditional and contemporary mediations which made for just such texts among all the possible ones to be written: the great role of some mediators such as Campbell is well-known but scarcely fully explored. But a history in which populist-cum-radical SF once upon a time sold at least as well as sterilized SF – the comparison of Mark Twain, Bellamy, Donnelly and Jack London with Frank Stockton, J. J. Astor, the antiutopians such as David Parry, or *Ralph 124C 41+* is immediately illuminating – makes it obvious that something changed radically in the North American 'reception aesthetics' around 1910, roughly with the advent of E. R. Burroughs. That not yet properly investigated 'something' amounts to an absorption of bourgeois ideology into SF. A group of ideological motifs now appears – sensational adventures dominated by physical conflict, technology as a force of good or evil divorced from who uses it for what interests, history as a catastrophic and meaningless cycle of barbaric rise and decadent fall, etc. – which was soon to give rise to the characteristic SF sub-forms defining the genre until the present day.

3.   RETROSPECT AND PROSPECT

3.1. Of course, all these tentative reflections do not in any way pretend to be a rounded-off theory of English-language SF, let alone modern SF in general. Important changes in SF came about in the 1960s which at least partly broke with the internalized consensus sketched above (and which itself had bright exceptions; many of them – Simak, Pohl, Tenn, Sheckley, some Heinlein, etc. – were noted but insufficiently explained in Amis's *New Maps of Hell*). One indicator of the change is the phoenix rebirth of concern with and for *utopias*, for the collective sociopolitical organization of human happiness. The repressive tolerance in 'rational', 'commonsense' politics and ideology had distorted this term into a landlord's sneer – Macaulay's 'an acre in Middlesex is better than a principality in Utopia'. More insidiously, conservative ideology and abstract escapism had infiltrated the texts themselves, turning too many (though never all) fictional utopias into static and untenable constructs. In fact, many of these stunted utopias presented quasi-religious and terrorist pseudo-paradises as isolated from dynamic social practice as the catastrophic SF narrations – the 'new maps of hell' dystopias – whose obverse and ideological complement they by that token became.

Moreover, all of this happened in an age when increased productivity led to both socio-political practice and powerful cognitive systems – such as Darwin's, Marx's or Einstein's – that were incompatible with an eternal stability. No doubt, too, the only very partial (displaced, isolated, and ideologized) success of radical hopes from, say, the Mexican and Bolshevik revolutions to the present day amounts to an overall temporary failure and deferral of utopian hopes. In spite of all this, the basic lesson of all such heroic attempts, including the tragic failures, has to our mind confirmed the unquenchability of utopian Hope-the-Principle (Bloch) as the horizon correlative to human strivings and in fact defining *Homo sapiens* as more than simply an animal, as a cultural or indeed a cosmic entity. Thus, a deeper lawfulness seems to be indicated by the fact that whenever SF began shaking off the repressive hierarchical and ideological consensus, and in direct proportion to the depth to which this was being shaken, SF was able to envisage the pros and cons of a dynamic, provisional – in old, static terms 'ambiguous' – utopia again. This held for the period from Bellamy to London, and it holds for the period from Yefremov, the Strugatskys, and Dick to Russ, Piercy, Le Guin, Delany, Callenbach and Nichols. In between those two periods, in the heyday of E. R. Burroughs and Asimov, utopia was philosophically neither more nor less possible or necessary, it was simply ideologically occulted and displaced, privatized and fragmented (for example, into psycho-history or Laws of Robotics). In these last half a dozen years, the utopianizing thrust of *c*.1961–73 has mostly run dry in response to socio-political backlash and disappointment. This is why we find a wave of demoralization, of commingling anti-cognitive fantasy with SF, of irrationality or banality, surging back into even the more significant SF texts.

3.2. All the more reason for SF criticism to begin considering *not only* the major achievements of the genre *but also* the reasons for the unease prevalent in SF today, which paradoxically (or lawfully?) corresponds to its marketing successes. In order to do so, SF criticism has to become able to look at its own blind spots as a prerequisite to illuminating the cognition and ideology in SF. Just as the human eye inverts external pictures in its working process, so products of intellectual work fashion their models not only by selecting from the raw materials of 'external' inputs but also by inverting the relationships of social existence and presenting their concepts as entirely thought-derived: in the actual artistic (or scientific) presentation the most abstruse or fantastic concept is as real as any other concept. It is thus not absolutely necessary that SF call things by their scientific names, but it certainly is that it calls things by their humanly cognitive – moral and political – names. SF criticism must be able to do justice to such specific characteristics of SF, and to avoid confusing the genre's utopian-cum-scientific pathos and cognitive horizon with a pragmatic demand for accurate scientific extrapolation, either technological or socio-political. In brief: SF criticism ought to be not only firm, but also flexible; not only systematic but also open.

(Originally published in 1979)

NOTE

1. Our title as well as some basic links in our argument derive from Brecht; see in English *The Messingkauf Dialogues* and *Brecht On Theatre*, but also the Methuen and Vintage *Collected Plays* editions in progress (New York, 1971ff.) which include much highly pertinent commentary of his – as well as the plays themselves and *Poems* I–III (London, 1976). Other as basic links derive from Ernst Bloch, whose encyclopedic opus is even less accessible in English – see his titles in all three sections of the Bibliography. From the numerous other methodological debts, those to Jurij Lotman's *Structure* (1977); Sartre's *Search* (1968); Prieto's *Pertinence* (1975); and Poulantzas's *Power* (1973), could be most directly felt in what sometimes amount to paraphrases of their positions. The best introductions to this whole complex of problems can be found in Jameson, *Marxism* (1971) and Williams, *Marxism* (1977); see also their and Solomon's bibliographies. The D. H. Lawrence quote is taken from L. C. Knights, *Explorations 3* (Pittsburgh, 1976), p. 113, and the Macaulay one from his *Critical, Historical and Miscellaneous Essays and Poems* (Albany,

1887) II:229; the use of Wells by the US press is illuminatingly documented in David Y. Hughes, '*The War of the Worlds* in the Yellow Press', *Journalism Quarterly*, 43 (Winter 1966). Our discussion carries on the arguments in our earlier works, for example, Angenot (1975). We are particularly grateful for valuable comments on an embryonic form of this essay by James Bittner, Samuel Delany, Fredric Jameson, Gérard Klein, Dale Mullen, Patrick Parrinder, Robert Philmus, Pamela Sargent and George Szanto.

5

Narrative Logic, Ideological Domination, and the Range of SF: A Hypothesis

1. NARRATIVE LOGIC AND INTERTEXTUALITY[1]

A literary text has at least two strange groups of properties pertaining to its extension and to its intension (I am here appropriating terms from logic as metaphoric suggestions only). Extensively, the text can in any sufficiently small period still be thought of as objectifying the central element of a circuit at whose ends are the original sender and the original receiver. However, this objectification – the apparent constancy of the text – lends itself to the creation of other communication circuits, with new receivers and often also new senders: synchronically and (more often) diachronically, a text can have different intensions – that is, result in a number of different messages for different social addressees. As to the latter, it is clear that Marvell's ode to Cromwell, for example, is read differently by monarchists, Puritans and Levellers, as well as by differing social addressees one, two or three centuries later; this also holds for, say, Dickens's *Hard Times* read by a factory owner, a liberal reformer and a socialist, or for Heinlein's *Stranger in a Strange Land* read by Charles Manson and by you, gentle critical reader. Perhaps less evident but no less significant is the series of strange metamorphoses undergone by the image of the implied writer, which is the only aspect of authorship relevant in a communication circuit (the 'everyday', never mind the 'true', personality of the writer is not known even to the original readership). Thus, while both receiver and sender change, giving rise to a family of messages, the text seems to remain unchangeable. Literary studies – even taken in the widest sense, as studies of the rhetorics of all 'printed matter' or even of all discourse, printed or oral – have therefore in a way rightly centred on the text as the one stable element of literary communication.

61

Yet if this is in a way right, it is also in a way wrong. More precisely, if it is *necessary* to focus on this link in the communicational chain – as against the temptation to dwell on readers or (more often) on writers – it is not *sufficient* to do so. The text is not an independent totality, a closed monad within or atom of social discourse. Rather, it is the frozen notation of a *producing* of meanings, values and structures of feeling, which results from the writer's work on given *materials* within a given socio-historical *context*. Outside of a context that supplies the conditions of making sense, no text can be even read (as distinguished from spelling out the letters). Only the insertion of a text into a context makes it intelligible; that is why changing social contexts bring different messages out of the same text. Any reading ineluctably invents a more or less precise and pertinent context for the text being read. Any critical reading has at its centre the interaction between text and context, the unique literary work and the collective social world of its addressees (a present world, and in case of scholarly reconstructions, a past world too). Thus, even the basic 'formal' identifications of significant features are possible only because we can approach a narration with some initial or 'zero' assumptions about people's relationships to each other and to their world.

Furthermore, as it was argued in the preceding chapter, these first identifications will remain of little use unless they are finally integrated into the identification of those narrative bonds that can be defined as the relation between the set of elements in the text and the larger set of elements from which the textual ones have been selected (for example, the relation of a blue sun to all other stars). In other words, the world that is excluded from the text cannot fail to be tacitly reinscribed into it by the ideal reader cognizant of that world: he will notice that the sun is not simply blue but blue-and-not-yellow. It is, of course, possible and not infrequent for readers to have a distorted perception of our common world, through ignorance, misinformation, mystification, or class interest: for them, literature will not be properly 'readable' until their interests change. None the less, a text contributes to the education of its readers more than is usually assumed.

The context indispensable for a text's intelligibility could be analysed at several levels. One could begin with the historical semantics of any term taken separately – a procedure whose pertinence is more than usually clear in the genre of SF, inevitably committed to new terms that sketch in its *novum*. Such a specialized analysis, however, will not be attempted here, not only because it would be too elaborate but primarily because its implications can be subsumed under those of the text's own presuppositions.

The *presuppositions* of an utterance or proposition and of a text are – together with the more strictly linguistic factors – a necessary condition of its coherence.[2] As such, they are not external to the statement, but necessarily implied in and by it: 'The presupposed (*le présupposé*) partakes of the literal meaning of an utterance just as the posed (*le posé*) does' (Ducrot, 1972, p. 24). In other words, the presuppositions of an utterance and statement are a most intimate mediation between what is 'inside' and 'outside' it, between text and context. To take a famous example, the statement 'The king of France is bald' implies a complex and articulated universe of discourse. Incompletely enumerated, in it one can find: (1) the anthropological presupposition that there is in this universe a collective entity called France (which means that we are not omitting a classification by anthropological entities, we are not talking about non-collective anthropological entities nor about any anthropological collective entity not called France); (2) the political presupposition that France has one male ruler (that is, we are not omitting political classification: France is not organized non-hierarchically; it does not have several rulers nor one female monarch); (3) the physiological presupposition that the king of France has no hair on his head (we are not talking about his non-physiological qualities, nor about any other of his physiological characteristics, etc.). The famous SF sentence 'The door dilated' presupposes – among many other things – that in this narration's universe of discourse there are intelligent beings (psychozoa) who use sight, locomotion and constructed edifices, that these edifices incorporate building techniques not used in human history up to the author's period, that the narration's 'otherwhere' locus is normal for the implied narrator, and that the categories of visual observation, locomotion, constructed edifices, building techniques and historical normality are relevant for understanding this universe of discourse. Obviously, presuppositions such as the existence of nations, kings, baldness, edifices, doors, sight, etc., exist *inside* these propositions: they may underlie the propositions but they are present within them (not extrapolated) and necessary for them (not conjectural). However, a synthesis of presuppositions implied in all the statements of a text amounts to more than finding the rules that hold for this universe of discourse. In so far as the presuppositions simultaneously and equally exist *outside* the propositions, they are also ideological maxims; in their most general form, they are *principles of verisimilitude or believability* – that is, the cultural invariants or ideological commonplaces of the context common to the text's writer and addressee, and necessary for understanding the text. The addressee's cultural commonplaces unfailingly supplement and indeed shape the 'information' offered in the text (for example, the Victorian taboos on the body as locus of sexuality and as source of physical labour-force).

The presuppositions, the ideological givens, are thus both logically prior and analytically posterior to the text: its emergence as well as its interpretation is impossible without them. They are crucial factors of the context; but they are also among the materials with which the writer has to work, the building bricks which he can manipulate in the text. Ideology is pre-eminently a compromise between the discursive and the non-discursive, a 'representation' of the imaginary relationship between a subject and the situation in which it practically exists. It is a negotiation between the subject's (the ideology's collective bearer's) inventing a place for her/himself in a historical process that largely excludes his/her fundamental desires and her/his accurate 'mapping' of the social reality 'which is itself basically non-representable and non-narrative' (Jameson, 1979, p. 12). Directly to the purpose of studying fiction, ideology is also a lived structure of feeling 'which simultaneously organize[s] the empirical consciousness of a particular social group and the imaginative world created by the writer.'[3]

The presuppositions, the ideological maxims, the particular or common 'places' (*topoi*) of a text as a sequence of coherent propositions, are thus always *intertextual* – taken over (possibly modified) from and shared with other discursive texts. In modern periods they are mostly (or at least most verifiably) shared with other printed matter that coexists with it in a given moment of ideological history. This intertextual context, or intertext, is therefore not only an important means for establishing the horizon of expectation of a text's ideal reader. It is also the privileged way of establishing the rules of believability or conventions of verisimilitude for a text or a group of texts.[4] This is particularly clear in Victorian fiction, strongly oriented as it was toward 'the structure, internal movement, and moral atmosphere of contemporary society. . . . The [major] novelists . . . were especially concerned with the anxieties, envy, insecurity, snobbery, and kindred psychological malaises that stemmed from the ambiguities of rank and wealth in a time of social flux.' Practically without exception, Victorian fiction took its themes from problems of the day, usually already formulated in the intertext of an 'enormous body of printed argument and exhortation . . . [that] provided the matrix for the masterpieces of social discussion . . .' (Altick, 1973, pp. 17 and 70).

Through such intertexts, various groups of texts may usefully be linked with differing verisimilitudes, each of which is the cultural invariant of another social group. In proportion to the richness of a text or group of texts (macro-text), this linkage is not a one-to-one correspondence between it and the ideology of a social group. Rather, it will shape the text as a battleground of competing ideologies or 'common senses'. In the society as a whole, one 'common sense' – the structure of feelings embodying the basic invariants of the ruling class(es) – is dominant or *hegemonic* (see Gramsci, 1957 and 1970; also Williams, 1980). This hegemony does not entail only 'the articulate and formal meanings, values, and beliefs, which a dominant class develops and propagates':

> It is a whole body of practices and expectations, over the whole of living: our senses and assignments of energy, our shaping perceptions of ourselves and our world. It is a lived system of meanings and values – constitutive and constituting – which as they are experienced as practices appear as reciprocally confirming. It thus constitutes . . . a sense of absolute because experienced reality beyond which it is very difficult for most members of the society to move, in most areas of their lives. It is, that is to say, in the strongest sense a 'culture', but a culture which has also to be seen as the lived dominance and subordination of particular classes.   (Williams, 1977, p. 110)

In brief, this hegemony is not simply a passive domination. 'It has continually to be renewed, recreated, defended, and modified. It is also continually resisted, limited, altered, challenged . . .' – either by pressures that do not challenge its overall social validity and power (an alternative ideology) or by pressures that do so (an oppositional ideology). But even such counter-pressures are shaped by the hegemonic ideology: 'the dominant culture . . . at once produces and limits its own forms of counter-culture' (ibid., pp. 112 and 114; see also Williams, 1980, pp. 37–40).

Intertextuality is thus not simply an intersection and mutual influencing of different texts. It is primarily a way of developing, from *within* texts, the crucial scrutiny of their meanings and values as structures of feeling in a differential dialogue with other structures of feeling within the all-pervasive, complex, and shifting field of social discourse and its ideological tensions. The privileged, the most pertinent and significant, mediations in such a dialogue are, for fiction, the fictional forms, conventions and genres. These mediations seem to be nearest to the actual processes of fictional production and reception. They make it possible to avoid both overly generalized concentration of ideology as direct, conscious and pragmatic manipulation (though this aspect of ideology must also be taken into account, especially in SF) and overly particularized examination of atomized 'influences' proceeding from a few texts isolated from the conditions that shaped their influences (though some works which are fountainheads and/or summations of widespread tendencies will also have to be taken into particular account when discussing a particular historical period). Further, it is also possible to use the intertextual approach to discuss central fictional devices – in SF, for example, the novum, the estrangement, the protagonist or certain themes crystallizing as sub-genres.

2. IDEOLOGICAL DOMINATION *VS.* THE NOVUM: THE RANGE OF SF

What, then, are the central characteristics of that formally and historically defined set of texts which I identified as Victorian SF in *VSF*? I have argued in *MOSF* that SF in general – through its long history in different contexts – can be defined as a literary genre whose necessary and sufficient conditions are the presence and interaction of estrangement and cognition, and whose main formal device is an imaginative framework alternative to the author's empirical environment, and that it is distinguished by the narrative dominance or hegemony of a fictional 'novum' (novelty, innovation) validated by cognitive logic. At the same time, I suggested that the notion of an ineluctably historical novum implies that SF in any particular period will only be understandable by integrating socio-historical into formal knowledge. Further, Angenot has rightly remarked that ' "the author's empirical environment" cannot be understood directly, that it is necessarily mediated by epistemic categories, so that it presupposes, outside the text, the contradictory whole of the social discourse' – in particular, taking into account both intertextuality and institutional status (Angenot, 1980, p. 651).

If an SF narration hinges on the presence of a novum which is to be cognitively validated within the narration, then this novelty has to be explained in terms of the *specific* time, place, agents and cosmic-cum-social totality of each narration – i.e., in terms of its 'possible world'. This means that, in principle, SF has to be judged – like 'realistic' fiction and quite unlike mythological tales, fairy tales and horror or heroic fantasy – by the richness, consistency and relevance of the relationships presented in any narration. In this chapter I shall focus on *consistency*, as an already fundamental criterion for analysis.

In a seminal theoretical essay, 'The Absent Paradigm', Marc Angenot has further shown that all SF tales suggest – in the very act of their reading as traced out in the text – the existence of a both delusive and indispensable 'elsewhere', a missing or phantasmatic paradigm (in the semiotic sense) bodying forth a differing world. The SF tale is constantly 'shifting the reader's attention from the syntagmatic structure of the text to a delusion which is an important element of the reader's pleasure' (Angenot, 1979, p. 12). This carries important implications. If the suggested alternative world, or the alternative formal framework, is not suggested *consistently* – if, that is, the discrete syntagmatic novelties are not sufficiently numerous and sufficiently compatible to induce a coherent 'absent paradigm', or indeed if the novelty is, without regard for its logically to be expected consequences, co-opted and neutralized into the current ideological paradigm – then the reader's specific SF pleasure will be mutilated or destroyed. 'An immanent aesthetics of SF is implied here: if the mechanical transposition of "this-worldly" paradigms is sufficient to account for every narrative utterance, we have a witless, even infantile, type of SF' (ibid., p. 116 *et passim*).

This tallies astoundingly well with an only recently published lecture of H. G. Wells's, 'Fiction About the Future', in which he distinguished (to use present-day terms) between the SF story 'at the lowest level', a middle range of SF, and its highest form. Wells begins with the necessity of achieving 'the illusion of reality . . . the effect of a historical novel . . . a collaboration [with the reader] in make-believe'. He then focuses on the propensity of the SF writer whose imagination breaks down to 'pretend that all along he was only making fun': this is why so much SF 'degenerates into a rather silly admission of insincerity before the tale is half-way through'. The lowest level of SF, he ironically notes, stops at the superficial or defensive 'first laugh' which is implied in the strangeness of 'every new discovery':

> Suppose – which is probably quite within the range of biological possibility – that a means is discovered for producing children – and feminine children only – without actual fathers. . . . Don't . . . probe into the immensely interesting problems of the individual or mass psychology that it would open up, but just suppose it done. Then you have the possibility of a comic, manless world. In order to be really and easily funny about it, you must ignore the fact that it would change the resultant human being into a creature mentally and emotionally different from ourselves. That would complicate things too much. You must carry over every current gibe at womanhood, jokes about throwing stones, not keeping secrets, lip-stick and vanity bags, into the story, and there you are.   (Wells, 1980, p. 249)

The middle range of SF comes about if the writer carries out his hypothesis 'to the extent of trying to imagine how such a possibility would really work' – how would women grow up and live in a manless world: 'That would be a much more difficult book to write; it would probably lose itself in dissertations and unrealities, but it would be a much finer thing to bring off if you could bring it off.' However, 'the highest and most difficult form' – and Wells wryly confesses that he has never written one – would be an account of the *struggle* between opposed opinions, values and social groups that constituted the change in human relations as a consequence of the novum (here, directed parthenogenesis). That would have to be a full-blown novel rather than his own 'romances or pseudo-histories', probably narrowed down to a small group of figures (ibid., pp. 247–9). One does not have to agree with all of Wells's details (there are other forms of evasive inconsistency besides 'I was only making fun', for example, the 'dissertations and unrealities' he also mentions; nor does one have to accept the usual self-disparagement of his SF 'romances') to see both how closely this agrees with the results of present-day narratology and, more importantly, how useful it is for an analytic grouping of the texts

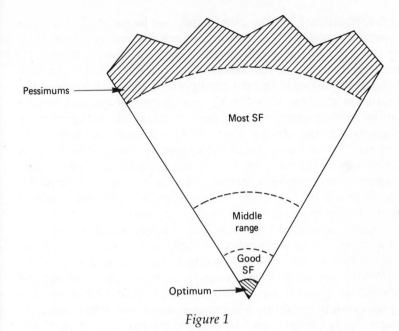

Figure 1

(As all models, this could be improved upon; for example, it should be a three-dimensional cone, not a fan.)

themselves. Wells, too – and who better qualified? – is here, clearly, pleading for logical stringency and consistency in developing the implications of the novum.

To systematize such leads: there is an immanent aesthetics to (at least the novel-size) SF tales, which fuses formal and value criteria. It can be represented as a fan-shaped spread with two limits, the optimal and the pessimal (see Figure 1).

In the *optimum*, a sufficiently large number of precisely aimed and compatible details draw out a sufficiently full range of logical implications from the central SF novum and thus suggest a coherent universe with overall relationships that are – at least in respect of the thematic and semantic field associated with the novum – significantly different from the relationships assumed as normal by the text's addressees. The narrative details (narremes) will therefore be neither too sparse, nor too disparate, nor too circumscribed. In order to bring about the most effective estrangement, their arrangement will, on the other hand, not be too explicit nor too repetitive, but will slyly enlist the reader's imaginative activity to fill in the gaps in the paradigm and create an 'illusion of reality', analogous to that of the historical or 'realistic' novel, by a wise balance of the posed and the presupposed. In such best cases, the balance or shuttling allows the SF estrangement to feed back into the reader's own presuppositions and cultural invariants, questioning them and giving him/her a possibility of critical examination. In optimal SF, the interaction of the vehicle (relations in the fictional universe) and the tenor (relations in the empirical universe), makes therefore for the reader's parabolic freedom: *this freedom is rehearsed, traced out and inscribed in the very act of reading, before and parallel to forming a conceptual system.* As Wells suggested, such a freedom is somehow connected both with personal relationships and with power-conflicts of social groups: a consistent narrative logic is not only formal but also informed by ethics and politics. Since freedom entails the possibility of something truly different coming about, the distinction between the consistent and inconsistent novum (as a special case of the distinction between a true and fake novum) is, interestingly enough, not only a key to aesthetic quality in SF but also to its ethico-political liberating potentiality. Finally, as of the nineteenth-century capitalist industrialization, the only consistent novelty is one that constitutes an open-ended or dynamic system (which will be argued further in the first chapter of Part Three).

If there is only one ideal optimum, there are several ways of falling short of it. Here, these worst cases can be divided into *the banal, the incoherent, the dogmatic* and *the invalidated pessimum.* In the banal pessimum – probably the most widespread type of SF tale – the narrative details or elements that deal with the novum are too sparse or too circumscribed. They are drowned in the non-SF details and/or plot gimmicks of a *banal* mundane tale – adventure story, love story, etc. Wells's lecture focuses on the SF being drowned in joke or whimsical inconsequentiality, a peculiar mode characteristic of English class snobbery from the seventeenth century on, and as such not without importance for Victorian SF. Beyond a certain minimum of SF narrative elements, the tale ceases to be SF and becomes another genre which contains a localized SF element that does not determine the tale's dominant narrative logic.[5]

In the second pessimum, the narrative details may be too disparate, and then the tale is just not clearly focused. In that case, genological judgments become difficult, relying as they do more on the writer's guessed-at intention than on the *incoherent* execution.

The third, *dogmatic* pessimum is (in different ways) the obverse of the first two. In it, the narremes are too explicit or too repetitive, so that the reader's return to the workaday world does not pass through an imaginary aesthetic paradigm. On the contrary, the reader is referred directly to the relationships in the empirical environment (which, conversely, severely limits the possible Other in the tale, the kind and radicality of the novum employed). In other words, these empirical relationships are redeployed so as to present merely a different conceptual grid or general idea. While a conceptual ideological field is always to be found in a work of fiction, it is (at the latest from the French Revolution on) in the significant cases not a static, preordained substitute for a specifically fictional insight or cognizing, but a questioning or problematic 'attitudinal field' *within* the overall fictional cognition. In significant SF this means that the novum will, as explained above, allow for the reader's freedom – in literary terms, that the story will be not a project but a parable. Any SF tale that is not a parable but a linear or panoramic inventory correlative to a general conceptual grid – most clearly the static utopias of the nineteenth century – thus to a degree partakes of non-fiction (of political, technological or other kind of blueprint) and loses to that degree the flexibility and advantages of fiction. If in the first pessimum a banal plot is almost all there is to the tale, in this third pessimum the conceptual blueprint does not allow for interaction with the plot: the plot is here merely so that the reader should traverse the blueprint, and the narration has constant trouble with balancing events and lectures. (It follows from this that all uses of SF as prophecy, futurology, program or anything else claiming ontological factuality for the SF image-clusters, are obscurantist and reactionary at the deepest level – for example, all of Cabet and most of Bellamy, much of Gernsback's and Campbell editorial policies, von Däniken and Manson, Scientology and Future Shock (see Elkins (1979); Nudelman (1979); Parrinder (1980)).

Finally, the *invalidated* pessimum is akin to the banal one and competes with it for the lead in SF statistics. However, it is more sophisticated: instead of the narrative details being quantitatively insufficient, they are qualitatively unsatisfactory in that they oscillate between a cognitive and a non-cognitive or anti-cognitive validation – in genological terms, between SF and fantasy, fairy tale or kindred metaphysical genres. The details are plentiful indeed, in a way too plentiful: for the strategy here is to induce in the reader an ambiguity concerning the status of the fictive novum inside the story. Is it explainable as a set of logical events on the same level as the story framework, or is it a delusion, dream or irruption of another level with different laws? An unambiguous decision for the second possibility would remove the story from SF and into delusional or horror fantasy, or into similar genres. The constant switching of indications and presuppositions, however, prevents any de-ambiguation and maintains a permanent hesitation between physical and metaphysical explanation. As the first pessimum is characteristic for British literature, so this last one is for US and French literature (for example, much of Poe, and Maupassant's 'Le Horla'). The estrangement is stressed but cut off from cognition or feedback into the reader's empirical world. Instead of a parable, the invalidated tale amounts at best to an unclear symbol suggesting the uncognizability of the reader's empirical reality. Like the old-fashioned and 'realistic' banal pessimum, it finally proclaims that the novum was not meant seriously; but it is a glossy, modernistic, non-mundane, occultist banality, whose model has advanced from the surface-world of joyous market competition to the more threatening mysteries in the hidden depths of the commodity logic.

All the pessimums, then – the broad peripheral arc of the SF genre envisaged as a fan – amount to the hegemonic ideology denying, repressing, circumscribing, dispersing, invalidating or otherwise neutralizing – and thus incorporating or coopting – the cognitive novum and the parable that allows estrangement to feed back into the reader's empirical environment.[6] In all cases, the novum is prevented from full logical development and full narrative domination; to use Fourier's appropriate term, the 'totally divergent' desire and cognition have been prevented. The wolf has been turned into a lapdog: tameness is all. Only the safe – indeed the deliciously titillating – memories of wolfdom are sometimes allowed to show through the dog.

No doubt, there is a middle range in between these good and bad extremes (which are ideal types rather than actually existing tales). One should in practice be thinking of how these models mingle and contaminate in each particular case. In the (inadequate) topological metaphor of the fan, most tales will be in a broad band say two-thirds of the way outward from the optimal fulcrum (see Figure 1), a minority in the central 'middle range', and a few, singular exceptions near the optimum. This state of affairs seems to me the handiest description of modern SF, from the rise of the commodified literary *epistémé* suggested in the introductory essay to this book and to the present day.[7]

(Originally published in 1982)

NOTES

1. This essay was originally written as an introduction to a much larger interpretive study of SF in the UK from 1848 to 1886, now Part II/C of *VSF*. Therefore, a number of details in the essay's second section (for example, those particular four pessimums) obviously apply directly only to the Victorian SF 'macro-text'. I trust none the less that even this section can help to both exemplify and develop the general theoretical approach to narrative logic and intertextuality of the essay's first section.
2. See for the following discussion Angenot (1982); Bellert (1972) (with further bibliography); and Ducrot (1972). See also Angenot, 'Paradigm'; *Communications*, no. 16; van Dijk (1976); Groupe Mu (1970); Lotman (1977); Segre (1974); Vološinov (1973); and Williams (1977). All these, and further titles adduced in this chapter, refer to the Bibliography.
3. Williams (1980) p. 23, quoting Lucien Goldmann.
4. See Angenot (1979 and 1983); Culler (1981); Jameson (1981); Jenny (1976); Kristeva (1966); Petöfi and Franck (1973); Stalnaker (1974); and Wilson (1975).
5. See a longer argument in Suvin (1978).
6. Beside the literary aspect, discussed theoretically in Williams (1977), and historically for paraliterature (beginning with Sue) in Marx and Engels (1956–68), Eco (1978), Angenot (1975 and 1978), and *VSF*, see on co-opting Marcuse (1966 and 1972).
7. See for this crucial problem-expanse of fiction and discourse in our age of market commodification the fundamental opus of Walter Benjamin (only a small part of which is available in English), in particular *Baudelaire* (1973); also Sohn-Rethel (1971); Jameson (1971); and some caveats in Williams (1977). I approached this area in *VSF*, 'Discours' (1985) and 'Commodities' (1985).

6

The SF Novel as Epic Narration: For a Fusion of 'Formal' and 'Sociological' Analysis

The preceding essays, dealing both with technical tools of narratology and indispensable value-judgements springing from the reading interests of given social groups, might have established the necessity to characterize SF texts by some ways of fusing these two approaches. As sundered in most criticism today, such approaches are – rather imprecisely – often labelled 'formal' and 'sociological'; taking a cue from linguistics, it would be better to call them 'syntactic' and 'pragmatic', since their necessary overlap in the intermediary 'semantic' or meaning-bestowing approach would then become apparent. This whole book arises out of a conviction – itself a feedback from the experiences culminating in Russia from 1910 to 1930 and retraversed in my previous work – that only such a fusion can lead to encompassing and verifiable positions. The formal, or better syntactical, approach can only be undertaken once we have decided which are the significant forms to be privileged as objects of our investigation; that decision necessarily intervenes into the text from 'outside'. The sociological, or better pragmatic, approach cannot bring to bear a social context on any proposition before we have decided which contextual elements or presuppositions are pertinent (cf. Prieto, 1975) to given textual aspects or positions; that decision interrogates the context from 'inside' the text. In fact, this chapter wishes to put into question the very metaphor of an 'inner' textual space closed off against the 'outer' world like a walnut or an orange. Such organicist metaphors are a fossil remnant from Romanticism. True, the great Romantics' shell-shocked encapsulation into a totally different aesthetic reality – a besieged fortress of the human heart – had good reason in the face of heretofore unknown alienating powers of mass capitalism.

But it is equally true that the market economy set free previously unseen productive potentialities. The interaction of the achievement with the price of the bourgeois age must therefore be carefully examined in each particular case, in the tradition of searching for its underlying truth so well established by Tocqueville and *The Communist Manifesto* (cf. on their pertinence Angenot and Suvin (1980), and Suvin, 'Le Discours' (1985)). This holds eminently for the rise of mass literary forms, such as SF, and in particular the SF novel.

The question of pertinent beginnings to SF is not only entirely dependent on its definition, but also recomplicated for the particular case of the SF novel. In the wake of the well-known positions of Eliot, Lukács and Benjamin, I argued in *MOSF* (as well as in Chapter 3) that genre traditions are legitimately established in retrospect and that SF can in that sense be said to begin at the latest with Plato and the Hellenic marvellous voyages and utopias (already satirized as a brittle repetition by Lucian, and later sublated by More). However, even if this is accepted, the tradition of the novel in the strict sense (as different from the anatomy, the romance, the short story and similar narrative forms) does not fully fuse with that of the SF genre until the second half of the nineteenth century (cf. *VSF*). I am therefore neglecting here such formally impure precursors of the SF novel as Samuel Gott's *Nova Solyma* (1648), Robert Paltock's *Peter Wilkins* (1750), Mary Shelley's *Frankenstein* (1818) or C. I. Defontenay's extraordinary *Star ou Psi de Cassiopée* (1854). If it is certainly incorrect to say that SF, even in the strictest sense, begins with Jules Verne and H. G. Wells, a case could be made for saying that *the SF novel*, if it does not begin then, at least becomes sustained and indeed dominant with these Dioscuri. My investigation will therefore begin with Wells. Further, it will be limited to a corpus of 13 novels written for a similarly wide or 'mass' readership from several social classes which arises in the age of high capitalism with its compulsory universal literacy, mass newspapers (and other forms of mass communication), global imperialisms and revolutionary movements against them, increasingly violent and widespread power-struggles culminating in World Wars, etc. – an age which is at its outset well characterized by Wells's *The War of the Worlds* in 1898.

The SF novels I have chosen – with inevitable simplification – as representative for world trends in the ensuing three-quarters of a century are (with date of first book publication unless otherwise indicated): H. G. Wells, *The War of the Worlds* (1898); H. G. Wells, *The First Men in the Moon* (1901); Evgeniy Zamyatin, *We* (*My*, written 1920); Olaf Stapledon, *Sirius* (1944); Isaac Asimov, *The Foundation Trilogy* (1951–3); Frederik Pohl and C. M. Kornbluth, *The Space Merchants* (1953); Ivan A. Yefremov, *Andromeda* (*Tumannost' Andromedy*, 1958); Robert A. Heinlein, *Stranger in a Strange Land* (1961); Stanisław Lem, *Solaris* (1961); Philip K. Dick, *Martian Time-Slip* (1964); Arkadiy N. and Boris N. Strugatsky, *Snail on the Slope* (*Ulitka na sklone*, magazine and anthology publication 1966–8); John Brunner, *The Jagged Orbit* (1969); Ursula K. Le Guin, *The Dispossessed* (1974). I am very conscious that other significant novels could be found – and are indeed discussed as such in my Part Three – but having done some homework on them, I think they would not change the broad overview which I am attempting here. It will be focused on two complementary elements of the SF novel which are so crucial that they permit some meritorious discussion of its 'formal' and 'sociological' aspects and of their inter-relation: extensively, on the *novum as plot generator*; and intensively, on the *ending*.

1. My argument starts with the *MOSF* conclusion that SF is distinguished by the narrative hegemony of a fictitional yet cognitive novum – a term adapted from Bloch to mean a totalizing phenomenon or relationship deviating from the author's and implied addressee's norm of reality. The (as yet) Unknown or Other introduced by the novum is the narrative's formal and cognitive *raison d'être* as well as the generator, validation and yardstick of its story or plot (*siuzhet*). Such a novum has as its correlate a fictional alternate reality, centred on deviant relations of the narrative agents to each other and to their world, and resulting in a different chronotope – different relationships developing in narrative time and space. Born in history and judged in history, the novum has an ineluctably historical character. So has the correlative fictional reality or possible world which, for all its displacements and disguises, always corresponds to the wish-dreams and nightmares of a specific sociocultural class of implied addressees. Finally, the novum can be differentiated according to its degree of magnitude (from one discrete new 'invention' to a whole radically changed locus and agents), according to the cognitive believability of its validation, and according to its degree of relevance for a given epoch and class of readers.

What consequences has such a premise for the plot structure of significant SF novels? Lotman has posited that all fictional texts can be thought of as lying on a spread between the extremes of mythological structure with cyclical world-time and (to adapt him) epic structure with developing world-time.[1] I would build on this to say that modern SF is then – in proportion to its meaningfulness – under the hegemony of the epic. True, this general finding can be resolved into a more complex set of situations. Some significant novels (Zamyatin's *We*, Stapledon's *Sirius*, Lem's *Solaris*) are noticeably influenced by the mythological 'revelation-as-inventory' or cataloguing technique, which uses a list of names as a fixed and limited type of cognition, and which is, as a rule, borrowed by SF through antecedents in utopian fiction. But even these novels can only organize their resulting descriptive panoramas by means of some variant of the epic adventure or voyage-of-discovery plot. In these cases, it is the frequent SF variant of the 'adventure of an idea' as it affects the protagonist and as it is, in fact, elucidated in his consciousness. In the above three novels this elucidation is, respectively: D-530 'discovering' he has a soul, Sirius discovering the dead-end character of the split between senses and intellect, Kelvin pursuing in spite of all a wary 'Holy Contact' with the Solaris Ocean. Correlative to such a plot is the unavoidable timeless instant or moment of epiphany, the obligatory scene in each of these narratives: D's intoxicating moment in the 'Ancient House', Sirius's 'hound of the spirit' letter, Kelvin's quasi-handshake with the Ocean. Each of them can only be arrived at as culmination of a richly orchestrated rhythm of *historical time* flowing, eddying, meandering and rushing forth. Only such a world-time, that limns the new configurations of reality in both inner and outer space, can validate the transcending vision as a this-wordly, inescapable and thus truly cognitive insight – as Bloch's intramundane transcendence ('innerweltliche Transzendenz': Bloch, 1959) – rather than an *a priori* dogma pretending to mythological status or a private impression. The chronicling of a unique series of events pivoting on the novum – instead of and as opposed to the mythic reconfirmation of cyclic processuality – demands a text connecting the addressee's Self with the Other. Therefore, an SF novel will (again in proportion to its meaningfulness) represent spatial and historical configurations as partly but irreconcilably different from the norm dominant in the author's age. The unity-in-diversity of a novel will, of course, demand that such agents and relationships be metaphorically or metonymically related. However, the real alternatives and choices of the 'epic' novel, teleologically connected with the unforeseeable outcome of the story in terms of success or failure of the central values (usually, of the protagonist), will refuse the mythological homeomorphy where all cycles and all agents are, centrally, such transformations of each other which can bring forth neither truly new values nor a hesitation as to the empirical success of existing values.

The magnitude and relevance of the SF novum is therefore crucially testable by the quality of the 'other' agents and relationships developed in the novel. My first example will confront the two novels by Wells. The Martians from *The War of the Worlds* are described in Goebbelsian terms of repugnantly slimy and horrible 'racial' alienness and given the sole function of bloodthirsty predators (a function that fuses genocidal fire-power – itself described as an echo of the treatment meted out by the imperialist powers to colonized peoples – with the bloodsucking vampirism of horror fantasies). This allows the reader to observe them only from the outside, as a terrifying object-lesson of the Social-Darwinist 'survival of the fittest'. These aliens are less developed, they repose upon less well explained and less mature presuppositions and they are more subsumed under sensationalist scaremongering, than Wells's aliens from *The First Men in the Moon*. No doubt, the Selenites are grotesque and, what is more, potentially dangerous – as any species or culture when menaced. Yet they finally approach the status of a subject on its own and can thus serve not merely as a rod with which to chastise the complacent Victorian bourgeois but also as an alternate reality with its own inner logic. That fictional reality's premises and values are testable in their effects – in this case, the insectoid biological specialization as a satirical analogue to social class and caste in the author's empirical actuality. Correlatively, the two awkward narrators from *War of the Worlds*, one too much involved and one too little involved in the events for cognitive purposes, are here recast into the significant oppositions of and interrelations between Bedford the 'imperial' adventurer and Cavor the 'pure' scientist.

For a second example I shall compare Asimov and Dick to the detriment of the former. The future previsions of Hari Seldon in Asimov's *Foundation Trilogy* are based upon the certitudes of 'psycho-history', an imaginary discipline supposed to be applying mathematical quantification to 'the reactions of human conglomerates' and thus to turn history and social psychology into a nineteenth-century-type of natural science – a poor man's version of 'vulgar Marxism' or Saintsimonism or a 'hard' form of futurology. Furthermore, this psycho-history is grafted upon the Spenglerian historiosophy of rise and fall of civilizations treated as monolithic individuals whose unavoidable, quasi-biological rhythms it can merely shorten. On the contrary, the 'decline and fall' previsions of the supposedly autistic boy, Manfred, in Dick's *Martian Time-Slip* grow out of a complex network of emblematic but closely pursued relationships between the politically powerful and powerless, the employers and employees, the men and women within an exemplary community. Similar to the example of *The First Men in the Moon*, in the course of the political and psychological articulation of these relationships, a whole logical gamut of forms of large-scale capitalism has been richly brought into relation with the growth of paranoia, schizophrenia and a sense of reality-loss. This fulness of Dick's possible world renders such forms and their effects verifiable or falsifiable within the novel (see further discussions in Chapter 9). The novum of an alternative vision of history is here not – as in Asimov – validated by the reader's belief into or disbelief of determinism, that is, on a purely ideological level. In Dick, the necessarily present conceptual categories can be judged within the fictional – imaginary but analogically applicable and therefore verisimilar – reality of representative agential relationships. This is what separates aesthetic cognition from fictional repetition of pre-existing, ideologized conceptual systems (in Asimov much poorer than in Wells's *War of the Worlds*).

These discussions point to the fact that a seemingly most 'intrinsic' or 'formal' analysis of significant SF novels cannot fail to use the concepts of *verisimilitude or believability*, and thus may be equally considered as partaking of an 'extrinsic' or 'socio-political' analysis. The paradox is only apparent: the SF novel, arising as it does in a genre 'at the outer limits of desire' (to adapt a phrase by Frye) and functioning, therefore, as a parabolic mirror to empirically possible relationships, simply shows most clearly that the compromise or balance between these two approaches – perhaps best codified in the Wellek-Warren *Theory* – is no longer a fruitful analytical tool or ideological horizon.

2. The novum may be conveniently materialized into the Aliens or the Future (which, by the way, often stand for each other, as alternative signifiers for the same signified: Wells's Martians are identical to his evolutionary 'Man of the Year Million'). But even then, the novum as a totalizing category can only be properly judged after a thoroughgoing analysis of each novel's syntagmatics. On the contrary, the *ending* is a short and relatively unambiguous segment of narrative, and lends itself more readily to a synoptic view and to exemplifying the novel's overall paradigm.

The ending is, of course, that special and often crucial segment of the story in which it both retrospectively makes sense of all the preceding segments and leaves the reader with a built-in directive of how to apply the reading to empirical actuality. Generally, it can be said that every coherent narrative is a system whose elements are unified by partaking of a common model or paradigm of relationships. But the epic *vs.* mythological distinction operates here with a vengeance. The epic events must be presented as historically contingent and unforeseeable (and thus as a rule historically reversible), while the mythological events are cyclical and predetermined, foreseeable descents from the timeless into the temporal realm. The verse or prose epic has, so to speak, foregrounded the plot, which was a foregone conclusion in mythology. In this epic plot, best developed in the novel, 'the "before" causally determines the "after", and the series of such determinations cannot be retraversed backward . . . but, according to the epistemological model by which we explain our empirical world, it is irreversible'.[2] Thus, an epic text, as distinct from a mythological one, will be meaningful only if each syntagmatically successive element is the result of an axiological paradigmatic *choice*, as opposed to axiologically pre-established or automatized sequentiality. That choice constitutes the poetry of post-mythological prose, opposed to the myth's incantatory repetitions of names. Choice shapes the agential relationships within the narration in unforeseeable and therefore potentially new and better ways. It is the precondition for a narrative rendering of freedom. The ending is so crucially important because it is, in principle, the place where *the sum of all the narrative choices* reaches its textual end-result, and from which all these choices can be retrospectively valorized. In mythological texts, there is no proper beginning or ending; obversely, as Aristotle remarked, the presence of a genuine beginning, middle and end defines a post-mythological text (so that 'epic' in this sense, as Brecht saw, includes drama).

Within such epic textuality, various historical ideologies have tended to stress the significance of one of these segments. Lotman remarks that in dominant medieval ideology it was the beginnings (whether an event came from God and how) which were most important. It is probable that the importance of endings, triumphing in Boccaccio and Renaissance laicization, denotes the rise of this-wordly success as the dominant ideology and validation in the textual cause-and-effect system (homologous to the new extra-textual system). In modern times, right-wing philosophy has proclaimed with Heidegger that 'the beginning is greater', and left-wing philosophy with Lenin's *Philosophical Notebooks* that 'the truth is not in the beginning but in the end, or better in the continuation' (Faye, 1972, pp. 77–8). In SF novels, again more explicitly and testably than in most other genres, the ending is the moment of truth for the novum's cognitive validation and the narrative's believability – for the coherence, richness and relevance of the text as significant SF.

Whereas the mythological structure is cyclically closed, the epic structure, ideally, should be open-ended.[3] However, socio-historical practice and ideologies constricted and even modified such an ideal type into a number of ending-types spanning the whole formal gamut. In SF, Verne's novels are almost perfect examples of a closed cyclical trajectory, allotting to the novum, paradoxically, a central but transient function and finally expunging it at all costs – including melodrama and even the breakdown of cognitive validity (often a natural catastrophe as an almost literal *deus ex machina*). I have argued in *MOSF* how this corresponds to the ideological paradox of Verne's 'utopian liberalism'. Wells made an aesthetic form out of ideological hesitations and fence-sitting about the radically Other. In *War of the Worlds* he used the conquering bacteria as a *deus ex machina* comparable to Verne's (but shifted from spatial physics into evolutionary biology), while in *The First Men in the Moon* he allowed an open ending to emerge from the complementarity of his two narrators' fate. In the wake of Wells and Dostoevsky, the plot of *We* still follows the late Realist trajectory described by Lukács as the hero's existential failure turned into the novel's aesthetic success. However, the root of Zamyatin's novel, written in the quintessentially 'chronicle' or epic form of modern science, the lab notes, as well as the unresolved public oppositions in *We* between entropy and permanent revolution, leave the reader with a hint of fragile open-endedness. The hero has noticed, agonized over, and finally been crushed by the devolved revolution frozen into entropy, by the reason irrationally fixed and impoverished into basic arithmetics and geometry (without the square root of -1). Yet his dystopian fate is perhaps an awful warning rather than the final defeat of the fiery novum of revolutionary desire: for there is no final number, and 0–90 is with child. A cognate ideological stance in *Sirius* registers the tragic destruction of the protagonist as an arrested balance between individual and society, between the novum of Sirius's alien intelligence and the unready world of repressive Britain; this balance is then rather disappointingly glossed as the biological dichotomy between the animal and the spiritual, which impoverishes the issues of the novel.

After the Second World War, the immense expectations raised by modern economics, politics and technology since the Russian Revolution and the New Deal have resulted in an overwhelming ideology of material open-endedness. This has also led to the hegemony of epic structuring in both main brances of the 'mass' SF novel, the Anglo-American and the Slavic. One could perhaps argue against this by pointing to the predominance of satirical-cum-dystopian SF in Čapek and much Lem, in the English language market from Orwell to the 1960s, and in many of the best Soviet texts (for example, in the Strugatskys' or in Varshavsky's later phases). However, I do not believe this argument would hold. On the contrary, the central device of these 'new maps of hell' (Amis, 1975) is to impress on the addressee that they are to be understood as black. The reader can only feel that these closed horizons are hellish (and not mythologically natural or even paradisiacal – as they are, for example, in Plato's *Republic* and most classical utopias) against an assumed bright background which is not only a thinkable alternative but an overriding human necessity in the name of which the dystopian reality is simultaneously perceived and judged. All the writers of more recent SF arose out of an open-ended tradition (often present in their own opus too), and the significant SF texts inflected toward dystopia also contain utopian elements, however banalized, perverted and co-opted: the psycho-historical rebuilding of the Galactic Empire in *The Foundation Trilogy*, the unspoiled

Venus as the alternative to polluted and admass-run Earth in Pohl and Kornbluth's *Space Merchants*, the 'grokking' transcendental psychosexual togetherness in Heinlein's *Stranger in a Strange Land*, the Rousseauist noble savages and the ineradicable decency of the little people in *Martian Time-Slip*, the 'sentimental materialism' of both protagonists in the Strugatskys' *Snail on the Slope*, the union of instinct and reason in Brunner's *Jagged Orbit*. The endings, then, will be defined by how they reconcile the principle of hope and the principle of reality. On the one hand, this can be shaped as a predetermined detection-adventure plot returning to mythological closure (Asimov) or as ideologized pulp escapism jettisoning the dystopic verisimilitude (Pohl–Kornbluth and Heinlein). On the other hand, this can be shaped into a more mature polyphony envisaging different possibilities for different agents and circumstances, and thus leaving the formal closure cognitively open-ended, regardless of whether at the end of the novel the positive values be victorious or defeated (Dick, the Strugatskys, Brunner).

The ideological and economico-political open-endedness was parallelled even formally in the rebirth of optimistic, utopian works. In different forms, such works had been characteristic of much early SF but had fallen into abeyance since the 1920s. The return of utopia – first in some Slavic writers of the 1950s 'thaw' and then in the USA during and slightly after the upswing of radical questioning and hopes of the 1960s – was, however, in turn a highly significant refashioning of the tradition of utopian fiction. It was marked by that shift from static to dynamic structure for which Wells had theoretically pleaded already at the beginning of the century and which he had tried out with imperfect success in *A Modern Utopia*. Utopian fiction turned now definitely from anatomy to novel, and its voyage-of-discovery plot was enriched by a doubly new consciousness of utopia. First, utopia as the idea of a radically more perfect life was understood as something to be achieved in a spiral and ongoing development rather than brought down once and for all from the heavens of dogma, as well as something to be accompanied by constant self-critical watchfulness against the temptation of the arrested moment, of the 'verweile doch, du bist so schön' by Goethe's Faust. Second, utopia as a fictional text was materialistically understood as such rather than a pure transparency of utopia as idea. In brief, for utopia as final locus a tension was substituted between the achievable locus and the never fully reached horizon (Somay, 1984). Mythological stasis turned into epic dynamics.

The isomorphic plot of physical, spatial marvellous voyage as analogue to the ideational discovery of the protagonist has been a permanent hallmark of the utopian tradition. But where earlier upon reaching the shores of Utopia this gave way to more or less pure description, a number of the best new utopian novels use an ongoing, complexly spatiotemporal voyage as analogue to the ongoing discoveries against a dynamically receding horizon (Yefremov's *Andromeda* and Le Guin's *The Dispossessed*, also Lem's *Magellan Nebula*, the early Strugatsky texts, Piercy's *Woman on the Edge of Time*, or Robert Nichols's wonderful *Daily Lives in Nghsi-Altai* tetralogy). Correspondingly, the ending will be open, but only ambiguously, not finally so. If in the dystopian works the closure can only be understood as a non-openness, in the utopian works the revolutionary openness can only by understood as a permanent struggle against entropic closure – whether the cosmic voyage of discovery (as in Le Guin) or left to stand on its own as the vehicle of the parable (as in Yefremov).

3. Summing up, I have discussed two of the most meaningful ways to characterize significant twentieth-century SF novels. The first is a cognitive novum, narratively actualized as an epic voyage of discovery toward and through a radical Otherness, and evaluatable by the richness of relationships presented and sustained in the fictional exfoliation. The second is an ending that takes into account both the principle of hope and the principle of reality. The best SF novels can on that basis be taken as equipollent to novels in any other genre. Further, neither the narrative development of the novum nor the axiological summation possible in the retrospective from the ending can, in my opinion, be rendered justice to by an analysis which does not use the pragmatic categories of societal believability within a given cultural and ideological system, as well as the syntactic categories of formalist narratology. Both kinds of categories are required if we wish to subsume 'the formal' as well as 'the sociological' into an integral aesthetic analysis refusing both of these ghettoes and accounting for the novels' meanings to the implied addressees. A central way to such an integral analysis is the distinction between epic and mythological types of narration, with all the new lights upon plot, ending, etc. that follow from this crucial distinction. The genre specificities of SF 'at the outer limits of desire' may lend themselves well to these discussions, which are of general interest for the evolution of the twentieth-century novel and its poetics or aesthetics.

(Original version 1982)

NOTES

1. Lotman (1974), in particular the part originally published as 'O modeliruiushchem znachenii poniatii "kontsa" i "nachala" v khudozhestvennykh tekstakh', in *Tezisi dokladov vo vtoroi letnei shkole po vtorichnim modeliruiushchim sistemam* (Tartu, 1966). Let me note that Lotman concentrates on the mythological *siuzhet*, and the binary opposition to epic (though I believe it is consonant with his indications) was developed by me as stimulated by Brecht, Lukács, and Propp's *Fol'klor* and *Epos*. For a complementary discussion of SF as epic cf. Parrinder (1980).
2. Eco (1964) p. 237. Cf. for the ending also studies of narrative semiotics beginning with Shklovskii (1929); e.g., Maria Renata Mayenowa, *Poetika teoretyczna* (Wrocław, 1974); and Jan Trzynadlowski, *Rozwazania nad semiologią powieści* (Wrocław, 1976). I cannot agree with the nihilist conclusions Barthes draws from his brilliant discussion of the 'hermeneutic story' which ends in revelation of the truth, and which he – disputing Brecht – believes to be tied to individualist metaphysics (Barthes, *S/Z*, 1976, pp. 82–3, 193–4, and 58).
3. Cf. on open-endedness Brecht (1966), Lotman (1974), Eco (1967), and Suvin (1984), and for SF the pioneering essays of Jameson, 'Discontinuities' (1976) and Nudelman, 'Approach' (1976); and for different approaches Robert M. Adams, *Strains of Discord: Studies in Literary Openness* (Ithaca, NY, 1958), and Alan Friedman, *The Turn of the Novel* (New York, 1966).

7

On Teaching SF Critically*

In this book there are many things which don't exist in reality at all, I like that.

> (15-year-old German girl, 1971)

Let's be realistic, let's demand the impossible.

> (Sorbonne students, May 1968)

I see what is, and ask: why? I dream of what could be, and ask: why not? That might be called critical daydreaming.

> (SF writer, July 1979)

The following reflections address some – not all – fundamental problems pertinent to teaching SF, and are intended to open discussion of those problems.

1. A RIGHT TO DAYDREAM: A DUTY TO DAYDREAM CRITICALLY

We take it that the twin axioms of a useful approach to SF – and therefore to SF teaching – are:

(1) Whatever else SF may also be, it is primarily and centrally *narrative fiction*, literature, a literary form or genre, a set of *stories told in writing*. Methods inappropriate for understanding a story may be used to illustrate this or that element within SF, but will be fundamentally inappropriate for approaching it.

(2) Though each short story or novel is – obviously – in our

* **Co-author: Charles Elkins**

civilization written by an individual author seeking his/her own voice, fictional literature as a whole is much more complex. Social behaviour and language itself, along with literary forms and conventions, are products of past traditions, present urgencies and intimations of possible futures, as well as a collective product created by the co-operation of the writers and their public (and the middlemen in between them). Looked at as a whole, therefore, the basic purpose of fiction is to make human life more manageable, more meaningful and more pleasant, by means of selecting some believable human relationships for playful consideration and understanding ('playful' being here not the opposite of 'serious' but of 'rigid'). Methods inappropriate for considering the interaction between particular stories and the audience's common social world may be used to illuminate this or that aspect of SF, but will be fundamentally inappropriate for approaching it.

The first axiom means that fiction is a *daydream*, with which it is, in principle, necessary and pleasant to identify, because doing so educates us in unactualized possibilities and relationships between people. The second axiom means that fiction is an *articulated and collective* daydream, toward which it is, in principle, necessary and pleasant to maintain a critical distance, because doing so educates us to compare its possibilities with historical actuality.

Only both of these approaches together – that is, an aesthetic modulating from identification to critical distance and back again – make full sense of fiction. Separated, each stunts it. Together, they make for a *cognitive horizon*, which incorporates the viewer (experimenter, reader) into what is being viewed (experiment, text). Only within this horizon can the reader become truly critical, correcting her/himself on the basis of information from social practice. Only within the cognitive horizon, thus, does fiction have a chance – if written and read intelligently – to show realistically both the now-possible (believable and existing) and the now-impossible but not-forever-impossible (believable though not existing here and now) relations between people in a material world.

2. ON PARALITERATURE AS AN OPEN TENSION BETWEEN IDEOLOGY AND UTOPIA

All fiction lies between the poles of playful simulation of *utopian* (i.e. radically better) relationships and *ideological* explanation as to why relationships are as they are and can change only for the worse. As a rule, utopian presentation has to be explicit since it presents an alternative, while ideological presentation will best be served by remaining implicit, as an unargued premise that this is how things are, were, and will be. Both the cognitively utopian and the mystifying horizons are intimately interwoven in most stories, often in the same paragraph or indeed the same sentence.

If this is true for all literature, it is most evident in the case of paraliterature ('popular' or 'mass' fiction), which does not reduce this constant tension to the straitjacket of individual psychology and experience. On the contrary, paraliterature deals with the tension set up between the utopian and ideological horizons in more or less openly communal, collective terms. In this way, 'popular' narrative – and in particular, SF narrative – can be considered as the concealed truth of all modern literature, that battleground of understanding and mystification.

How did this two-headed monster literature/paraliterature arise? Historians are in substantial agreement that the complex and often contradictory development of the nineteenth century novel is intimately related to the triumph of the bourgeoisie and modern capitalism, which reshaped all areas of human life. Consider, for instance, the significant and indeed crucial change in the nature of authorship: whereas earlier a writer was working at the behest of a patron and addressing a relatively small, homogeneous readership, by the nineteenth century he/she was working on her/his own but under the influence of an economic gatekeeper (promoter, publisher, agent) and facing an impersonal, heterogeneous mass market. This market, dependent on the mass production of cheap and diverse reading material, changed literary production, the product, its distribution and its consumption. Writing became a branch of commerce; by the end of the nineteenth century, *writers had become wage earners.* Some integrated into affluent bourgeois life; others lived in garrets and eked out livings as hack writers for firms bent on capturing the mass market with its insatiable mechanisms of ephemerality and quick turnover. Mass production of fiction thrived under the tyranny of calculatingly induced and promoted fashion. Railway novels, 'penny dreadfuls', gothic and romantic fiction were mass-produced in an assembly line manner, where the writer was paid by the sheet if not browbeaten to accept a pittance for a whole manuscript.

At the same time, many bourgeois – especially in England – denounced the democratization of literature and the relative ease of access to it for the poor and working classes. Spokesmen warned against allowing the masses to waste their leisure time reading novels; they criticized those who thought the 'lower orders' responsible enough to read essays and fiction dealing with politics or religion, or those novels which favoured the lower orders at the expense of their betters. By the time of the Boston Brahmins or of Matthew Arnold, the ideologists agreed that 'real' literature was not accessible to all, that it took a degree of culture and 'taste', that only a connoisseur could appreciate it. Literature would (and should) be inaccessible to the masses. Only the initiated who possessed a certain education, social and economic status could respond appropriately to literature. Conversely, the possession of this sensibility was in itself a sign that one was a member of an elite. Culture became quite openly a mode of domination.

Caught in these developments, the writers – whether lionized by their society or consigned to oblivion – increasingly exhibited various forms of alienation. Some, such as Scott, Fenimore Cooper and Bulwer-Lytton, simply denied their vocation, preferring the title of 'gentleman'. Others, such as Dickens, George Eliot and Mark Twain, were able to write novels of high quality for a popular audience and to integrate – at a very high psychic price – into bourgeois society, while criticizing many of its aspects. Still others withdrew from the popular audience and social meanings in fiction, either by retreating into the self as the sole source for authentic experience and denying the validity of an external reality, or by treating art as pure form with its own inner logic. For these writers, the major artistic problems became technical, and their techniques, conventions, and language grew increasingly more elaborate and inaccessible to the lay reader. 'Art' was seen as a personal expression of a private vision.

However, the creator of paraliterature could afford no such luxury. She/he had to write fiction which, though the author might see it as an end in itself, could nevertheless be used by the audience to deal with the world it confronted every day. One solution to this dilemma was to write fantasy, which allowed readers to express their hopes, dreams, aggressions and lusts in symbolic terms. Such 'popular' fiction furnished an escape from the squalor and drudgery of everyday life and permitted readers a gradual release and displacement of emotional tension, which if contained might have become intolerable. At the same time, these works often drew attention to the discrepancy between the reality of their readers' lives, their ideological underpinnings, and the ideal, the utopian longing. Or the writer could furnish his/her readers with roles for identification, especially those the bourgeoisie felt necessary for maintaining the social order: ideals concretely represented by images of elegance, power, romance and success, inspiring the reader to overcome obstacles standing in the way of success or to endure what she/he could not change. Again, these depictions often underscored the tension between the reality of the present and the possibility of change.

The author of paraliterature thus expressed what her/his consumers needed or wanted to believe about everyday life or offered them an alternative to the commonplaces of routine existence in the guise of fantasy, adventure, romance, etc. Yet whatever else this author had to do, he/she had to communicate. Thus the tension between the real and the ideal, between the ideological and the utopian horizons, had to be drawn in sufficiently open terms, with formulaic plots and representative heroes. The author had to respond to the capabilities and needs of his/her audience, to name its situations in such a way as to allow it to use fiction for the pleasurable exploration of the possibilities of human relationships.

3.   ON SOME SPECIFIC CHARACTERISTICS OF SF

SF shares with other paraliterary genres some aspects very important, indeed crucial, for the teacher and student. First, a *large number of people actually read it* – regardless of the official educational requirements. Therefore, assigned texts will usually be presented to a group of students heterogeneous in respect of their previous familiarity with that kind of text: some will be familiar with whatever books are chosen, some will not. More importantly, some will have notions (sometimes strong notions) about what kind of writing – what characteristic genre or category – these books belong to.

Second, the economically and indeed anthropologically (philosophically) crucial aspect SF shares with other paraliterature is that *it is primarily a commodity*. (Every book published under capitalism is a commodity; but remnants of pre-capitalist notions of prestige, glory, etc., qualify the commodity status of much 'high lit.'.) This means that the book publishers and the TV and movie producers have to enforce certain strongly constricting lower-common-denominator cliches in strict proportion to the capital invested and profits expected (rather than to a mythical audience-taste); the constricted narrative patterns, plots, characters, language, etc., in turn prevent paraliterature from giving a full and lasting satisfaction to its consumer. However, this also means that the book-as-commodity acquires a certain financial independence of its ideological content: it will be subject to promotion, hypes, etc., and conversely it will be excused anything as long as it brings in the profits. Third, this makes for its twofold *dominant societal function*: financially, that of selling well (to many readers); ideologically, that of momentarily entertaining and pacifying its readers. This helps the social status quo both economically and politically, by addicting the reader and/or viewer to further reading/viewing for further momentary compensation (see Russ, 1978) and by defusing active or at least radical civic discontent, in favour of mass social mythologies of an anti-rational kind (see Barthes, 1970).

However, while this can be said of SF too, along with such crass ideologies this genre has also in a small minority of its most significant texts managed to preserve cognitive aspects opposed to this market ideologization (as is argued at length in *MOSF*). In its basic technique of evoking the possibility of different relationships among people (even if these are masked as nautiloids and cosmic clouds), SF breaks down the barriers of a closed and immutable world. If its action is simply a substitute for the reader's activity, if relations among its figures are simply escapist surrogates for different relations in the reader's life, then that SF is much the same as other kinds of paraliterature – ideological and mystifying. It can, however, be faulted *because* it is SF, because it wastes the chances for presenting genuinely different possibilities which are latent in the genre's basic assumptions. *Bad, mystifying SF can – and should – be criticized by criteria taken from inside the SF genre*. The universe of the SF narrative does not necessarily – in all significant cases does not – make the reader a passive escapist. The wish gratifications of SF *can* be critical of reality, even if they rarely are.

Thus, we see SF as a genre in an unstable balance between the cognitive potentialities (political, psychological, philosophical) growing out of its subversive (and historically lower-class) tradition of inverting the world, on the one hand, and, on the other hand, powerful upper and middle-class ideologies that have sterilized the bulk of its texts. This means, first, that a teacher will have to disentangle in each text the elements or aspects belonging to pleasurable cognition from those belonging to ideology, and second, that she/he will have to be severe with the latter in proportion to the chances presented by the former.

4.   ON THE GOALS OF SF TEACHING

The main and the highest goal of SF teaching – as of all teaching – ought, in our opinion, to be *a specific form of civic education*. We propose that, though SF can be used for popularizing science or religion or city planning, or for promoting cathartic togetherness, this does not do justice to its possibilities.

First, it is quite possible that SF can be used for awakening interest in science (hard or soft) or religion, in literary form or sociology, or in anything else one cares to mention. But we deny that this is its most efficacious and most fruitful use, and we therefore deny that this should be its *main* use. Second, by civic education we don't mean an instrumental use of literature and art as 'a disguise for morality or prettification of knowledge' but (to continue the quotation from Brecht's *Messingkauf Dialogues*) 'as an independent discipline that represents the various other disciplines in a contradictory manner'. This emphatically does not mean propagating uncritically any values taken for granted today. It means something that can be heard in the very word 'civic' if one listens to it carefully: that we are all *cives*, 'citizens', of the same Earthly City, which will not survive unless we learn that we all belong to one another, and that this belonging in our scientific age is to be demonstrated by understanding how the science which deals with people living together ought to inform all the other sciences. This ideal of civic education would thus be located somewhere between Jesus of Nazareth's 'Love thy neighbour as thyself' and Karl Marx of Trier's 'The world has been merely explained, the point is to change it'. But even such an ideal cannot be 'served' by SF texts; they can only be explained as (in the best cases) *in their own way* leading to it (if and when they do).

In any event, we trust that even those who do not share this goal – which we are aware of having expressed in a provocative, because abbreviated, fashion – will agree that no good teaching can come about unless the teacher in her/his daily practice knows what the goals of his/her teaching are. These goals shape the teaching from the beginning; they influence the choice of texts we teach, our scholarly and pedagogical approaches to those texts, our role as teachers and our criteria of evaluating class success. Therefore, at least in this explicit discussion, we would articulate our purposes as clearly as possible.

No doubt, a fair number of questions still remain to be asked: Who establishes these goals? If there are any conflicts over them with administration, students, parents, etc., who has the power to resolve such conflicts? How are the goals related to students' goals and to the traditional or non-traditional functions of education? And what methods are adequate to the goals desired?

5. ON OUR ROLES AS TEACHERS

SF is (as all literature) taught within an institutional context – a university, college, high school, evening school or writing course. The institutional regulations – teacher qualifications, registration fees, the category and number of students who take the course, its duration and frequency, course requirements if any, etc. – are, as a rule, basically beyond the control of the teacher and the students. Most frequently, the students can only take or refuse to take such a course, while the teacher, even should he/she consider some important regulations such as class size, composition, or timing to be stultifying, often does not have the option of refusing to hold it. The undoubtedly greater flexibility of, say, North American university teaching in the last 20 years did not change this basic context. For, institutions as well as individuals are shaped by the larger social environment within which SF is being taught, and are permeated by its values. Writers, teachers and students do not exist in a vacuum. Our attitudes toward matters dealt with by SF, and toward SF itself; our roles as teachers or students and our concepts of these roles; all of these are – to an extent much greater than most of us are willing to acknowledge – determined by the society within which we live and our relationships within that society. They are meanings and values which are organized and lived as social practices, and which constitute for us that 'reality' on which any personal variants of ours will be grafted.

In particular, we would like to put up for discussion the following propositions:

(1) SF is being taught within a particular dominant culture, which is not god-given but the result of a social choice among possible alternatives.

(2) Teaching SF either reinforces, questions, or rejects the dominant culture by (tacitly or openly) endorsing the values and norms upon which the dominant culture rests or by endorsing alternative norms and values of past, residual cultures or future, emerging cultures (see for those concepts Williams's overview in *Marxism and Literature*).

(3) The acceptance, doubting or rejection of a dominant culture will be overwhelmingly influenced by the teachers' and students' positions within that culture, their class, status, role, sex, age, financial position, etc.

None the less, for all the constraints upon us as teachers, in this age of doubt and of faltering or competing value-systems there is sometimes enough manoeuvring room for us to make our pedagogical decisions important, and thus practically and ethically meaningful. In that situation, our understanding of our own role as teachers is of crucial importance. True, our independence is most often illusory, for our role is for the most part not personally created but given by a particular social system to suit its own interests (which upon closer inspection turn out to be the interests of a particular dominant group within that society). That teaching role is then further shaped by our audience, which determines the limits of what we can intelligibly say: for all their important individual differences, our students' roles and values will produce a few groups, each of which will have its own fixed response to SF – as we have all experienced. Teaching nevertheless remains always a drama of communication, with the teacher as one of the protagonists struggling to establish meanings (cognitive cum imaginative cum emotional), to evaluate them and to communicate them to the class.

Teaching SF, we would like to propose, involves description and assessment, interpretation and evaluation; *teaching SF is an act of literary criticism fused with the communication of that criticism.* Thus, the teacher of SF is centrally dealing with the interaction between text and context, the unique literary work and the class's common social world: she/he is doing so, because even not dealing explicitly with this interaction is a very effective form, the 'zero form', of dealing with it – and 'zero form' or limiting messages get to the class most quickly ('in this class we don't do such-and-such'). In this situation, we believe it is both the more honest and the more fruitful course to relate literary production explicitly to its social meanings, so that these may be opened up to everybody's scrutiny and contestation. A first step in literary analysis, on paper or in class, is of course to identify the actual development of significant features in the story. But even this beginning is only possible because there are some prior assumptions about people and the world with which all of us approach the act of literary analysis itself. And furthermore, such an indispensable first logical step will remain useless if it is not integrated with identifying at least summarily what has been *excluded* from the text at hand. If we are dealing with an SF text where a matriarchy develops on the planet of a blue sun, a full reading of it must note that it is *not only* a matriarchy *but also* not a patriarchy or egalitarian society, that it is *not only* the planet of a blue sun *but also* not the planet of a yellow sun or any other star type (see on this technique Chapter 4). All modern sciences, from linguistics to physics, are not absolute but relational: any element in a structure receives its significance from its relative position toward and differences from other elements, whether we are speaking of a phoneme or a space/time island. In other words, against all 'positive' common sense, *a text is constituted and characterized by what it excludes as well as by what it includes.* In practice, of course, one has to start from what is in the text; but as we have just argued, it is impossible to evaluate/understand it unless by comparison with other elements – both those inside and those outside the text. In direct parallel to its value, a literary text contains its historical epoch as a hierarchy of significances *within itself.*

This means that the teacher of SF, just like the critic, cannot simply be the writer's or even the text's advocate. No doubt, he/she has to be able not only to function on the text's wavelength in order to understand it but also to point out its strengths (if it has no strengths, it should not be taught). But the teacher should, we believe, properly be neither for nor against the writer, and the cult of personalities so rife in SF should be staunchly resisted, whether we are dealing with Asimov or Le Guin. The teacher's loyalties are not even to the text, except as the text is the privileged tool of class investigation. In our opinion the teacher should finally be the advocate of the provisional yet meaningful truth and value that she/he and the class will come to at the *end* of the investigation which started from the text, but passed through its confrontation with our common social reality in order to return to the text with a full understanding of its values. Since there is no eternal truth in and by itself but only a truth-in-context and truth-for-a-historical-group, we believe *the teacher should be the advocate of an ideal non-alienated and libertarian reader who has the right to receive all the evidence of how, why and in whose interest the text has interpreted our common universe.* Such an ideal reader is only an imaginative heuristic construct, yet we believe it to be an indispensable one in order to counter both shipwreck in day-to-day pragmatic concerns and flying off at private, quite eccentric and idiosyncratic, tangents.

All of this means, in other words, that *the teacher cannot choose not to be the advocate of some values*: all presentations of human relationships (however disguised these may be in SF parables) are heavily fraught with values. The teacher can only choose which values to identify, stress or deny, and how to go about it – first of all, implicitly or explicitly. This should stand, of course, at the opposite pole from preaching or indoctrination, which would mean picking out only those value-systems one agrees with for explanation and for proclamation as valid. Though we believe the teacher should declare her/his ideological or value-positions early on in the course, he/she should have the fundamental intellectual honesty and loyalty to point out, in the discussion of any particular point, alongside those arguments she/he would agree with also the strongest arguments that could be presented against such an evaluative position. Only from this stance, practising what is 'preached', can the teacher be the advocate of the ideal libertarian reader described above.

(Originally published in 1979)

Part Three
Positions in SF Practice:
Seven Writers

8

Three World Paradigms for SF: Asimov, Yefremov, Lem

The best works of SF have long since ceased to be crude adventure studded with futuristic gadgets, whether of the 'space opera' or horror-fantasy variety. If SF is (as posited in *MOSF*) a literary genre of its own, whose necessary and sufficient conditions are the interaction of *estrangement* (*Verfremdung, ostranenie, distanciation*) and *cognition*, and whose main formal device is an imaginative framework alternative to the dominant motions about the implied addressee's empirical environment, then such a genre has a span from the *romans scientifiques* of Jules Verne to the social-science-fiction of classical utopias and dystopias. Its tradition is as old as literature – as the marvellous countries and beings in tribal tales, *Gilgamesh* or Lucian – but the central figure in its modern renaissance is H. G. Wells. His international fame, kept at least as alive in Mitteleuropa and Soviet Russia as in English-speaking countries, has done very much to unify SF into a coherent international genre. Yet, no doubt, these three major cultural contexts – discussed in this essay – their traditions and not always parallel development in our century, have also given rise to somewhat diverging profiles or paradigms for SF. I shall here briefly explore those paradigms in the most significant segment of post-Wellsian SF development, that after the Second World War.

Since a general overview of even the most compressed kind is impossible, short of a fat volume (I estimate that at the beginning of the 1970s about 200 new book titles of SF in the strictest sense are being produced yearly in the world, of which 160 are in English), I am choosing one representative example for each of the three paradigms, namely Isaac Asimov's *I, Robot* for Anglophone SF of the so-called 1938–58 'Golden Age', Ivan Yefremov's *Tumannost' Andromedy* (*Andromeda*) for the Soviet SF revival in the late 1950s, and Stanisław Lem's *Solaris* for Mitteleuropean SF. Two of the three choices should raise no methodological doubts: Yefremov's novel is universally acknowledged as not only the bearer of the Soviet SF thaw but also as the supreme achievement of its first phase, and Lem is even more universally acknowledged as the most important SF writer west of the Bug. As for Asimov, he is very probably the most popular US SF writer in the world. In a richer national and linguistic micro-climate, he is, no doubt, not as central as Yefremov and Lem are in theirs; a significant part of Anglophone SF did not share his faith in science and technocracy. However, the hypothesis of this paper is that this SF was, on the whole, characterized by a failed search for solutions outside of human creativity. If this can be substantiated for Asimov, whose optimism is seemingly at the farthest possible remove from the 'new maps of hell' of so much other US and British SF, my proof will be applicable *a fortiori* to at least the characteristic tendency for his whole generic micro-climate. I have chosen his book *I, Robot* instead of the equally famous *Foundation Trilogy* because it is more manageable, and yet not dissimilar in the final horizons (as can be seen in Chapter 6). I shall proceed with a brief analysis of the American and the Russian book and the social consciousnesses they imply, in order to end with a comparison to Lem's *Solaris*.

1. *I, Robot* (1950) is a series of 9 short stories detailing the development of robots 'from the beginning, when the poor robots couldn't speak, to the end, when they stand between mankind and destruction' (p. 192). The stories are connected thematically and chronologically, and also supplied with a flimsy framework identifying them as glances backward from 2057–58 by 'robo-psychologist' Susan Calvin; she is being interviewed after 50 years of pioneering work at US Robots and Mechanical Men, Inc., during which time the robots have won out against reactionary opposition from labour unions and 'segments of religious opinion' (p. 8). On the surface, this is a 'future history' on the model of Bellamy's sociological or Wells's biological extrapolations. It is based on two premises: first, that except for one factor, human behaviour and the social system – for example, press reporters and giant corporations – will remain unchanged; second, that the new, change-bearing factor will be the epoch-making technological discovery of 'positronic brain-paths', permitting mass fabrication of robots with intelligence comparable to human. The robots are constructed so as to obey without fail Asimov's famous Three Laws of Robotics: '1 – A robot may not injure a human being, or, through inaction, allow a human being to come to harm. 2 – A robot must obey the orders given it by human beings except where such orders would conflict with the First Law. 3 – A robot must protect its own existence as long as such protection does not conflict with the First or Second Law' (p. 6). Now Lem himself has persuasively demonstrated that such robots are *logically* unrealizable.[1] This ingenious mimicry of the Decalogue and the Kantian categorical imperative in the form of Newtonian laws cannot therefore be taken at all seriously as a basis of prophetic extrapolation, and the stories can be read only as *analogies* to very human relationships. The nine stories form a clear sequence of growing robotic capacities. In the first story, 'Robbie', an early model is mute playmate for a little girl, and functions as a huge doll – and yet, melodramatically, as the girl's saviour. In 'Runaround', the next model is a drunken servant who functions as a stereotyped plantation 'darkie'. In 'Reason', the robot is a comic-opera idolater who functions as an immature philosopher. In 'Catch That Rabbit', an adult, 'head of family' robot collapses under stress, analogous to a psychotic. The fifth and central story, 'Liar!', is a pivot in this progression of robotic power in relation to people: by now, the robot model is a telepath who is capable of turning the tables on them, and severely perturbing the life even of the leading expert Susan (incidentally, this proves the Laws of Robotics wrong). In 'Escape', the new model is a 'child genius', steering a spaceship to unknown galaxies (a feat conveniently dropped as factor of change in later stories), who behaves as a superior practical joker. In 'Evidence', a robot undistinguishable from man becomes city mayor in a career that will lead him to president of the Federated Regions of Earth. Finally, in 'The Evitable Conflict' the positronic brains have grown into not only a predicting but also a manipulating Machine 'in absolute control of our economy' (p. 192) – literally, a *deus ex machina*. Thus, this clever sequence of 'the Nine Ages of Robot' leads from the doll of the first to the god of the last story: and doll turning into god is a good approximate definition of fetishism, a topsy-turvy kind of technological religion. As in Saint-Simonism, of which it is a variant, there are no workers in Asimov's universe, the army and corporation bosses are only figure-heads, and the real lovable heroes are the efficient engineers, including Susan Calvin, the 'human engineering' expert of behaviourist psychology. In fact, all humans are cardboard stereotypes compared to the more vivid robots who act as analogies to traditional human functions. This view of the benevolent, sometimes comic but finally providential robots and their rise to absolute power amounts to a wishful parable of the socio-political result correlative to presumably perfect scientific ethics. Like Dostoevsky's Grand Inquisitor, it chooses security over freedom in post-Depression USA.

Yefremov's work is representative of another classical utopian vision which looks forward to a unified, affluent, but (different from Saint-Simonism) also classless, stateless and humanist world.[2] In *Andromeda* (1958) mankind has established informational contact with inhabitants of distant star-clusters and lives in year 408 of the Era of the Great Ring. The Earth is administered – in analogy to the associative centres of the human brain – by an Astronautic Council and an Economic Council which tallies all plans with existing possibilities. Within this framework of the body politic, Yefremov concentrates on new ethical relationships of de-alienated agents. The novel's strong narrative sweep, full of action (from a fistfight to an encounter with electrical predators and a robot spaceship from the Andromeda nebula), allots the highest value to creativity, a simultaneous adventure of deed, thought and feeling resulting in physical and ethical harmony. Even his title signifies not only a constellation but also the chained Hellenic beauty rescued from a monster (in Yefremov, class egotism and violence, often with hallmarks of Stalinism) by a flying hero endowed with superior science. Astronautics thus does not evolve into a new uncritical cult but is claimed as a humanist discipline, in one of the most significant fusions of physical sciences, social sciences, ethics and art that the novel establishes as the norm for its agents. Such a cross-connecting is also the basis of the compositional oscillation between cosmic and terrestrial chapters, where the 'astronautic' Erg-Nisa subplot is finally integrated with the 'earthly' Darr-Veda subplot through the mediation of creative beauty arising out of science allied to art (Mven-Chara and Renn-Evda). Furthermore, this future is not the arrested, pseudoperfect end of history that constituted the weakness of optimistic utopianism. Even when freed from economic and political hinderances, people must still redeem time, which is unequal on Earth and in space, through a conflictual though humanist dialectics of personal creativity and teamwork united – in a clear harking back to the ideals of the Soviet 1920s – in the beauty of functionality. This is best shown in such scenes as Darr's listening to the 'Cosmic Symphony in F-minor, Color Tone

4.75 μ' or in the catastrophic but finally vindicated 'null-space' experiment of Mven. Creativity is always countered by entropy, and self-realization paid for in effort and even suffering. In fact, several very interesting approaches to a Marxist 'optimistic tragedy' or *felix culpa* can be found in *Andromeda*; for example, the destructive experiment in Mven's 'Happy Fall' finally leads to the great advance of establishing direct contact with friendly aliens. Also, very importantly, the accent on beauty and responsible freedom places into the centre of the novel female heroines interacting with the heroes and contributing to the emotional motivation of new utopian ethics. Though their characterization is still condescending, it is in strong contrast to US SF of the time, with which Yefremov was in a well-informed polemical dialogue.

No doubt, *Andromeda* is today somewhat dated. In a number of places the novel's dialogue, motivation and tone flag. Just as in Asimov, Yefremov then tends to fall back on melodrama and the quantitatively grandiose. Where Asimov's agents are often breezily folksy, Yefremov's tend to be plaster-of-Paris statuesque. Thus, Mven blows up a satellite and half a mountain, Veda loses the greatest anthropological find ever; Erg is manly, Nisa is pure. Most of this can be explained, if not justified, by the story's having to achieve several aims at once. It was the first work to burst open the floodgates closed for 25 years, and it overflowed into clogged channels. This possesses both interesting parallels and differences to Asimov's incongruous insertion of bold speculation into the wooden prose and characterization of pulp SF (both of them build on that tradition, for example, on Hamilton). One feels in *Andromeda* as well as in *I, Robot* the presence of an unsophisticated addressee who is, as Yefremov wrote, 'still attracted to the externals, decorations, and theatrical effects of the genre' – in other words, one feels the presence of Russian respectively US clichés and taboos of the time, hindering fast orientation toward a radical novum. The difference is that while Yefremov has been allotted his proper place as a pioneer of Russian SF, Asimov is still uncritically adulated by most US fans and critics.

In sum, as *I, Robot* is a clever textualization of US engineering technocracy, so is *Andromeda* – epistemologically wedded to a naive anthropocentrism – an engaging textualization of Russian fieldwork scientism. Just as Asimov lives in the notional universe of nineteenth-century science, from thermodynamics to behaviourism, and believes in its leading ever onward and upward without basic social and existential changes, so Yefremov lives the complementary nineteenth-century view of man as subject and the universe as object of a cognition that is ever expanding, if necessary through a basic social change yet without major existential consequences. In both writers, doubt and the menace of entropy enter human life only as an external enemy – for example, the electric predators of a far-off planet in Yefremov, or the uppity 'lost robot' in Asimov. If any epistemological opaqueness ever becomes internalized in a reasonable creature, then it is a melodramatic villain (Pour Hiss in Yefremov) and simply abnormal (Cutie, the religious maniac in Asimov, whose problem is blatantly evaded).

2. A distinctively modern approach, pertinent to the age of Einstein and Eisenstein, of world wars and revolutions, began gaining ground in mass-published SF only in the 1960s. Even in the rather conservative commercial SF the realization took hold that modern human as well as natural sciences are open-ended, and that SF will be the more significant the more clearly it emancipates itself from both classical utopia and classical dystopia as static and closed paradigms. The possibilities of such sophisticated SF have so far been most closely approached by the Polish writer Stanisław Lem. The Asimov thesis that 'Man is limited and not to be trusted' (or, robots are 'a cleaner better breed than we are', p. 8), and the Yefremov antithesis 'Man is unlimited and must be trusted', are both transcended in Lem's novel *Solaris* (1961).[3] Lem's dialectical conclusion is that people are very limited and yet have to be trusted, because they are capable of understanding their limitations, and slowly and painfully evolving to a higher level.

Solaris is a scientific puzzle (as Asimov's writings are), a story about human emotions (as Yefremov's are), but also a parable showing that anthropocentric criteria and 'final solutions' of the absolutist, religious kind are inapplicable to the complex situations of modern man. As opposed to Asimov's string of short glimpses and Yefremov's polyphonic blocks, *Solaris* unfolds around a first-person narrator who is gradually and tentatively piecing together the evidence about the strange planet Solaris. The planet is completely covered by an organic Ocean; in *Summa Technologiae* Lem defined Reason or Intelligence as a 'second-degree homeostatic regulator able to counteract the perturbations of its environment by action based on historically acquired knowledge', and in that sense the Solaris Ocean is undoubtedly an intelligent entity. It finally reacts to the activity of a human research station by synthesizing for each scientist a living person, which it had in some uncomprehended way 'read off' his deepest memory encoded in the brain cerebrosides. Since that memory is – by Lem's not wholly convincing hypothesis – a trauma of erotic guilt, each scientist is visited by the woman he has in some way lost or slighted. At least – since Lem is on purpose unclear on this point – that is the case with the protagonist Kelvin and his wife Harey, who had died after being estranged from him. Much as with van Vogt's Gosseyn, the resurrected 'Doubles' (or Phantoms, as Lem calls them) are human, although the Ocean has constructed their albumens from neutrinos and not from atoms. They evince some non-human traits, such as a compulsion to stay near the 'source' person, and super-human strength when impeded in that; yet they not only possess human emotions and self-consciousness, they also quickly become socialized in human company, growing increasingly independent of the Ocean. Kris Kelvin soon becomes emotionally attached to the 'phantom' Harey as strongly as he was to his wife – though in a subtly different way.

Such a biopsychological puzzle is characteristic of a whole group of US SF tales. Lem uses this convention in a masterly way, applying its cognitive bias to the most intimate and painful personal relationships rather than to exotic xenobiological oddities. This endows his novel with its particular warmth and immediacy. However, he uses the convention also as a means to a richer, multi-level novel. The detection-mystery model suggests and connects with one of Lem's basic themes – the erroneousness of pretending to a final solution or total knowledge of any complex situation. Humans always project their mental models upon the foreign universe: on Solaris, the universe obligingly materializes one projection. Thus, the stars are for Lem in a way what Utopia was for More and Brobdingnag for Swift: a parabolic mirror for ourselves, a roundabout way to understand our world, species and times. The Ocean – the basic device of this novel – is a magician more potent than the sorcerers of Glubbdubbdrib, who materialized the past for Gulliver in order to teach him the true history of mankind. Lem's Ocean materializes, in a very Swiftian way, the central moral trauma of each person. It shows thus to Kelvin a country stranger than Solaris or Laputa: the back of his own mind. There be tygers in that country: 'we can observe, through a microscope as it were, our own

monstrous ugliness, our folly, our shame!' (p. 82) proclaims one of
Kelvin's fellow-sufferers. On the other hand, that is also the country
of lambs, indeed, of resurrection of slaughtered lambs: the age-old
dream of a second change for our mismanaged personal encounters
in the role of slaughterer or slaughtered, can also materialize on
Solaris. All depends on the particular personality: Gibarian commits
suicide, Sartorius goes into seclusion, Snout is more than half
paralysed, but the narrator-protagonist Kelvin wins through to a
painfully gained, provisional, and relative new faith in an 'imperfect
god' (p. 204). The science of solaristics as a search for the Grail of the
'Holy Contact' between cosmic civilizations has been a tragicomedy
of errors, yet the true Holy Contact between bloody but unbowed
personalities such as Kelvin's and Harey's is still possible. The
novel's *parable* aspect implies that such resurrection and contact is a
materialist rather than a spiritualist mystery, a matter of history and
earthly people rather than of abstraction and heavenly stars. It
draws its potency from some of the deepest life-affirming heresies
about human relations in European history, from the tradition
flowing through Gnostics and Joachimites to the warm utopian
socialism of Fourier and Marx.

Most noteworthy, perhaps, this is a parable without transference
or reference to any ruling system; diachronically, to Asimov's
Saint-Simonian technocracy or Yefremov's Chernyshevskian
revolutionary romanticism, or synchronically – in the Polish cultural
context – the sacred books of Yahwe or of Stalin. The truth it teaches
through its fable is an open and dynamic truth. Lem's major novels
have at their *cognitive core* the simple and difficult realization that
there is no end to history: no closed reference system, however
alluring to the weary and poor in spirit, is viable in the age of
Zamyatin's permanent revolution, of relativity theory and Gödelian
post-cybernetic sciences. Now twentieth-century sciences are
polyvalent and can be used for widely differing purposes. The only
sure thing about their methodology is that they lead into vast
unfathomed areas of new findings, techniques and orientations – to
new cognition, which gives mankind new sets of contingencies to
choose from. *Modern sciences are open-ended*, and anticipation in our
age will be the more significant the more clearly it rejects both the
classical utopia of the Plato–More type and the whilom fashionable
dystopia of the Huxley–Orwell type. Both of them are static and
closed; neither does justice to the immense possibilities of modern
SF in an age polarized between the law of large numbers and ethical

choice. Of course, SF has adopted a vaguely materialist philosophy of history ever since Wells; but without dialectics, this can easily lead back to the old antinomy of facile optimism or cynical despair. Therefore, the pet horror of the dialectical artist, Lem, is eschatology – a claim to final static perfection, be it religious in the Christian sense or a lay myth in the liberal or pseudo-Marxist way. Reliance on familiar imaginative frameworks is erroneous in radically new situations; even a whole new science such as solaristics – whose description, with all its twists and turns and a complete history of saints, heretics and buffoons, makes for some of the most brilliant pages of modern SF – can become simply a sublimation of mystic nostalgias for a final Revelation, 'a liturgy using the language of methodology' (p. 180).

This also means that the nineteenth-century image of man and world cannot be accepted as an eternal, static form. An important motif within Lem's refusal of final solutions is the stripping of illusions about human and cosmic reality. This is what makes self-knowledge so imperative; refashioning the tradition of 'educational novels' dear to Rationalism, Lem's major novels feature a single or group protagonist learning painfully the truth about himself, his limitations, and central strengths, by way of investigating a new SF situation. The puzzle-plot and the parable form both flow organically out of this central concern for a Copernican or Brunoan dethroning of anthropocentric theory. Man is not the measure of all things except for other people, and human mental models cannot be usefully projected on to the universe. It is especially pitiful, Lem notes, to limit the possibilities of new worlds to the anthropomorphic role of our rulers or our subjects – a swipe at western SF projecting the Cold War into cosmic warps.

One might call this enmity of Lem's to the two-valued either-or logic and to the closed horizons of history anti-Aristotelian (in a sense much wider than van Vogt's 'Null-A' approach, which quickly bogs down into plot gimmicks). However, as Lem once remarked, if history has no beginning, middle or end, a play or novel certainly has. But the ending or upshot of a novel that is to be adequate to the open-ended cognition, demanded by modern natural and anthropological sciences, will also have to be open. Therefore, neither an Asimovian technocratic nor a Yefremovian politocratic faith prevails at the end of *Solaris*. In the final chapter, the protagonist, who came from Earth with his notebook, his apartment key and his certainties, has once and for all time been shown how useless they all are. The eschatological illusions have been shattered, man can rely only on himself and the dialectics of reality: 'I shall never again give myself completely to anything or anybody. . . . And this future Kelvin will be no less worthy a man than the Kelvin of the past, who was prepared for anything in the name of an ambitious enterprise called the Contact. Nor will any man have the right to judge me' (p. 203).

This renunciation can be sociologically traced to the bitter experiences of Central European intellectuals in this century. For Lem comes from the region, coextensive with the old Habsburg empire, which has in our century bred so many great writers attuned to the indifferent march of history: Musil and Svevo, Krleža and Andrić, Hoffmansthal and Kafka, Hašek and Čapek come immediately to mind. The baroque tradition of this environment is unmistakably present in Lem's imagination. Yet this has also been the region of great hopes, exploding after both World Wars. Lem's unique place in SF is due to his personal genius in fusing the bright hope with the bitter experience, the vision of an open road into the future with the vision of sure dangers and possible defeats inseparable from the risk of openness. This 'double vision' subverts both the 'comic inferno' approach of most American SF and the deterministic utopianism of most Soviet SF, using the strengths of both; it juxtaposes the black flickerings of the first with the bright horizons of the latter, so that each colour shows up the other. Lem's dialectics envision in each endeavour first of all its internal contradictions: he is a writer in the great tradition of *wit*, which is a shifting between different cognitive levels. No wonder his favourite book is *Don Quixote*, and the epoch that haunts him is the seventeenth and eighteenth centuries. If Kelvin is at the end of the novel a wiser and a sadder man, sadness has been a high but perhaps not unfair price to pay for the wisdom gained. It is expressed in theological terms by the final parable of 'the imperfect god . . . whose ambitions exceed his powers' (p. 204). We may disagree with Lem philosophically, but we have seen too many alluring gods of history turn into all-devouring monsters because of their pretended infallibility to shrug off his insight. National and religious ideologies of all kinds are still too much with us for that. The brightest hopes of humanity, we know, are liable to degenerate into justifications for the Inquisition, the Stalinist purges, or the My Lai massacres and the organizing of assassinations of Nicaraguan peasants. The imperfect, despairing, but also evolving god is a concept close to the 'Star Maker' of Stapledon, one of the rare SF writers Lem admires and is comparable to in scope. This cosmological metaphor as insight, correlative to the earlier quoted ethical declaration of independence, is what Lem's protagonist Kelvin has provisionally learned from the planet Solaris. We, the readers, may learn more from the novel *Solaris*: we may learn how cognition can become parable – and wisdom, aesthetic pleasure. We might have begun to doubt whether SF can be equal to our often depressing but also exciting times. Lem's work is a persuasive testimony that such doubts can be laid to rest. For *Solaris* – puzzle, parable and cognition of freedom – is neither a warning nor a solution. It is an example of what science fiction can do: show us our age as 'the time of cruel miracles' (p. 211), the time of keeping a sceptical faith. As such, it is a prime witness for the regaining of a maturity which SF possessed in the best works of Wells (not to mention More, Swift or Mary Shelley) but which it had lost by consenting to be confined into the 'Indian reservation' of pulp magazines and anthologies.

Such a maturation, accompanied by a sharp rise of literary qualities, is not confined to Mitteleuropa: in and after the 1960s it can be found in such Soviet writers as the Strugatsky brothers, or such US ones as Dick, Le Guin, Disch or Delany. Yet Lem was the first and is still at least equal to the best of that group, and there is little doubt that his personal talent was decisively furthered by his cultural context. The Asimovian social consciousness is one of a neo-capitalist technocratic elite, substituting clean robots for human creativity. The Yefremovian social consciousness is one of a specifically inflected 'scientific socialism', receptive only to certain romantically codified forms of creativity. Lem's is a consciousness committed to the philosophical Left by its emphasis on human reason and creativity, and yet acutely aware of the political Left's failures and errors, of the gap between ideas and power – not only the attainment but also the wielding of power – and therefore properly sceptical. It seems to me that Lem in the 1950s and 1960s holds a position all of his own in the intellectual 'Internationale' delimited on the left, say, by Bertolt Brecht and Jean Genet, and on the right by Claude Lévi-Strauss and Buckminster Fuller. If the term had not been abused for more limited purposes, I would risk calling the horizon of at least the first half of Lem's opus a New Left consciousness. Or, more prudently, a kind of creative post-Nietzschean consciousness that any new Left will have to absorb[4] –

rather than to simply refuse it by optimism and political rejection, as in the case of Asimov and Yefremov.

(Originally published in 1979)

NOTES

1. Stanisław Lem, 'Robots in Science Fiction', in Thomas D. Clareson (ed.), *SF: The Other Side of Realism* (Bowling Green, OH, 1971). Asimov's robot stories were first published in SF magazines between 1940 and 1950, and collected into his book with some adjustments to make them fit each other and the 'Laws of Robotics' excogitated in the meantime with the help of John W. Campbell, Jr. Because of such complex and, for the present purpose, irrelevant textual histories, the year referred to in the chapter is (for all three writers) that of first book publication. All quotes to Asimov are from the Signet Book edition (New York, 1964) by page number in parenthesis. See also on Asimov Joseph F. Patrouch, Jr, *The Science Fiction of Isaac Asimov* (Garden City, NY, 1974); James Gunn, *Isaac Asimov* (New York, 1982); and the brilliant essays by Charles Elkins, 'Asimov's "Foundation" Novels', *SFS*, no. 8 (1976)26–36, and Alessandro Portelli, 'The Three Laws of Robotics', *SFS*, no. 21 (1980)150–6. For a discussion of Saint-Simonism as fountainhead of a whole SF stream see *MOSF*.
2. For Russian SF in general, cf. *MOSF* and the annotated bibliography of criticism in my *Russian Science Fiction 1956–1974* (Elizabethtown, NY, 1976), with a continuation in *Canadian–American Slavic Studies*, 15 (1981) 533–44, in particular the works of Gurevich, Britikov, Liapunov, Tamarchenko, Chernysheva and Rullkötter. To this should now be added the special issue on SF of the same journal, 18, no. 1–2 (1984), especially the theoretical surveys by Nudelman and Tamarchenko. Besides these, on Yefremov in particular see the works of Brandis-Dmitrevskii, Siniavskii, Gromova, Nudel'man, Franklin and Zvantseva in my 1976 book, and my entry on him (and eight other Russian SF writers) in Curtis C. Smith (ed.), *Twentieth-Century Science-Fiction Writers* (New York, 1981).
3. *Solaris* is quoted from the Berkeley edition (New York, 1971), which has an afterword of mine. Cf. on Lem, Ryszard Handke, *Polska proza fantastyczno-naukowa* (Wrocław, 1969); Ewa Balcerzak, *Stanisław Lem* (Warsaw, 1973); Werner Berthel (ed.), *Insel Almanach auf das Jahr 1976: Stanisław Lem* (Frankfurt, 1976); and in English – beside Lem's own writing on SF and himself – Michael Kandel, 'Stanisław Lem on Men and Robots', *Extrapolation*, 14 (1972), and 'Lem in Review', *SFS*, no. 11 (1977)65–8; David Ketterer, *New Worlds For Old* (Garden City, NY, 1974), *passim*; Ursula K. Le Guin, 'European SF', *SFS*, no. 3 (1974) 61–5; Edward Balcerzan, 'Seeking Only Man: Language and Ethics in *Solaris*', in R. D. Mullen and Darko Suvin (1976) pp. 141–5; Jerzy Jarzębski, 'Stanisław

Lem, Rationalist and Sensualist', *SFS*, no. 12 (1977)110–26; Patrick Parrinder, 'The Black Wave', *Radical Science J.*, no. 5 (1977)37–61, and his *Science Fiction* (see Bibliography to Part Two), pp. 122–30; John Rothfork, 'Cybernetics and Humanistic Fiction', *Research Studies*, 45 (1977)123–33; Dagmar Barnouw, 'Science Fiction as a Model for Probabilistic Worlds', *SFS*, no. 19 (1979)153–63; Mark Rose, *Alien Encounters* (Cambridge, MA, 1985) pp. 82–95.

4. See Nietzsche's comments on the shadow of dead God and the chaotic universe, at the beginning of part 3 and in part 5 of *Die fröhliche Wissenschaft* (The Joyous Knowledge) (Munich, s.a.); Lem is, however, free of the misogyny and other proto-fascist elements in Nietzsche. As to a creative fusion of Nietzschean and Marxian horizons, cf. Lem's essays *Dialogi* (Cracow, 1957 and 1972), which were, in the characteristic guise of 'cybernetic sociology', an interesting discursive explication of a potentially new and Left consciousness. I am here not at all characterizing the civic *persona* of Lem, nor his development after, say, 1968.

9

Philip K. Dick's Opus: Artifice as Refuge and World View

The chronology of Dick's publications, taking into account only his books, looks as follows:[1]

	1952	1953	1954	1955	1956	1957	1958	1959	1960	1961	1962	1963
S	2	12	13	6	2	—	—	1	—	—	—	2
N	—	—	—	1	2	3	—	1	2	—	1	1

	1964	1965	1966	1967	1968	1969	1970	1971	1972	1973	1974
S	2	1	1	1	—	—	—	—	—	—	1
N	5	1	3	2½	1	3	1	—	1	—	1

Though I rather enjoy some of Dick's stories, from 'The Preserving Machine' (1953) and 'Nanny' (1955) to 'Oh To Be a Blobel' (1964), they are clearly secondary to his novels, where the themes of the most interesting stories are developed more fully. The novel format allows Dick to develop his peculiar strength of alternate-world creation by means of arresting characters counterposed to each other in cunningly wrought plots. Therefore, after 1956 Dick returned to writing notable stories only in his peak 1962–5 period; his later tries at forcing himself to write them are not too successful, e.g. the story in *Dangerous Visions*. In this chapter I shall concentrate on discussing his novels.

I would therefore divide Dick's writing into three main periods: 1952–62, 1962–5 and 1966–74. The first period is one of apprenticeship and limning of his themes and devices, first in short or longer stories (1952–6) and then in his early novels from *Solar Lottery* to *Vulcan's Hammer* (1955–60), and it culminates in the mature polyphony of *The Man in the High Castle* (1962). Dick's second, central period stands out to my mind as a high plateau in his opus. Following on his creative breakthrough in *MHC*, it comprises (together with some less successful tries) the masterpieces of *Martian Time-Slip* and *Dr Bloodmoney*, as well as that flawed but powerful near-masterpiece *The Three Stigmata of Palmer Eldritch*. The latest phase of Dick's writing, beginning in 1966, is in many ways a falling off. It is characterized by a turning from a fruitful tension between public and private concerns toward a simplified narration increasingly preoccupied with solitary anxieties and by a corresponding concern with unexplainable ontological puzzles; and it has clearly led to the creative sterility of 1970–4 (*We Can Build You*, though published in 1972, had appeared in magazine version by 1970). However, *Ubik* (1969), the richest and most provocative novel of this phase, testifies to the necessity for a closer analysis of even this downbeat period of Dick's. Thus, an overview of his opus can, I trust, find a certain logic in its development, but it is not a mechanical or linear logic. Dick's work, intimately influenced by and participating in the great processes of the American collective or social psychology in these last 20 years, shares the hesitations, the often irrational though always understandable leaps backwards, forwards and sideways of that psychology.[2] It is perhaps most understandable as the work of a prose poet whose basic tools are not verse lines and poetic figures but (1) the agential and spatial, i.e. semantic and axiological, relationships within the narrative; (2) various alternate worlds, the specific political and ontological relationships in each of which are analogous to the USA (or simply to California) in the 1950s and 1960s; and (3) – last but not least – the vivid characters on whom his narration and his worlds finally repose. In this essay, I propose to deal with these three areas of Dick's creativity: some basic relationships in Dick's story-telling – a notion richer than, though connected with, the plotting – will be explored by an analysis of narrative foci and power levels; Dick's alternate worlds will be explored in function of his increasing shift from mostly political to mostly ontological horizons; finally, Dick's allegorically exaggerated characters will be explored in their own right as fundaments for the morality and cognition in his novels.

1. PILGRIMAGE WITHOUT PROGRESS: NARRATIVE FOCI
AND POWER LEVELS

'Amazing the power of fiction, even cheap popular fiction, to evoke.
(*MHC*, ch. 8)

In order to illuminate the development of Dick's story-telling, I shall follow his use of narrative agents as *narrative foci* and as indicators of *upper and lower social classes or power statuses*. The concept of narrative focus seems necessary because Dick as a rule uses a narration which is neither that of the old-fashioned all-knowing, neutral and superior, narrator, nor a narration in the first person by the central characters. The narration proceeds instead somewhere in between those two extreme possibilities, simultaneously in the third person and from the vantage point of the central or focal character in a given segment. This is always clearly delimited from other segments with other focal characters – first, by means of chapter endings or at least by double spacing within a chapter, and second, by the focal character being named at the beginning of each such narrative segment, usually after a monotony-avoiding introductory sentence or subordinate clause which sets up the time and place of the new narrative segment. The focal character is also used as a visual, auditive and psychological focus whose vantage point in fact colours and limits the subsequent narration. This permits the empathizing into – usually sympathizing with but always at least understanding – all the focal characters, be they villains or heroes in the underlying plot conflict; which is equivalent to saying that Dick has no black or white villains and heroes in the sense of Van Vogt (from whom the abstracted plot conflicts are often borrowed). In the collective, non-individualist world of Dick, everybody, high and low, destroyer and sufferer, is in an existential situation which largely determines his/her actions; even the arch-destroyer Palmer Eldritch is a sufferer.

The novels before 1962 are approximations to such a technique of multifocal narrative. Its lower limit-case and primitive seed, the one-hero-at-the-centre narrative, is to be found in *Eye in the Sky* and, with a half-hearted try at two subsidiary foci, in *The Man Who Japed*. *Solar Lottery* has two clear foci, Benteley and Cartwright, with insufficiently sustained strivings toward a polyphonic structure (Verrick, Wakeman, Groves). Similarly, though there are half a dozen narrative foci in *Time Out of Joint*, Ragle is clearly their privileged centre; in fact, the whole universe of the book has been constructed only to impinge upon him, just as all universes impinged upon the protagonist of *Eye in the Sky*. *Vulcan's Hammer* is focused around the two bureaucrats Barris and Dill, with Marion coming a poor third; the important character of Father Fields does not become a narrative focus, as he logically should have, nor does the intelligent computer though he is similar, say, to the equally destructive and destroyed Arnie in *MTS*. However, in *MHC* there is to be found for the first time the full Dickian narrative articulation, surpassed only in *MTS* and *Dr B*. With some simplifying of secondary characters and sub-plots, and taking into account the levels of social – here explicitly political – power, *MHC* divides into two parallel plots with these narrative foci (marked by caps, while other important characters are named in lower case – see Figure 2):

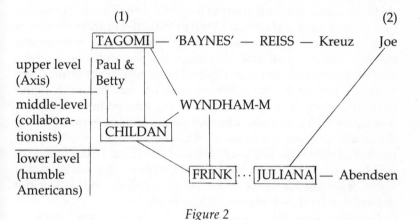

Figure 2

The upper level is one of politico-ethical conflict between murderous Nazi fanaticism and Japanese tolerance (the assumption that a victorious Japanese fascism would be radically better than the German one is the major political blunder of Dick's novel). In (1), the San Francisco plot, the two sympathetic focal characters are Frank Frink, the suffering refugee Jew and creative little man, and Mr Tagomi, the ethical Japanese official. In (2), the locomotive plot, the sole focal character is Juliana. Tagomi helps 'Baynes' in trying to foil the global political political scheme of Nazi universal domination, and incidentally also foils the extradition of Frink to the Nazis, while Juliana foils the Nazis' (Joe's) plot to assassinate Abendsen, the SF writer of a book postulating Axis defeat in World War Two; they both turn out to be, more by instinct than by design, antagonists of the fascist politico-psychological evil. But the passive link between them is Frink, Juliana's ex-husband, and his artistic creation, the silvery pin mediating between earth and sky, life and death, past and future, the *MHC*-universe and the alternate universe of our empirical reality. Tagomi's reality-change vision in Chapter 14, induced by contemplating Frink's pin, is a Dickian set scene which recreates, through an admittedly partial narrative viewpoint, the great utopian tradition that treats a return to the reader's freeways, smog and jukebox civilization as a vision of hell – exactly as at the end of *Gulliver's Travels, Looking Backward* or *News from Nowhere.* But it is also an analogue of the vision of Abendsen's book: the book and the pin come from chthonic depths but become mediators only after being shaped by the intellect, albeit an oracular and largely instinctive one. For Dick, a writer (especially an SF writer) is always first and foremost an 'artificer', both in the sense of artful craftsman and in the sense of creator of new, 'artificial' but nonetheless possible worlds. Frink and Abendsen, the two artificers – one the broodingly passive but (see Figure 2) centrally situated narrative focus of the book, the other a shadowy but haunting figure appearing at its close – constitute with Tagomi and Juliana, the two instinctive ethical activists, the four pillars of hope opposed to the dominant political madness of Fascism. Though most clearly institutionalized in German Nazism, it can also be found in middle-class Americans such as Childan, the racist small shopkeeper oscillating between being a helper and a deceitful exploiter of creative artificers such as Frink.

The second or plateau period of Dick's opus retains and deepens the *MHC* narrative polyphony. It does so both by increasing the number of the narrative foci and by stressing some relationships among the focal characters as privileged, thereby making for easier overview with less redundancy and a stronger impact. The two culminations of such proceeding are *MTS* and *Dr B.* In *MTS*, three of the focal characters stand out (see Figure 3). Of the three privileged characters, the labour boss Arnie is powerful and sociable, the autistic boy Manfred politically powerless and asocial, while the central character, Jack Bohlen, mediates between the two not only in his socio-political status but also in his fits of and struggle against psychosis. However, Jack and Manfred, the time-binding precog and the manual craftsman, are allied against the tycoon Arnie. This is the first clear expression in Dick's opus of the alliance and yet also the split between Rousseauist personal freedom, realized in Manfred's final symbiosis with the totally asocial, noble-savage Bleekmen, and an ethical communal order, implied in Jack. The politically powerless turn the tables on the powerful – as did Juliana in *MHC* – by means of their greater sensitivity. This

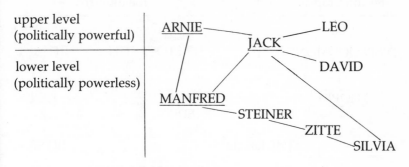

Figure 3

allows them a much deeper understanding of people and things, inner and outer nature (which they pay for by greater suffering). Therefore, the set-piece or obligatory situation in *MTS* is again a visionary scene involving Manfred, Jack and Arnie in several interdependent versions of nightmarish reality-change (chs 10–11).

The oppositions are aggravated and therefore explored more fully in *Dr B*, Dick's narratively most sophisticated work. Nine personal narrative foci are here, astoundingly, joined by two choral focal groups – the secondary characters who get killed during the narrative but help decisively in Hoppy's defeat, such as Fergesson, and the post-Bomb-community secondary characters, such as June. The double division in *MTS* (powerful/powerless plus personal freedom/ethical order) is here richly articulated into (1) the destructive dangers which are opposed to the new prospects of life and vitality, further subdivided into (2) the search for a balanced community, and (3) the search for personal happiness. Very interestingly, Dangerfield, the mediator of practical tips and past culture, provides the link between all those who oppose the destroyers. In this most optimistic of Dick's novels, Bloodmoney's Bomb was a Happy Fall: the collapse of American socio-political and technological power abolishes the class distinctions, and thus makes possible a new start and innocence leading to the defeat of the new, anti-utopian would-be usurpers by the complementary forces of a new communal and personal order. These forces are aptly symbolized by the homunculus Bill – perhaps Dick's most endearing character – who is both person and symbiotic creature (see Figure 4):

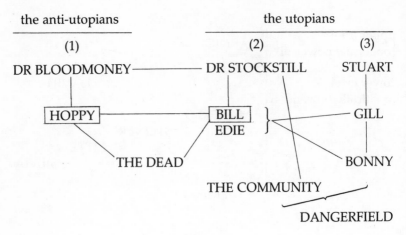

Figure 4

In this light, the ideological movement of the book is complete when Bonny, the all-embracing Earth Mother figure, has forsaken the old danger, Bloodmoney, and when her son Bill – coeval with the innocence and power of the new order (much as his feebler prototype, Mrs Grayles in Miller's *A Canticle for Leibowitz*) – has defeated the new danger, Hoppy. Jameson identifies (in the *SFS* Dick issue) the new danger convincingly with a neo-pragmatic stance connected with modern electronics and the USA, just as the old danger was the classical mad scientist of the Dr Strangelove type connected with nuclear physics and Germany. Jameson's essay, as well as the analyses of *MTS* by Aldiss and Pagetti, make it possible to cut short here the discussion of narrative foci in these two masterpieces of Dick's. It only remains to notice that a Rousseauist utopianism cannot finally fuse personal happiness and harmonious community – at the utmost it can run them in tandem, or as the horizons of two successive generations and historical stages.

2.　AM-WEB: POLITICS AND ONTOLOGY

The disintegration of the social and economic system had been slow, gradual, and profound. It went so deep that people lost faith in natural law itself.

(*Solar Lottery*, ch. 2)

There remains, in Dick's middle period, the important if ambiguous *3SPE*, the discussion of which will require shifting the emphasis to what are for Dick the horizons of human destiny. *3SPE* is the first significant Dick novel to allot equal weight to politics and ontology as arbiters of its microcosm and its characters' destinies. I shall deal first with politics.

Up to the mid-1960s Dick could be characterized as a writer of anti-utopian SF in the wake of Orwell's *1984* and of the menacing world-war and post-Bomb horizons in the pulp 'new maps of hell' by Bradbury, Heinlein, Blish and Pohl (to mention those who, together with Vanvogtian plotting and Besterian Espers, seem to have meant most to him). The horrors of Cold War politics, paranoiac militarism, mass hysteria organized by politicians and encroaching government totalitarianism are broached in the stories of the mid-1950s such as 'Breakfast at Twilight', 'War Veteran' or 'Second Variety'; in one of the best, 'Foster, You're Dead', the militarist craze for bomb-shelters is further seen as a tool for commercial twisting of the everyday life of little people. In Dick's early novels the dystopian framework is developed by adding to a look at the dominated humble people an equally inside look at the ruling circles – the telepaths and quizmasters in *Solar Lottery*, the secret police in 'The Variable Man' and *The World Jones Made*, the mass-media persuaders in *The Man Who Japed*, the powerful bureaucrats in *Vulcan's Hammer*. Indeed, *Eye in the Sky* is the formalization of a literally 'inside' look at four variants of dystopia, and carries the message that in the world of modern science we are all truly members of one another. Up to *3SPE*, then, the novels by Dick which are not primarily dystopian (*The Cosmic Puppets, Dr Futurity, The Game-Players of Titan*) are best forgotten. Obversely, political dystopia has remained a kind of zero-level for Dick's writing right to the present day (for example, in *Flow My Tears, the Policeman Said*), at times even explicitly connecting the early stories to the later second-line novels by taking over a story's theme or situation and developing it into the novel's mainstay (for example, 'The Defenders' and *The Penultimate Truth*, or 'Shell Game' and *Clans of the Alphane Moon*).

The culmination and transmutation of political horizons occur in what I would call Dick's 'plateau tetralogy', from *MHC* to *Dr B*. *MHC*, with its superb feel of Nazi psychology and of life in a world of occupiers, occupied and quislings overshadowed by it, is the high point of Dick's explicitly political anti-utopianism. Paradoxically if precariously balanced by ethical optimism, it is, because of that confident balance and richness, in some ways Dick's most lucid book. It is also the first culmination of the Germanic-paranoia-turning-fascist theme which has been haunting Dick as no other American SF writer (with the possible exception of Vonnegut) since 'The Variable Man' with its Security Commissioner Reinhart, and the seminal *Man Who Japed* with its German–American Big Brother in the person of Major Jules Streiter, founder of the Moral Reclamation movement. The naming of this shadowy King Anti-Utopus is an excellent example for Dick's ideological onomastics: it compounds allusions to the names and doctrines of Moral Rearmament's Buchman, Social Credit's Major Douglas, and the fanatic Nazi racist Julius Streicher. The liberalism of even the seemingly most hard-nosed dystopian SF in the American 1940s and 1950s, with its illusions of Back to the Spirit of 1776, pales into insignificance beside Dick's pervasive, intimate and astoundingly rich understanding of the affinities between German and American fascism, born of the same social classes of big speculators and small shopkeepers. This understanding is embodied in a number of characters who span the death-lust spectrum between political and psychological threat. Beginning with the wholly American Childan (who is, correspondingly, a racist out of insecurity rather than fanaticism, and is allowed a positive conversion) and the German assassin Joe masquerading as an American in *MHC*, through Norbert Steiner and Otto Zitte as well as the vaguely Teutonic-American corrupt bigwigs Leo Bohlen and Arnie Kott in *MTS*, such a series culminates in Dr Bruno Bluthgeld/Bloodmoney (descended from Von Braun, Teller, *et sim.*, both through newspapers and through Kubrick's mad German scientist Dr Strangelove). It finally leads to a German takeover of the Western world by means of their industries and androids in *The Simulacra*, and of the whole planet through the UN in *The Unteleported Man*. In this last novel, the revelation that UN boss Horst Bertold (whose name and final revelatory plea are derived from Bertolt Brecht, the anti-fascist German whose name would be most familiar to the music and drama lover Dick) is a 'good' German, on the same side of the political fence as the hounded little man Rachmael ben Applebaum, effects a reconciliation of powerful German and powerless Jew.

These politico-national roles or clichés had started poles apart in *MHC*. But by the end of Dick's German-Nazi theme and cycle the year was 1966, and the sensitive author quite rightly recognized that the world, and in particular the USA, had other fish to fry: the ubiquitous fascist menace was no longer primarily German or anti-Jewish. Already in *MTS*, the lone German killers Steiner and Zitte were small fry compared to the Americans of Teutonic descent, Leo and Arnie. In *Dr B*, therefore, the Bluthgeld menace is supplanted by the deformed American obstinately associated with the product of Bluthgeld's fallout – the Ayn Rand follower and cripple Hoppy, wired literally up to his teeth into the newest electronic death-dealing gadgets. Clearly, Bluthgeld relates to Hoppy as the German-associated World War Two and Cold War technology of the 1940s and 1950s to the Vietnam War technology of the 1960s. It is the same relation as the one between the Nazi-treated superman Bulero and the reality manipulator Eldritch, and finally between the Krupps and Heydrichs of *MHC* and the military-industrial complex of American capitalism: 'it was Washington that was dropping the bombs on [the American people], not the Chinese or the Russians' (*Dr B*, ch. 5). The transformation or transubstantiation of classical European fascism into new American power is also the theme of two significant stories Dick wrote in the 1960s, 'If There Were no Benny Cemoli' (read – Benito Mussolini) and 'Oh, To Be a Blobel' (where an American tycoon turns Alien while his humbler employee wife turns human). The third significant story, 'What the Dead Men Say' – which stands halfway between *3SPE* and *Ubik* – features half-life as a non-supernatural hoax by American economic and political totalitarians on the make.

By the *MTS* phase, Dick's little man is being opposed not only to political and technological but also to economic power in the person of the rival tycoons Leo (representing a classical big speculators' syndicate) and Arnie (whose capital comes from control of big trade union funds), while on the horizon of both Terra and Mars there looms the big cooperative movement, whose capital comes from investments of members. In the corrupt microcosm of *MTS* these three variants of capitalism (classical *laissez-faire*, bureaucratic and demagogically managerial), together with the state capitalism of the superstate UN disposing of entire planets, constitute what is almost a brief survey of its possible forms. The slogan of the big cooperative-capitalist movement, which Manfred sees crowning his horrible vision of planetary future in decay, is AM-WEB, explained in Dick's frequent record-jacket German as 'Alle Menschen werden Brüder' – 'All men become brothers' (from Schiller through Beethoven's Ninth). But of course this explanation is half true and half disingenuous – the proper acronym for the slogan would, after all, be AMWB with no 'E' and no hyphen. Thus, within Dick's normative Germano-American parallelism, AM-WEB is also, and even primarily, an emblem of the ironic reversal of pretended liberty, fraternity and equality – it is the *American Web* of big business, corrupt labour aristocracy and big state that turns the difficult everyday life of the little man into a future nightmare. As Brian Aldiss remarks in the *SFS* Dick issue, the whole of *MTS* – and beyond that, most of Dick – is a maledictory web. The economico-political spider spinning it is identified with a clarity scarcely known in American SF between Jack London's Oligarchy and Ursula Le Guin's Propertarians. The Rousseauist utopianism of *Dr B* is an indication that the urge to escape this cursed web is so deep it would almost welcome an atomic holocaust as a chance to start anew: 'We are, Adams realized, a cursed race. Genesis is right; there is a stigma on us, a mark' (*The Penultimate Truth*, ch. 13).

The three stigmata of Palmer Eldritch, the interplanetary industrialist who peddles dope to enslave the masses, are three signs of demonic artificiality. The prosthetic eyes, hands and teeth allow him – in a variant of the Wolf in Little Red Riding Hood – to see (understand), grab (manipulate), and rend (ingest, consume) his victims better. Like the tycoon in 'Oh, To Be a Blobel', this Eldritch Palmer or uncanny pilgrim towards the goal of universal market domination is clearly a 'mad capitalist' (to coin a term parallel to mad scientist), a miraculous organizer of production wasted through absence of rational distribution (ch. 1) who turned Alien on a power trip. But his peculiar terrifying force is that he turns his doped manipulees not only into a captive market (see Dick's early story of that title) but also into partial, stigmatized replicas of himself by working through their ethical and existential weaknesses. The Palmer Eldritch type of super-corporative capitalism is in fact a new religion, stronger and more pervasive than the classical transcendental ones, because 'GOD PROMISES ETERNAL LIFE. WE CAN DELIVER IT' (ch. 9). What it delivers, though, is not only a new thing under the Sun but also false, activating the bestial or alien inhumanity within man: 'And – we have no mediating sacraments through which to protect ourselves. . . . It [the Eldritch Presence] is out in the open, ranging in every direction. It looks into our eyes; and it looks *out* of our eyes' (ch. 13). Dick moves here along jungle trails first blazed by William S. Burroughs: for both, the hallucinatory operators are real.

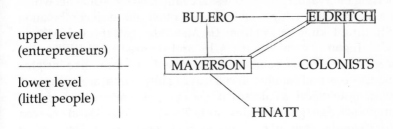

Figure 5

The narrative structure of *3SPE* combines multifocality with a privileged protagonist–antagonist (Mayerson–Eldritch) axis and with the division into power levels (see Figure 5). However, the erstwhile normal conflict between the upper and the lower social levels is here superseded by the appearance of a new-type antagonist, Eldritch, who snares not only the little people – Mayerson and other Mars colonists – but also the established power of Bulero, and indeed subverts the whole notion of monadic, Individualistic characters of the nineteenth-century kind upon which Dick's, like most other SF had so far reposed. The appearance of Eldritch, signalized by his stigmata, *inside* the other characters shifts the conflict into their psyches – can they trust their reality perceptions? The political theme and horizon begin here to give way to the ontological. While the ontological dilemmas have a clear genesis in the political ones, they shift the power relationships from human institutions to mysterious entities, never quite accounted for or understood in the narration. *3SPE* is thus that first significant station in Dick's development where the ontological preoccupations begin to weigh as heavily as, or more heavily than, the political dystopianism.

Such preoccupations can, no doubt, be found in Dick's writing right from the beginning, 'Foster, You're Dead', the story of a boy alienated by conformist social pressures, is already halfway between Pohl's satires (it was published by Pohl in *Star SF 3*) and the suffering alienated boy Manfred in *MTS* who erects an alternative reality as refuge, and can serve as a key to Dick's theme of mental alienation connected with reality changes. Parallel to that, 'Adjustment Team' is a first tentative try at evolving the 'Tunnel Under the World' situation of total manipulation – also the kernel of *3SPE* – toward metaphysics. The mysterious failure of memory, or missing interval of consciousness accompanied by headache, which is a sign of dissolving realities and is often found in combination with drug-taking, recurs from *The Man Who Japed* through *MTS* to *3SPE*. Tagomi's great vision in *MHC* and Manfred's AM-WEB vision in *MTS* can already be interpreted not only as trance-like insights but also as actual changes in collective reality. These are changes in being (ontological, as already in *Eye in the Sky*) rather than only in foreknowledge (gnoseological, as in *The World Jones Made*) or, even more simply, fraudulent-cum-psychotic ones (as in *Time Out of Joint*). Indeed, the story-telling microcosms, the depicted planetary realities of both *MHC* and *MTS*, are analogies for reality changes immanent in the author's here-and-now and already showing through it, like Eldritch's stigmata. *MHC* is an alternative world explicating a California, USA, and globe fallen prey to fascism. *MTS* substitutes the more general physical category of entropy for its political particular case; Dick's Mars is a run-down future, 'a sort of Humpty-Dumpty' where people and things have decayed 'into rusty bits and useless debris' (ch. 6), a space and time leading – in ironic repudiation of Ray Bradbury's nostalgia for the petty-bourgeois past and Arthur C. Clarke's confidence in liberal scientism – to the dialectical interplay between Manfred's devolutionary vision of 'gubble' (rubble, rubbish, crumble, gobble) invading everybody's reality and vitality and Jack's struggle against it. The total manipulation and the entropic human relations are to be found in *3SPE* together with and flowing into a false, profit-making religion.

However, the shift from politics to ontology, which was only hinted at in *MHC* and will culminate in *Ubik*, is in *3SPE* not consistent. The referents of this lush novel are over-determined: Eldritch, the allegorical representative of neo-capitalism, is at the same time the bearer of an 'evil, negative trinity of alienation, blurred reality and despair' (ch. 13) of demonic though unclear origin. An orthodox religious and an orthodox politico-economic reading of *3SPE* can both be fully supported by the evidence of the novel; but neither of these complementary and yet in some ways basically contradictory readings can explain the full novel – which is to boot overburdened with quite unnecessary elements such as Mayerson's precog faculties, the garden-variety theological speculations, etc. Politics, physics and metaphysics combine to create in *3SPE* a fascinating and iridescent manifold, but their interference also, to my mind, makes for an insufficiently economical novel. It starts squarely within the political and physical field (clash of big drug corporations, temperature rise, colonization of Mars) and then drags across it the red herring of ontologico-religious speculations grafted upon Vanvogtian plot gimmicks (here from Leigh Brackett's *The Big Jump*, 1955) which shelve rather than solve the thematic problems.

3. ALL WE MARSMEN: CHARACTEROLOGY AS MORALITY AND COGNITION

We do not have the ideal world, such as we would like, where morality is easy because cognition is easy.

(*MHC*, ch. 15)

In Dick's anthropology, the differentiation between upper and lower politico-economic power statuses is correlative to a system of correspondences between profession, as relating to a specific type of creativity, and ethical goodness or evil. This reposes on a more general view of human nature and species-specific human conduct, for which morality and cognition are closely allied, and which will be discussed in this section. Such an alliance breaks down in *Ubik*; this is to my mind the explanation of Dick's difficulties after 1966.

From Dick's earliest writings, aggressiveness is identified not only with militarism but also with commercialism (as in 'Nanny'), and villainy with either dictatorial or capitalist rulers (as in 'A Present for Pat', and in the stories of the 1960s mentioned in section 2). Opposed to the unscrupulous tycoons and other bigwigs (Verrick in *Solar Lottery*, the terrifying roster of Führer candidates in *MHC*, Leo Bohlen and Arnie Kott in *MTS*, Leo Bulero and Palmer Eldritch in *3SPE*, the Yancy Men in *The Penultimate Truth*, etc.) are the little people. The two ends of the politico-economic and power scale relate as 'havenots' to 'titans' (*The Unteleported Man*, ch. 4), but also as creators to destroyers. For, Dick's protagonists are as a rule some variant of immediate producer or direct creator. They are not industrial workers engaged in collective production – a class conspicuous by its absence here as in practically all modern SF. On the contrary, Dick's heroes are most often the new individual craftsmen, producers of art objects or repairmen of the most sophisticated (for example, cybernetic) Second Industrial

Revolution products. They are updated versions of the old-fashioned handyman (who is celebrated in the 'Fixit-cart', non-statistical, unquantifiable, 'variable man' of the eponymous story) for a contemporary, or near-future, highly industrialized society; and their main trait is a direct and personalized relationship to creative productivity as opposed to standardized mass-production with its concomitant other-directedness, loss of self-reliance, and shoddy living (a key to this is to be found in the story 'Pay for the Printer', a finger-exercise for *Dr B*).

This characterology is not yet quite clear in the earlier novels, which deal more with the Ibsenian theme of social deceit versus individual struggle for truth than with the theme of destruction *vs.* creation. Of *Solar Lottery*'s two heroes one, Benteley, is a classical 'cadre', a biochemist, and only the other, Cartwright, is 'electronics repairman and human being with a conscience' (ch. 2). Similarly, the hero of *Eye in the Sky* turns only at the end of the book from chief of missile lab to builder of phonographs, switching from Dick's chief dislike, militarism, to his chief love, music. But already in his early works there appears a populist or indeed New Left tendency to distrust rational intelligence, contaminated as it is by its association with 'the cult of the Technocrat . . . run by and *for* those oriented around verbal knowledge' (*Vulcan's Hammer*, ch. 14), and to oppose to it spontaneous action guided by intuition – a politics of the 'do your own thing' type. Thus, in *Time Out of Joint* Ragle is a creative personality who dislikes the nine-to-five drudgery of the huge conformist organizations, regimented like armies (ch. 1), and who can 'sense the pattern' of events through his artistic abilities (ch. 14). Though the traces of this dichotomy can be felt even in the *MHC* heroes Tagomi and Frink – who are juxtaposed as mind and hand, intellectual visionary from the upper power level and intuitive creator from the powerless depths – it is fortunately absent from his most mature creations, the 'plateau masterpieces' in which his ethico-professional pattern of characters emerges most clearly. In *MTS*, Steiner and Zitte are small speculators who exploit the work of others, just as the small shopkeeper Childan in *MHC* exploited the creativity of the artificer Jew–Gentile pair, Frink and McCarthy; like him, Steiner and Zitte are unable to face reality and so resort to sexual fantasies alternating with suicidal/homicidal moods. At the other end of the power scale, Arnie fuses the financial role of big speculator, represented in pure form by Leo, with Zitte's role of sexual exploiter.

This quasi-robotic role of a sexually efficient but emotionally uncommitted *macho*, for Dick an ethical equivalent of economic exploitation, is to be found in his negative characters from the android of 'Second Variety' to such 'titans' as Verrick in *Solar Lottery* or Arnie in *MTS* who use their female employees and mistresses as pawns in power manoeuvres. Opposed to them are the sincere little people, here the repairman Jack Bohlen, who fight their way through the sexual as well as the economic jungle step by laborious step. In *3SPE*, the character spread runs from the capitalist destroyer Eldritch to the suffering artist-creator Emily; and the central hero Mayerson's fall from grace begins by his leaving Emily for success's sake and is consummated when he refuses her creations for personal revenge, thus becoming an impediment to human creativity and falling into the clutches of Eldritch's false creations. Emily's husband Hnatt is midway between her and Mayerson: he is her co-worker, the vendor of her products, but his ambiguous position in the productive process finally brings about her creative regression in the novel's rather underdeveloped sub-plot of false creativity through forced intellectual evolution (this sub-plot is carried by Bulero, the old-fashioned tycoon). Similarly, in *The Penultimate Truth* the weak and less sympathetic characters are the wordsmiths who have forsaken personal creativity to be abused for the purposes of a regressive political apparatus (Lindblom). This novel divides into two plots, the ruling-class and the subterranean one. The first centres, alas, around a Vanvogtian immortal and the intrigue from *The House That Stood Still* (1950), marring one of Dick's potentially most interesting books. For the hero of the other plot, Nick, is the democratically elected president of an oppressed community, whose creativity is manifested by political persistence in securing the rights of an endangered member. Thus, Dick's concept of creativity, though it centres on artists, encompasses both erotical and political creative ethics.

Beside the professional roles, Dick has three basic female roles, also clearly present in *3SPE* as Roni, Emily and Anne around Mayerson. The first role is that of castrating bitch, a female *macho*, striving to rise in the corporative power-world (also Kathy in *Now Wait for Last Year*, Pris in *We Can Build You*, etc.); the second that of weak but stabilizing influence (also Silvia in *MTS*, etc.); and the third, crowning one that of a strong but warm sustaining force. Although Dick's female characters seem less fully developed than his male ones, such an Earth Mother becomes the final embodiment of ethical and political rightness in his most hopeful novels, *MHC* and *Dr B* (Juliana and Bonny); conversely, the Bitch is developed with increasing fascination in his third phase.

As suggested above, the totally unethical and therefore inhuman person is often an android, what Dick, with a stress on its counterfeiting and artificial aspect, calls a *simulacrum* (see his very instructive Vancouver speech in *SF Commentary*, no. 31). Already in his first novel, this is associated with modern science being manipulated by power-mad people, who are themselves the truly reified inhumans and therefore in a way more unauthentic than their simulacra. An interesting central anthropological tenet is adumbrated here, halfway between Rousseau and Marx, according to which there is an *authentic core* identical with humanity in *Homo sapiens*, from which men and women have to be alienated by civilizational pressures in order to behave in an unauthentic, dehumanized way, so that there is always an inner resistance to such pressures in anybody who simply follows his or her human(e) instinct of treating people as ends, not means. That is why Dick's heroes rely on instinct and persistence (several of them, such as Jack in *MTS* or Nick in *The Penultimate Truth* are characterized as permanently 'going to keep trying'). That is why social class is both a functionally decisive and yet not an exclusive criterion for determining the humanity of the characters: the more powerful one is, the more dehumanized one becomes, and Dick's only real heroes tend to be the creative little people, with the addition of an occasional visionary; yet even the literally dehumanized alien such as Eldritch has inextinguishable remnants of humanity within him which qualify him for suffering, and thus for the reader's partial, dialectical sympathy for his (now alienated) human potentialities. That is why, finally, there emerges the strange and charmingly grotesque Dickian world of semi-animated cybernetic constructs, which makes stretches of even his weaker novels enjoyable light reading: for example, the fly-size shrilling commercial and the hypnotic surrogate-'papoola' of *The Simulacra*, the Lazy Brown Dog reject carts in *Now Wait for Last Year*, the stupid elevators and grumpy cybernetic taxis such as Max the auto-auto in *The Game-Players of Titan*, etc. Together with a few interesting aliens, the all-too-human inhumans culminate in the menace of *3SPE* and in Dick's richest spectrum of creatures in *Dr B*, which runs from the stigmatic psi-powers of Bluthgeld and cyborg booster-devices of Hoppy to the zany and appealing new life-cycle of homeostatic traps and evolved animals. At the centre of *Dr B* is the homunculus Bill, who is in touch with humans, animals and even the dead, and unites the kinaesthetic and verbal powers in the universe of that novel.

I have left *Ubik* for the end of this discussion both because it seems to me Dick's last major work to date and because in it the analogies between morality and cognition suffer a sea-change. The Dickian narrative model, as discussed in this essay, is in *Ubik* extremely simplified and then recomplicated by being twisted into a new shape. The character types remain the same and thus link the new model with Dick's earlier work; the bitch Pat, the redeemer Ella, the bewildered old-fashioned tycoon Runciter, the shadowy illusion creator Jory, losing in precision but gaining in domination in comparison to Eldritch, and, most important, the buffeted but persistent *schlemiel* Joe Chip. But the shift from social to ontological horizons around the axis connecting the two main narrative foci of Runciter and Chip results in a world without stable centres, or peripheries, where the main problem is to find out who is inside and who outside the unstable circles of narrative consciousness, liable to an infinite receding series of contaminations from other – often only guessed at – such centres. The characterological equivalent of this uncertainty is the half-life, a loss of sovereignty over one's microcosm. After the explosion on the Moon, is Chip, or Runciter, or neither, or both in that state? The most all-embracing explanation would be that both are in the moratorium with different degrees of control, and acted on by the rival forces of destruction and redemption of Jory and Ella. However, no explanation will explain this novel, about which I have to differ fundamentally with what seem to me the one-sided praises of Lem and Fitting. No doubt, as they convincingly point out, *Ubik* is a heroic effort with great strengths, particularly in portraying the experiences of running down, decay and senility, the invasion of entropy into life and consciousness, amid which the little man yet carries on: *impavidum ferient ruinae*. This experience of manipulated worlds, so characteristic of all our lives, is expressed by a verbal richness manifest, first, in a whole fascinating cluster of neologisms connected with the half-life, and second, in the delicious satire centred on the thing Ubik – the principle of food, health and preservation of existence, of anti-entropic energy – which is promoted in kitschy ad terms parodying the unholy capitalist alliance of science, commercialism and religious blasphemy. Dick's basic concern with death and rebirth, or to put it briefly with *transubstantiation*, has here surfaced perhaps more clearly than anywhere else in his opus. Yet it seems to me that – regardless of how far one would be prepared to follow Dick's rather unclear religious speculations – there is a serious loss of narrative control in *Ubik*. The 'psi-powers' signifier has here become not only unnecessary but positively stultifying – for example, has anybody in the book ever got back on the original time-track after Pat's first try-out?; did Pat engineer also her own death? etc. Further questions arise later: why isn't Pat wired out of the common circuit in the moratorium?; why isn't Jory?; etc. There is a clumsy try at subsidiary narrative foci with Vogelsang and Tippy (chs 1 and 5); Jory 'eats' Wendy just when Pat was supposed to have done it; etc. The net result seems to me one of great strengths balanced be equally great weaknesses in a narrative irresponsibility reminiscent of the rabbits-from-the-hat carelessness associated with rankest Van Vogt if not 'Doc' Smith: the false infinities of explaining one improbability by a succession of ever greater ones.

The deconstruction of bourgeois rationality for which Professor Fitting argues seems thus not to result in a new form but in a nihilistic collapse into the oldest mystifying forms of SF melodrama, refurbished, and therefore rendered more virulent, by some genuinely interesting new experiences. This is, of course, not without correlation to Dick's ideologies after the mid-1960s, his drug-taking experiences, and his (often very ingenious) God-constructions; and one must assume that this was validated by the feeblest and least useful aspects of the late-1960s counterculture, by the mentality despising reason, logic and order of any kind – old or new. Thus, the heroic effort of *Ubik* seems to me, in spite of its many incidental felicities, to be the *3SPE* experience writ large: in some ways among the most fascinating SF books of its time, it is finally, I fear, a heroic failure. In art, at least (and I would maintain in society too), there is no freedom without order, no liberation without controlled focusing. A morality cut off from cognition becomes arbitrary; as Dick's own words in the epigraph to this section imply, it becomes in fact impossible.

My argument may perhaps gain some additional strength if it is accepted that Dick's writing around and after *Ubik* has not been of the order of his first-rate novels. From *Now Wait for Last Year* on, it has withdrawn from the earlier richness into an only fragmentary use of his already established model, it has centred on one protagonist and his increasingly private and psychoanalytic problems, or, as the other side of the coin, on a Jungian collective unconscious. In *We Can Build You*, for example, the erstwhile characteristic Dickian theme of the simulacrum Lincoln is left to fizzle out in favour of the Jungian theme of Pris – though the conjuring up of the past probity from the heroic age of the US bourgeoisie against its present corruption cries out for more detailed treatment. While the touch of the master shows in incidental elements of these late novels (for example, the comics society of *The Zap Gun*, or the imitations of Chaplin's *Great Dictator* in *Now Wait for Last Year*) there are also outright failures, such as *Do Androids Dream of Electric Sheep?*, with its underlying confusion between androids as wronged lower class and as inhuman menace. Indeed, Dick's last novel, *Flow My Tears . . .* , raises to my mind seriously the question whether he is going to continue writing SF or change to 'realistic' prose, for its properly SF elements (future Civil War, the reality-changing drug, the 'sixes') are quite perfunctory in comparison to its realistic police-state situations.

4. THE TIME IS OUT OF JOINT: INSTEAD OF A CONCLUSION

> 'Oh no', Betty disagreed, 'no science in it. Science fiction deals with future, in particular future where science had advanced over now. Book fits neither premise'.
>   'But', Paul said, 'it deals with alternate present. Many well-known science fiction novels of that sort.'
>   (*MHC*, ch. 7)

A number of very tempting subjects have to be left undiscussed here: the uses and transubstantiations of stimuli from movies and music (especially vocal music concerned with transcending the empirical world, for example, in Bach, Wagner, or Verdi); the uses of literature – from Shakespeare, Aesop, and Ibsen through Hemingway, Wells, Orwell and the comics to the SF of the 1940s and 1950s; the strange coexistence of dazzling verbal invention with sloppiness and crudities; etc. Also, no conclusion will be attempted here. That would be rather an impertinence in the case of a writer hopefully only in the middle of life's path, who has grown and changed several times so startlingly, outstripping consistently most of his critics (so that he will, hopefully, also prove my gloomy opinions about his latest phase wrong). Instead of a conclusion, I would like to stress that in his very imperfections Dick seems typical. All his near futures and alternate presents are parabolic mirrors for our time, which he has always deeply felt to be out of joint. His political acumen was a good dozen years in advance of his fellow-Americans, not so much because he mentions Nixon both as President and as FBI Chief in his earliest works as because, for example, in his first novel he asked: 'But what are you supposed to do in a society that's corrupt? Are you supposed to obey corrupt laws? Is it a crime to break a rotten law . . .?' (ch. 14). His ontologico-religious speculations, while to my mind less felicitous, have the merit of taking to some logical SF limits the preoccupations a great number of people have tried to express in more timid ways. It is when Dick's view is trained both on Society and Reality in their impact upon human relationships, with the ontology still clearly grounded in the sociology, that I believe Dick's major works, from *MHC* to *Dr B*, have been written. His concerns with alienation and reification, with one-dimensional humans, parallel in SF terms the concerns of a whole generation, expressed in writings such as those of Marcuse or Laing. His concerns with a social organization based on direct human relations parallel the movements for a radical democracy from the Berkeley Free Speech movement (the scene of his most fully utopian work, *Dr B*) to the abortive youth-New Left movement of the late 1960s. His deep intuitive feeling for decline and entropy raises the usual Spenglerian theatrics of space-opera SF to the 'Humpty-Dumpty' landscapes of *MTS*, *3SPE* and *Ubik*. He always speaks directly out of and to the American experience of his generation, most so when he uses the parabolic mirror of Germans and Nazis. He has the strengths and limitations of his existential horizons, which are identical to that of his favourite hero – the artificer, including the verbal craftsman. His books are artefacts, refuges from and visions of reality – as are Abendsen's book *The Grasshopper Lies Heavy* in *MHC* and Lederman's *Pilgrim Without Progress* in *3SPE*. In fact, only a fiction writer could have embarked on the Pirandellian ontology of *Ubik*, whose characters search not only for their Author but also for their world. Explicating the message in terms of the form, half a dozen works by Dick, at least, are SF classics. That is equivalent to saying that they are significant humanistic literature.

(Originally published in 1975)

NOTES

1. *S* means stories collected or otherwise published in books, namely nos 2, 7, 27, 32, 38 and 42 in R. D. Mullen's bibliography in *SFS*, no. 5 (1977) 5–8, with the lead story from no. 7 somewhat arbitrarily classified as a novel; *N* means novel. The 1967 *Ganymede Take-Over*, written in collaboration, is counted as one half of a novel and will not be further considered here. The most frequently used titles of Dick's are abbreviated, after their first mention, as follows: *MHC* for *The Man in the High Castle*, *MTS* for *Martian Time-Slip*, *3SPE* for *The Three Stigmata of Palmer Eldritch*, and *Dr B* for *Dr Bloodmoney*. My thanks for help in procuring books by Dick are due to Fredric Jameson, L. W. Currey, Mr Martinas Yčas, and to Doubleday and Co. for *Flow My Tears . . .*; and for first forcing me to look closer at Dick to Dr Alison Gopnik, then a McGill student. I have also profited from the contributions to the special Dick issue of *SFS* mentioned above, which I edited – both where I largely agree (as with Jameson) and where I largely disagree (as with Lem and Fitting).

2. Dick died half a dozen years after this essay was published, and I could have expanded it into a retrospect on his whole opus. I decided not to do so: first, because the strictly limited size of this book meant that another essay would have had to be dropped. But second, and more to the point, because I feel his development after 1974 – though with characteristic Dickian ups and downs, the rarer ups being wonderful – has confirmed my fears about the effects of a runaway inflation of ontological orgies. It would be no fun and no use to pull an even longer face at a wondrous, unfortunate and now dead creator. Rather than detailing where the real unreality of his society destroyed him – as so many other Californians, from Scott Fitzgerald to Marilyn Monroe – let us remain thankful for what he, in spite of all (or, thinking of Palmer Eldritch, in the teeth of it all) gave us. And obversely, let this practically unchanged essay also testify to its own historicity.

10

Parables of De-Alienation: Le Guin's Widdershins Dance

0. Why, of all the numerous interesting US SF writers, focus on the opuses of Philip K. Dick in the preceding essay and of Ursula K. Le Guin in the following one? No doubt, the first reason is my personal limitations of time, money, etc. But given that I was only writing on two of them, I shall put forward a justification adopted from Rafail Nudelman's remark (in the *SFS* issue on Le Guin) that Dick and Le Guin seem to be the two extremes among the significant English-language SF writers of the 1960s and early 1970s: the dominant movement in Le Guin's possible world(s) is toward oneness as the natural condition of the world, while in Dick it is toward disintegration of order and unity, toward destruction of all forms as the condition of his world(s). I would translate this general syntax as follows: both of these leading writers write out of and react against a historically identical – psychological and sociopolitical – situation: the experience of the terrible pressures of alienation, isolation and fragmentation pervading the neo-capitalist society of the world of the mid-twentieth century. But while Dick is a 'romantic' writer, whose energy lashes out in a profusion of incandescent and interfused narrative protuberances, Le Guin is a 'classical' writer, whose energy is as fierce but strictly controlled within a taut and spare architectural system of narrative cells. While both have – as any significant writer must – a fixed creative focus, Dick writes centrifugally, as it were in revolving sectors (say of a radar sweep) whose apex is always the same but whose field may differ, whereas Le Guin writes centripetally, in a narrowing spiral (say of a falcon circling to a swoop) delineating ever more precisely the same object. The main strength of the first lies in the recording of breakdowns in the old individualist system of interhuman relationships; of the second, in the quest for, and indeed (in the very midst of such a breakdown) in the first sketching of, a new collectivist system.

(Dick's fascination with simulacra or super-aliens and Le Guin's with time or the forest-minds do not at all contradict the assertion that their subject is interhuman relationships, to which – as in any writer – all other relations can only be analogies; I argued that for Dick in Chapter 9 and will argue it for Le Guin here.) Conversely, Dick gets less believable when he tries to focus on undegraded human relationships, a new collective (as in *Galactic Pot-Healer*) – he is not a bearer of good news; and Le Guin when she tries to focus on a Dickian world in degradation from which the individual must secede (as in *The Lathe of Heaven* and 'Those Who Walk Away from Omelas') – she is not a bearer of bad news. Both writers seem to have felt this, and *Galactic Pot-Healer* is finally negated by a down-beat ending just as the Le Guin novel and story are by upbeat ones – types of endings really more congenial to the basic creative vision of each. Characteristically, the three works mentioned are those in which the visions of Dick and Le Guin have been invaded by a not wholly assimilated alien vision: by Jung's in the case of Dick, by Dick's in the case of *LoH*, and by Dunsany's in the case of 'Omelas'. Concurrently, the stylistic danger for Dick is murkiness and prolixity, for Le Guin brittleness and curtness. Or, to simplify: Dick sees a world of addition and multiplication, so he reproduces it in his narrative forms; Le Guin sees a world of subtraction and division, and she also started by reproducing it – but it seems to me (see also the special *SFS* 1975 issue) that as of *The Left Hand of Darkness* she has increasingly expressed the complementary urge toward integration. At any rate, we need seers of both the Le Guin and the Dick type, for their visions help us to define and thus master our common world.[1]

1.   THE DISPOSSESSING

My thesis is that *the main thrust and strength of Ursula K. Le Guin's writing lies in the quest for and sketching of a new, collectivist system of no longer alienated human relationships, which arise out of the absolute necessity for overcoming an intolerable ethical, cosmic, political and physical alienation.* That this is the root experience present in the whole of Le Guin's opus could best be proved by an analysis of that whole. Here I shall have to content myself with a few – but I hope fundamental – indications.[2] However, it seems clear that such an analysis would, already in the sundered and dispersed races and communities of what could be called her 'apprentice trilogy' (*RW*, *PE* and *CI*) no less than in its metaphorical system of coldness and depopulated landscapes, find an 'objective correlative' of the alienation. Each of her novels is centred on a redeeming hero whose fierce loyalty to his companions and his task is an attempt to counteract the Fall of the symbolic territory – as is the development of mind-speech. In the apprentice trilogy, the hero is a stranger superior to the primitive territory. In *LHD*, the point of view of the stranger is for the first time shown as fallible, and the territory – though still cold and only artificially implanted with a human-yet-physiologically-inhuman population – has produced its own hero, the territorial traitor with a higher loyalty to humanity. This is exacerbated in *WWF*, where the well-meaning but sterile outsider can survive – both as narrative agent and narrative focus – only as part of the fertile indigenous liberation; and it is completely overcome in Le Guin's culminating masterpiece *TD* where the hero and the territory are for the first time adequate to each other: both the creative scientist-philosopher and classless society are a dynamically evolving vanguard of humanity so that higher loyalty to humanity does not have to be treason to its exemplary territorial manifestation in this novel. Parallel to the evolution of the hero from outsider to characterological embodiment of the territory is the evolution of the social habitat. Except for *LoH*, which for reasons explained at the outset I shall here slight, it is a strictly non-capitalist habitat. It is first presented as a barbaric simplification within which direct human relations can still be shown as meaningful, using but already largely refunctioning SF and heroic fantasy clichés (in *RW* a mixture of Tolkien or even Dunsany with SF feudalism of the Poul Anderson type, in *PE* the abandoned colony and the savage onslaught, in *CI* the post-Catastrophe social reversion, the Vanvogtian two-minded hero unconscious of his superpower, the Tolkienian bad guys, and a decadently refined enemy city strongly reminiscent of Buck Rogers' place of captivity under the Han Air Lords). In *LHD* – the hinge and divide of Le Guin's opus, the novel within which she broke through the apprenticeship to mastery and which because of that groans under the richness of dazzling and not fully integrated or clarified concepts – the social habitat is not so much a regression to uncluttered earlier social formation, but rather a simplified alternative to the capitalist or commodity-economics model (see Jameson's *SFS* article). All of Le Guin's opposed discords – foreignness and identity, loneliness and togetherness, fragmentation and connection, and a number of others all rooted in the split between I and Thou, Self and the Other – emerge in *LHD* in an up to then most concentrated and articulated form, materialized in the huge ice plateau of the novel's culmination. But at the same time, that culmination becomes a 'place inside the blizzard' engendering its own values; the habitat has thrown up its own weavers of unification, personal and political – Estraven the Traitor and his appropriate successor, Faxe the Weaver.

None the less, the fact that the ethical and the politico-religious strands of *LHD* still demand two (or three) bearers; or, that the Foretellers' religion and the other Gethenian myths with their metaphors of creation and still centre emerge as the main support unifying the novel's disparate thematic strands of geography, anthropology and political intrigue; or, in still other words, the richness yet fragmentation of the points of view, sundering narrator and hero – all these loose ends, though here turned to excellent formal account, admit of further conceptual and therefore also narrative stringency. In *WWF* a hero was found who could – at a price – unite action and reflection, world-time and dream-time, and show forth both vertical (relation of conscious-unconscious) and horizontal (relation of self and society) de-alienation. Very significantly, de-alienation is brought about by a liberating struggle against imperialist colonialism. Yet, though imperialist oppression is in our age the sabre's edge of the crassest, crudest and physically most murderous alienation (so that the characters of Ho Chi Minh or of doctors Ernesto Guevara and Frantz Fanon are quite relevant to that of Selver), unfortunately alienation within the all-pervading psychical eco-system of modern capitalism is not always so conveniently embodied in a malevolent Other. In everyday life within the imperial powers, the malignance of alienation lies largely in its insidious power to be internalized into the Self – and the defence of a balanced Self against death-bringing alienation of its own powers is the subject of Le Guin's *Earthsea Trilogy*. Seen from a purely formal viewpoint of internal consistency and stylistic clarity, that trilogy is her best work up to *TD*. But there is a price to pay for the pitiless simplification inherent in even the best heroic fantasy, and in particular when it is the parable of the Proper Namer, the artist-creator: his lonely sin can only be irresponsible playing with a world whose sole arbiter he is. Beautiful, polished and self-enclosed like a diamond necklace, *The Earthsea Trilogy* thus in the end deals with what a creator (say a writer) must do in order to live and create, and Ged's Dunsanian Taoism seems to me at a second – propaedeutic or therapeutic – remove from what Le Guin is trying to write about in her SF of collective practice. Therefore, the malevolent alienation, which comes from the outside but is mirrored inside the territory and the hero, was not disposed of in Earthsea. Even *WWF* only showed the emergence of the 'translating' or mediating hero; the territory of *WWF*, the forest which is the word for the world in the language of Selver's people, is in a static balance, a closed circle of unhistorical time. Selver's horizontal, collective de-alienation is achieved at the price of a partial vertical, personal alienation into what Le Guin here still calls 'the dead land of action' (ch. 2).

Only Urras and Anarres in *TD* are a twin system, able to account for the threats and forms of both external and internal alienation; only *TD* reconciles linear and circular time – or cosmic, historical and personal sense – in Shevek's simulsequentialist physics, politics and ethics. And this is, if not caused by (one hesitates to say, just as in Shevek's physics, which is cause and which effect), certainly correlative to the ideologico-political breakthough of Le Guin's identifying the root and the privileged forms of alienation as propertarian possession (i.e. capitalism). 'The Dispossessed' is already in its title so much richer than the territorial titles of the 'apprentice trilogy' or the Taoist mythopoetics (somewhat hollow in 'The Lathe of Heaven', and beautifully pivoted in 'The Left Hand of Darkness') of her middle-period book titles. The dispossessed are those who have no more possessions, the non-propertarians, but also those who are no more possessed (in the Dostoevskian sense of demon-ridden) or obsessed by the principle of Having instead of Being, no more ridden by profiteering possessiveness whether applied to things, other people, nature, knowledge (Sabul's and Urrasian physics) or to oneself (Urrasian – for example, Veia's – sexuality). From a propertarian point of view, the Anarresians have voluntarily dispossessed themselves of life-sustaining property, of their very planet; from an anarchist or socialist/communist/utopian point of view, they have rid themselves of the demon possession. The Dispossessed means thus literally – in its more beautiful, semantically richer, and thus more forceful English – the De-Alienated, those rid of alienation both as physical reification (by things and impersonal apparatuses) and as psychical obsession (by demons and what Marx calls fetishes). The things that are in the saddle and ride the reified Possessed recur in the imagery of barriers between individuals as well as between people and things on Urras – its walls and wrappings. The fetishes or idols of the obsessed Possessed are ideological pseudo-categories such as freedom *from* rather than freedom *for* (ch. 5) and linguistic idols such as the hierarchical 'higher' or 'superior' standing for excellent (ch. 1). Of course, obsession and reification are only two faces of the same pale rider, in the sense suggested by the fundamental Marxist category of 'commodity fetishism,' which uses the most modern philosophical vocabulary to properly name the most ancient enslavement or alienation of humanity. Thus, the ideological pseudo-categories and idols in *TD* are themselves also walls and wrappings, and vice versa. Therefore Anarres is at least ideally committed to being the place of naked, open, not compartmentalized (for example, professionally or sexually) and almost thingless human relationships. Its name testifies to its being not only the country of An-Archy (non-domination) and the negated (*an*) or reinvented (*ana*) Urras, but also (see Bierman in *SFS*) the Country Without Things (*res*); and Urras is not only a phonetically heightened shadow of Earth, but the primitive (*Ur*) and stunted (only disyllabic) opposite of Anarres; it is the place which has not yet got rid of *res*. The very real shortcomings and backslidings of Anarres do not ultimately detract from but instead reaffirm the exemplarity of its original, Odonian impulse.

2. THE NEW ATLANTIS

To pursue and perhaps clinch this argument, let me analyze Le Guin's latest story, 'The New Atlantis' (*NA*). In all evolutionary processes, in the Darwinian phylogenetic tree, in the spiral of social history, or in a writer's opus, the future – the latest point to which evolution has arrived, and the use of that point for a retrospective – is the justification and explanation of the past, and thus in a sense its cause. If this at first sight fairly abstruse story can be deciphered by using the theory that the centre of Le Guin's creation is the double star of identifying the neo-capitalist, individualist alienation and juxtaposing to it a sketch of a new, collectivist and harmonious, creation, then the theory will be shown to work.

NA is divided into two interlocking narrations, which gradually and parallel to each other define themselves and their mutual correspondences. As in *TD*, this is correlative to their presenting an

old and a new world – here a declining or subsiding and an
ascending or emerging one. Analogous to the parallelism of physics
to ethics and politics in *TD*, the informing metaphor of *NA* is the
substitution of geology for history. The old world, the old Atlantis of
NA rushing headlong toward the chasm which engulfed the
legendary Atlantis, is a somewhat extrapolated USA of advanced
political and ecological breakdown, rather similar to one of Orr's
alternative futures in the 2002 of *LoH* (and equally laid in Portland,
Oregon, *LoH*'s – and Le Guin's, who lives there – 'centre of the
world'). A 'corporative State', a well-identified American variant of
admass fascism, is conjured up simply by integrating into a
seamless governmental totality all the already existing
bureaucracies (as the Nazis did): stock-market and unions, health,
education and welfare, credit-cards and mass-media, with
interstices for regulated and parasitic 'private enterprise'. The
system makes lavish use of the twentieth-century habits of false
naming: the 'Supersonic Superscenic Deluxe Longdistance bus' is a
dilapidated coal-burner which breaks down when it tries to go over
30 mph; the 'Longhorn Inch-Thick Steak House Dinerette' serves
meatless hamburgers; the All-American Broadcasting Company
confidently announces that the war in Liberia is going well for 'the
forces of freedom' and peace is at hand in Uruguay, interspersing
this with weekly 'all-American Olympic Games' and catchy
commercials for 'coo-ol, puu-uure USG [i.e. canned] water'; and so
on. Also, a repressive bourgeois legality is only somewhat extended
to cover Solzhenitsyn-like Rehabilitation Camps and Federal
Hospitals for dissidents, compulsory full employment, reduction of
universities to trade schools, etc. But within this fairly standard
American radical nightmare, whose aspects can be found in a
number of SF works from Orwell and Pohl to Spinrad, there are two
new elements. First, in the sinking world there is a story of the
narrator's scientist-husband Simon and a group of friends, not too
dissimilar from Shevek's group (Simon publishes in Peking!) but in
USA rather than Anarres and, correspondingly, incomparably more
repressed. Working illegally, they invent direct energy conversion,
which would in sane circumstances stop the ecological breakdown
and thus obviate the economic necessity for the corporative – or any
centralized – State and its way of life. But the circumstances are the
opposite of sane, and, though the scientist-creators have found how
to use physical power, they have no clue to how to find and use
political power. This typical Leguinian ambiguity already makes the

story superior to either the unfounded optimism by which technological inventions automatically save the world bringing about decentralization and similar (for example, the same device in early Simak), or the gloom and doom arising from exclusive concentration – sometimes with an almost morbid satisfaction – on an ecologico-political breakdown (for example, in Brunner's very similar environment of *The Sheep Look Up*).

However, the second specifically Leguinian element is embodied in the very composition and style of the story, and therefore much more important. It is the parallel picture of a new creation – alternating with the old as the Anarres chapters do with the Urras ones in *TD* – which is arriving at self-consciousness and self-definition, a bit as if Plato's or Butler's souls of the not-yet-born were being incarnated and were gradually defining their senses by defining their environment: an extraordinary beautiful new Genesis of perception and cognition – of time, space, number and universe – by means of fitful lights. It is an (extremely un-Baconian) New Atlantis, an undersea creation which rises from a dark and cold pressure through mysterious tides to a final breakthrough into life. But the Genesis is, as always in Le Guin, an impure and ambiguous one. The light-bearing, Luciferic creatures announcing and inducing it are dwarfish and misshapen: ' . . . all mouth. They ate one another whole. Light swallowed light all swallowed together in the vaster mouth of the darkness.' Yet these cruel and poor 'tiny monsters burning with bright hunger, who brought us back to life' define by their hungry lights the coordinates of collective space, the planes and towers of a city which had existed earlier but had fallen. The city is now being recreated through the act of beholding and remembering it, and raised by irresistible geological pressures. At the end, the dawn still arrives as a dark blue and cold, a submarine one – the awareness of light itself rather than of the objects lit – but the metamorphosis of light above the tops of the towers indicates that the city's emergence is at hand.

I have paraphrased the much more puzzling 'submarine' strand of the narration as closely as I could in order to argue about its meaning in itself and within the whole story. Now, only second-rate writings in SF are rigid allegories with a one-to-one relationship of each item described to some dogmatic scheme. However, I would maintain that any significant writing in SF is necessarily analogical or parabolical – a parable being a verisimilar narration which has a determinable meaning or tenor outside of narration, but whose plausibility is not based upon such a transferred meaning but upon internal narrative consistency. Thus the classical (say New Testament) parable is ideologically closed or univocal, but stylistically always open-ended, waiting for the reader's application; its ultimate aim is the shock of estrangement reorienting the reader's perception – in modern times, making her recognize the alienated world she lives in. It is not an allegory in that it does not substitute one thing for another (in the case of *NA*, alienation for the dark pressure which had so long prevented fallen Atlantis from rising again) but *sets one thing by the side of another*, the explicit by the side of the implicit. Therefore, in a parable the literal narrative and the meaning 'do not coincide, as in an allegory; it is only parallels that exist between the two'.[3] And though the direction of the meaning is clear and univocal, there may be several levels of meaning; a parable is usually polysemous. All this seems particularly applicable to Le Guin, whose Anti-Queen Utopa – Odo (in *TD*) – wrote two books, *Community* and *Analogy* (her analogies, if I understand the Anarresians well, have four 'modes' – ethical, physico-technological, religious and philosophical – not unlike Dante's four modes of allegory): Le Guin is one of the most consciously analogical or parabolic writers around. What, then, does the analogy of the New Atlantis stand for?

If the story *NA* is to have any unity, the emerging new City must be an analogy – here by contraries – to the dying US society, a new republic, community or life-form germinating up from the depths, symmetrically opposed, as it were, to the perishing republic of the first strand. One key is supplied by the personal pronoun: the declining narration is in first person singular, the 'I' being that of Belle, the disloyal but suppressed citizen of the corporate State and wife of the only momentarily freed concentration-camp prisoner Simon. The ascending narration is in first person plural, the 'we' being a new community (shades of Odo!) which relates to that of the USA as collectivism does to individualism and also – in view of the cognition and colour imagery – as beauty and knowledge to pollution and ignorance of both self and universe. The Atlantis collective has been submerged and unconscious for ages, just as has the idea of a true and beautiful collective or classless society; the Fall of Atlantis, then, is here something like the fall from tribal into class society and the concomitant alienation of man into social institutions. A condition of pristine unity is presupposed in the whole of Le Guin's opus as a past Golden Age; it echoes through the present alienation from the unsplit Ancient One in *RW*, through the direct, unalienated communication he gives to Rocannon – mind-speech (whose development is the primary red thread of her writing up to *LHD*, rather than the Hainish chronology so ingeniously worked out by Watson in *SFS*, no. 5), to Selver's integral forest in *WWF* and the other forest-minds and tree images in her opus. But by 1975, in *NA*, there is a New Atlantis rising: the forces of de-alienation are on the rise in Le Guin's writing, parallel to what she (one hopes rightly) senses as the deep historical currents in the world. Having achieved a balance with darkness in *LHD*, a partial victory in *WWF* and the first large-scale victory in *TD*, these forces of a new and better creation are now ready to rise in full stature to the surface of our Earth. We cannot tell exactly who they are and what they will be like: we can only tell that they are being raised up by tides stronger than even the ultimate class society of the corporate State, by the slow and inexorable geological tides of history so to speak; that they have just begun to remember the past glories of their City; and that the Luciferic goads and precursors (the lantern-creatures, whom I would interpret as the revolutionary political and ideological movements of the last century or two, say since 1789 and 1917, swallowing each other up in fierce infighting and 'all swallowed together' by the still stronger alienation), although themselves twisted and stunted, have awakened the new creation to self-awareness.

All this can be confirmed by the correspondences existing between adjoining sections of the two narrative strands. The American strand is divided into six segments, each of which precedes the corresponding segment of the New Atlantis strand; and each group of two segments from the juxtaposed strands has a correspondingly parallel or inverse motif. For example, the two no. 1 segments (pp. 61–4 and 64–6) are introductions to the world and theme of the segment – to American degradations *vs*. Atlantean creation; the two no. 4 segments (pp. 76–9 and 79–80) present the 'cold sunrise' – the invention of direct conversion of solar power frustrated by the lack of political power *vs*. the deindividualized blue sunrise 'the color of the cold, the color farthest from the sun'; the two no. 5 segments (pp. 80–3 and 83–5) balance the American dissidents' frustrated vision of a possible New (the solar cell and its implications) with the Atlantean collective's wondering memory of the wonderful Old (the jewel-like gracious city and its implications); and finally, the last two segments (pp. 85–6) present the end of the

American narrator's private world-cell (the re-arrest of her husband) and the nearing end of the USA in earthquakes combated by atomic bombs, opposed to the breakthrough of the new Atlantis.

However, one final element reintroduces the realistic, bitter-sweet Leguinian ambiguity. For after all, it may be very well to know that the end of our creation means, at the same time, the beginning of a new and more colourful one; yet this is not a full consolation for our passing – for the passing of the courageous and well-meaning group of Simon's, and of the whole old continent with its future Schuberts (such as the Forrest whose compositions are also surreptitiously played by Simon's wife). And indeed it is the 'yearning music from far away in the darkness, calling not to us [i.e. not to the Atlanteans but to the Americans – and to the reader] "Where are you? I am here"', which is echoed in the final segment spoken by the Atlanteans:

> Where are You?
> We are here. Where have you gone?

For the music of the 'lonely ones, the voyagers' (like Schubert) called out for non-alienated man all along, through our whole history of fallen Atlantis. This music is not only the harmony of sounds – I would further interpret – but all harmony of art, science and philosophy, always harking back or looking forward to human unity: unity of a person within himself, of people in society, of humanity on Earth, and of people with nature. By that same token, such music of sounds, concepts, shapes or formulas is a witness to the unborn potentialities and unfulfilled promises of the race that produced this music. That is why it calls to it, and not to the Atlanteans. But that is also why the Atlanteans' last question-segment – the end of their strand and of the whole *NA*, which is rendered all the weightier for consisting of only three sentences – must, subsuming as it does the voices of the old creation's music, be taken as a lament for lost potentialities, as an acknowledgement that the New will, paradoxically, be lonely without (and because of the failure of) the Old. In my interpretation, even the classless society, the more beautiful humanity, will always miss the lost potentialities of ours, all our mute, inglorious Miltons or unburned Brunos or 40-year-old Mozarts. In simpler and less elitist terms, it will always yearn for all the life-patterns lost in our unnecessary hungers, diseases and wars. Le Guin's future is lonely for the past, as ascetic

Anarres is for the promises (the plant and animal creation as well as the people) of Urras.

I fail to see how else one can make full sense of *NA*.

3. THE PRICE AND THE HOPE

As the above analysis of *NA* and the elegiac tone (Nudelman) of Le Guin's whole opus indicate, the ambiguities never absent from it do not primarily flow from a static balancing of two yin-and-yang-type alternatives, two principles or opposites (light-darkness, male-female, etc.) between which a middle Way of wisdom leads. This may be an aspect or a 'middle phase' (Porter) of Le Guin's, but I would think the attempts to subsume her under Taoism (which has undoubtedly had an influence) are in view of her development after *LoH* not only doomed to failure but also retrospectively revealed as inadequate even for her earlier works (*LoH* being, here again, an exception, but as Watson argued a purgative one). Rather, the Leguinian ambiguities are in principle dynamic, and have through her evolution become more clearly and indubitably such. That means that to every opposition or contradiction there is, as Mao Tse-tung[4] would say, a principal aspect which is dominant or ascendant and by means of which that contradiction renders asunder the old, transforming it into the new. That principal or dominant aspect is Selver's 'godhood' translating new and terrible dreams into a new world-time, or Odonianism, the principle of classless and non-antagonistic community, analogically applied to man and the universe, transforming the old politics, ethics and physics. The synthesis of linear, sequential progress and cyclical, simultaneous fulness of being into spiral simulsequentialist dialectics is balanced only in the way a master skater or a hovering falcon is – in permanent revolution and evolution, which fails as soon as it is arrested. And it is always a left-hand skate or swoop, a counter-clock helix, a widdershins dance that goes against the dominant and alienated received ideas of our civilization.

Le Guin's heretic protagonists are culture heroes, in that each founds a major cultural concept, translating it from unnamed to named existence. The ingathering of races and recuperation of mind-speech which permits the naming of Rocannon's World, Estraven's 'treason', Selver's liberation warfare, Shevek's unifying ansible, Simon's direct power conversion, are such concepts. In the long run, they assert themselves in the Hainish universe; but not necessarily in the short run. Realistically, the heroes pay a stiff price for their victories, though the price decreases through Le Guin's opus down to Shevek, the first Founding Father who is also a biological father and whose collective or *comitatus* is not destroyed at the end of the story – another way of saying he can live on to enjoy his victory. Almost everybody else, from Rocannon and Falk to Selver and Simon, is an ambiguous questing figure 'lonely, isolated . . . out on the edge of things'.[5]

Sometimes, especially in early Le Guin, this is almost an existentialist stance of envisaging the creator as necessarily lonely in the *a priori* alien world of practice, a stance which sociologically corresponds to a petty-bourgeois intellectualism. Thus, an elementary text of capitalist economics bores Shevek, and no doubt Le Guin, 'past endurance' (ch. 5), as can be gathered from the political economics – what and how people work, cook, buy or distribute, what share of social product they create and control – absent from *LHD* and *LoH*, even from *TD* and *NA*, and replaced at their centre by shifting counterpoints of ethics, politics, and 'direct contact' with nature. Mythology and some forms of quasi-religious (though atheist) mysticism are a logical ground bass to these counterpoints. This is accompanied by a deep distrust of organized mass politics which (though historically understandable) even in *TD* leads to such half-truths as the 'You cannot make the Revolution. You can only be the Revolution. It is in your spirit, or it is nowhere' (ch. 9), explaining why the Urras revolt is the weakest link in that novel. Obversely, it also means a certain naïve dissolution of politics into ethics as in *CI* which is ideologically based on the conflict of the Shings' lie with Falk's truth. Indeed, mind-speech itself is (as in all SF) a kind of individualistic substitute for de-alienation or metaphor for a unifying collectivism, so that the Shings' possibility of mind-lying corresponds to a false collectivism (politically something like Fascism, Stalinism or – in its insistence on not taking life – Christianity) – which is why it is so horrifying. But this is a mystifying metaphor which translates the de-alienation into terms of the self rather than of the society. When the self is projected on to rather than taken as an analogy of the society or indeed the universe, narrative and ideological difficulties arise. A good example for projection *vs.* analogy are the two Portland tales, *LoH* and *NA*, the second of which seems to me to achieve what the first did not.

On the other hand, however, the insistence on personally meaningful ethics, on means commensurate to ends, is much more than petty-bourgeois sentimentality or liberalism. Though in actual practice things can never be as neat as in abstract planning, this is to my mind that demand of the old society, of radical and revolutionary middle-class (bourgeois and petty-bourgeois) traditions, for which the new society – or at least the movements toward socialism in the last 100 years – has to yearn as much as the New Atlanteans do for the old creation's Schubert-like music. In insisting upon it, Le Guin is taking up her characteristic dialectical position of being the devil's advocate not so much against the alienated old as against the insufficiently or ambiguously de-alienated new. Her political position can be thought of as a radical critic and ally of socialism defending its duty to inherit the heretic democratic, civic traditions, for example Jefferson's or indeed Tom Paine's. This would explain her great ideological affinity for the Romantics and the post-Romantic nineteenth-century democrats, especially for the left-wing 'populists' culminating in Tolstoi, Hugo, and Thoreau (whose *Walden* is the 'New Canon' of *CI*). That stance has some contradictions of its own (see Jameson, 1976), but when taken as being itself an Old Canon flowing into the New Canon of libertarian socialism, it represents a precious antidote to socialism's contamination by the same alienating forces it has been fighting so bitterly in the last century – by power apparatuses and a pragmatic rationality that become ends instead of means. Le Guin's anarchism, then, can be malevolently thought of as the furthest radical limit at which a disaffected petty-bourgeois intellectual may arrive, a leftist Transcendentalism, or benevolently as a personal, variant name for and way to a truly new libertarian socialism. A choice between these two interpretations will be possible only in retrospect, a few years hence; and no doubt, judging from her own spiral development in the last six or seven years, both interpretations of such an anarchism are partly right. But to my mind, in spite of elements discussed in the preceding paragraph, the dominant or ascendant aspect of Le Guin's contradictory ideology is a useful one. It not only claims for socialism the self-governing tradition of the citizen (as opposed to that of the bourgeois),[6] for example, the New England town-meeting tradition; it is not only a politically realistic warning; it also shapes accurate and therefore pleasurable *artistic analogies to the contemporary situation of the liberating New*. Just as her lonely heretics, the forces of the New are in truth – under the terrible pressures of the totalizing neo-capitalist commodity-economy (see Jameson, 1976) and of their own mistakes and dead ends (primarily the Russian example) – in an isolated minority within the North Atlantic if not the New Atlantean world. Their position and vicissitudes seem to me to explain not only the clear-eyed elegiac atmosphere of Le Guin's, but also the retrenchment she austerely – almost puritanically – operates in all of her work, culminating in *TD*. This 'world-reduction' (Jameson, 1976) is not only a reaction to the polluted American abundance and a realistic diagnosis of a better model of life but also the sign of a situation where the bearers of the New, the Lucifers, are separated from the large majority of those for whom this New is intended. In this situation, the aridity – like that of Anarres – is a retrenchment from the 'living flesh' (*TD*, ch. 4) of a natural community, a harsh but clean acceptance of asceticism. The beautiful passages of Shevek's recognition of animals (ch. 5) no less than the end of *NA* seem to me to signify that gulf of unrequited brotherhood. (In a somewhat more melodramatic form, the power of the clone break-up in 'Nine Lives', whose survivor, metamorphosed from being part to being alone, has to learn the lesson of alienation, surely also comes from this cluster of concepts.)

In an earlier article,[7] when faced with a group of 1969 novels including *LHD*, I noted that a clear group of 'New Left' SF writers (a term that, as used here, has to do more with sensibility and world view than political affiliation) had emerged. Their common denominator is a radical disbelief in the individualist ideology – that is, that a stable and humane system can be built upon a sum of individual, Robinson Crusoe greeds as the measure of all values. They deal with a changed neo-capitalist society of mass disaffection, mass media and mass breakdowns in a perceptive form for which – as different from earlier SF – Joyce, Dos Passos, Malraux, Faulkner, Brecht and intermedia in art, or Marcuse and Mao in philosophy of history, are living presences though not sacred texts. Ursula Le Guin, with her unsentimental warm concern with collective humanism, is the clearest and most significant writer of this group, allowing us to recognize our central concerns through a detour of estrangement. Already, *LHD* spoke – to use the words of that novel – to our 'strong though undeveloped sense of humanity, of human unity. I got quite excited thinking about this' (ch. 8). Since then she has evolved through Lao Tze to Kropotkin and Goodman. Le Guin is less flashy and abrasive than most other 'New Left' writers – such as Brunner, Delany, Russ or Spinrad – and the major presences in her writing are rather poets from Marvell and Coleridge on, and social novelists from Dickens, Stendhal and Dostoevsky to Solzhenitsyn and Virginia Woolf. In that way, she is the most European and – in her sense of human relationships being determined by human institutions – most novelistic writer in present-day American SF.

This blend of nineteenth-century Realism and a discreet Virginia Woolf-type adoption of some techniques of lyric poetry with the ethical abstraction of American romances may account for much of her stylistic power and accessibility. Her clear and firm but richly and truthfully ambiguous Leftism situates her at the node of possibly the central contemporary contradiction, that between capitalist alienation and the emerging classless de-alienation. Because of that, Le Guin is today not only one of scarcely half a dozen most important SF writers in the world, but her SF parables from *LHD* to *NA* are to my mind among the most penetrating and entertaining explorations of the deep value shifts of our age. Like the basic image in her work, that of two different hands meeting the dark, her writings touch us gently and firmly, reminding us that across the gulfs of otherness our brothers not only can but must be met. Her widdershins dance, denying alienation, figures forth a de-alienated humanity. That, I believe, is the basis for her wide popularity. Saying 'no' to the old, she also says 'yes' to the new – witness *TD* and *NA*. And if these tales were written a dozen years after she began publishing, what cannot we hope for from her in the future arising from such a past?

(Originally published in 1975)

NOTES

1. As in my comment to Dick, I decided not to update this essay from 1975. The reasons are similar but, fortunately, symmetrically obverse to those adduced for Dick's case: Ms Le Guin is still very much with us, and the major work of her uneven phase after *TD* and *NA* (which I still believe were her clear culminations as SF writer), the novel *Always Coming Home*, is just due to be published. I am using the following abbreviations for the titles of Le Guin's works: *CI = City of Illusions; DBR = The Day Before the Revolution; LHD = The Left Hand of Darkness; LoH = The Lathe of Heaven; NA*

= *The New Atlantis*; PE = *Planet of Exile*; RW = *Rocannon's World*; TD = *The Dispossessed*; VTE = *Vaster Than Empires and More Slow*; WWF = *The Word for World is Forest*.

2. On alienation, see two introductory anthologies: Erich Fromm (ed.), *Socialist Humanism* (Garden City, NY, 1966), and Eric and Mary Josephson (eds), *Man Alone* (New York, 1964). See further Meszaros (1970) – details in Bibliography to Part One; and a long bibliography in Herbert Aptheker (ed.), *Marxism and Alienation* (New York, 1965), especially the works by Fromm, Goodman, Marcuse, Marx and Mills.

   For secondary literature, cf. first of all the essays by Nudelman, Jameson and all the others from *SFS*, no. 7 (1975), a special issue on Le Guin's SF which I edited (now in Mullen and Suvin (eds) – see Bibliography to Part Two) and from which I learned much. Further, some pioneering works – for example, by Douglas Barbour, David Ketterer, Stanisław Lem, Robert Scholes and Ian Watson – were extant by the time this essay was written. A great spate of comments followed on the above *SFS* issue. Those until 1979 are usefully commented on by James W. Bittner, 'A Survey of Le Guin Criticism', in Joe de Bolt (ed.), *Ursula K. Le Guin* (Port Washington, NY, 1979) pp. 31–49; that book itself and the essay by Gérard Klein, 'Le Guin's "Aberrant" Opus', *SFS*, no. 13 (1977) pp. 287–95, reprinted in R. D. Mullen and Darko Suvin (eds), *Science-Fiction Studies, Second Series* (Boston, MA, 1978), should be singled out.

3. Eta Linnemann (1966) (see Bibliography to Conclusion) p. 26. See also both on parable and estrangement, Brecht (1966) and Bloch (1972) (both in Bibliography to Part Two), and further on parable and reference Bultmann (1968), Dodd (1971) and Via (1967) (in Bibliography to Conclusion); Abraham Kaplan, 'Referential Meaning in the Arts', *J. of Aesthetics and Art Criticism*, 12 (1964) pp. 457–74; and Louis MacNeice, *Varieties of Parable* (Cambridge, UK, 1965). I began to apply such insights – with due attention to the significant differences between various historical modes of parable – in *MOSF* and *VSF*, and I discuss this quite central matter of parable also elsewhere in this book, in greatest theoretical detail in the concluding essay. Later theoretical studies of mine on theory of narrative and theatre (for example, 'Performance' (1985; see Bibliography to Conclusion) are focused on the Possible World as parabolic vehicle.

4. Mao Tse-tung (Cedong), 'On Contradiction', in his *Four Essays in Philosophy* (Peking, 1968), especially part 4.

5. Le Guin's prefatory note to her story 'The Masters', where such a figure first appears, in her *The Wind's Twelve Quarters* (New York, 1975).

6. See, on this basic historical dualism, Karl Marx, 'On the Jewish Question', in Lloyd D. Easton and Kurt H. Guddat (eds), *Writings of the Young Marx on Philosophy and Society* (Garden City, NY, 1967).

7. D. Suvin, 'The SF Novel in 1969', in James Blish (ed.), *Nebula Award Stories Five* (New York, 1970).

11

On the SF Opus of the Strugatsky Brothers

One of the most useful ways of discussing a relatively unknown but prolific writer (and SF writers usually are prolific – this is, indeed, one of the crucial determinants of their work, where economics and aesthetics uneasily embrace) is to combine an overview with a depth-probe. I shall approach the Strugatskys' opus by this bias, trusting the approach will be justified by its yield.

1. THE DEVELOPMENT OF THE STRUGATSKYS' FICTION

The Strugatsky brothers, who collaborate in their writing, are on the whole the best and most significant Soviet SF writers who began publishing after the breakthrough of Yefremov's *Andromeda* in 1957–8.[1] Arkady, born in 1925, is a specialist in Japanese and English and worked first for the Institute for Technical Information and later for the State Publishing House in Moscow. Boris, born in 1933, was a computer mathematician at the Pulkovo Astronomical Observatory near Leningrad, but seems to have abandoned work in natural sciences for writing. A number of their works have by now been translated into English and other languages, but little context has been provided for placing such works, which come from various phases of their development.[2] In order to supply such a context, particularly necessary in a foreign context, I shall begin by listing their book-length publications; a full list of their works and the available translations into English, French and German can be found (within the limits imposed by the publication date) in my bibliography and article mentioned in notes 2 and 6. The order followed is: Russian title (followed by literal translation), place, publisher, then year of first publication in book form that I know of (unless otherwise indicated). The list is my best guess at the chronological order of actual composition, which in a few cases departs from the order of publication.

(1) *Strana bagrovykh tuch* (The Country of Crimson Clouds) (Moscow: Detgiz, 1959).

(2) *Shest' spichek* (Six Matches) (Moscow: Detgiz, 1960).

(3) *Put' na Amal'teiiu* (Destination: Amaltheia) (Moscow: Mol. gvardiia, 1960).

(4) *Vozvrashchenie. (Polden'. 22-i vek)* (The Homecoming: Noon, 22nd Century) (Moscow: Detgiz, 1962); revised edition expanded to 20 stories as *Polden', XXII vek (Vozvrashchenie)* (Noon, 22nd Century: The Homecoming) (Moscow: Detskaia lit., 1967).

(5) *Stazhery* (The Apprentices) (Moscow: Mol. gvardiia, 1962).

(6) *Popytka k begstvu* (An Attempted Escape), in anthology *Fantastika, 1962 god* (Moscow: Mol. gvardiia, 1962); reprinted together with number 9.

(7) *Dalekaia Raduga* (Far Rainbow), in anthology *Novaia signal'naia* (Moscow: Znanie, 1963); reprinted together with number 8.

(8) *Trudno byt' bogom* (Hard to be a God), in their *Dalekaia Raduga* (Moscow: Mol. gvardiia, 1964).

(9) *Khishchnye veshchi veka* (Predatory Things of Our Times) (Moscow: Mol. gvardiia, 1965).

(10) *Ponedel'nik nachinaetsia v subbotu* (Monday begins on Saturday) (Moscow: Detskaia lit., 1965).

(11) *Ulitka na sklone* (The Snail on the Slope) – (see further in the text. 'Kandid' part published in anthology *Ellinskii sekret* (Leningrad: Lenizdat, 1966); 'Pepper' part published in magazine *Baikal*, nos. 1 and 2 (1968). Book published in Estonian SSR in 1972; the 'Pepper' part alone was published in *Ulitka na sklone – Skazka o troike* (Frankfurt and Main: Possev, 1972) in an unauthorized edition).

(12) *Vtoroe nashestvie marsian* (The Second Martian Invasion), in their *Stazhery – Vtoroe nashestvie marsian* (Moscow: Mol. gvardiia, 1968).

(13) *Gadkie lebedi* (Ugly Swans) (Frankfurt and Main: Possev, 1972), an unauthorized edition (no publication in the USSR).

(14) *Skazka o troike* (Tale of the Triumvirate), in the magazine *Angara*, nos 4 and 5 (1968).

(15) *Obitaemyi ostrov* (The Inhabited Island) (Moscow: Detskaia lit., 1971).

(16) *Otel' 'U pogibshego al'pinista'* (Hotel 'To the Lost Climber') (Moscow: Znanie, 1982).

(17) *Malysh* (The Kid), in anthology *Talisman* (Leningrad: Detskaia lit., 1973); reprinted in their *Polden'* . . . – *Malysh* (Leningrad: Detskaia lit., 1976).

(18) *Piknik na obochine* (Roadside Picnic), published together with number 20.

(19) *Paren' iz preispodnei* (The Guy from Hell), in anthology *Nezrimyi most'* (Leningrad: Detskaia lit., 1976); as *Prishelets iz preispodnei* (The Alien from Hell) (NY: Advent, 1984), most probably an unauthorized edition.

(20) *Za milliard let do kontsa sveta* (A Billion Years Before the End of the World) (Moscow: Sov. pisatel', 1984).

(21) *Zhuk v muraveinike* (Beetle in the Anthill), in the magazine *Znanie-sila*, nos 9–12 (1979) 1–3 and 5–6 (1980).

In 1980, the folktale-like fantasy tale 'Of True and False Friendship' was published, and from 1981 on several rather different scenarios for the movie *Stalker*.

In English, besides a few short stories in various SF anthologies and magazines, the following have appeared (I give the English titles only if they significantly, in some cases weirdly, differ from the original): the long story 'Destination: Amaltheia' from no. 3 in the anthology of the same title (Moscow: FLPH, 1962); no. 4 (the enlarged edition) as *Noon: 22nd Century* (New York and London: Collier Macmillan, 1978); no. 5 as *Space Apprentice*, ibid. (1981); nos 6, 19 and 17 as *Escape Attempt – The Kid from Hell – Space Mowgli*, ibid. (1982); nos 7 and 12, ibid. (1979); no. 7 (Moscow: Mir, 1967); no. 8 (New York: Seabury, 1973 and DAW Books, 1974; London: Eyre Methuen, 1975); no. 9 as *The Final Circle of Paradise* (New York: DAW Books, 1976); no. 10, ibid. (1977); no. 11 (New York: Bantam, 1980; London: Gollancz, 1980); no. 12 in C. G. Bearne (ed.), *Vortex* (London: MacGibbon & Kee, 1970; London: Pan, 1971) and as *The Second War of the Worlds* (New York: Macmillan, 1979); no. 13 as *The Ugly Swans*, ibid. (1979); nos 14 and 18 as *Roadside Picnic – Tale of the Troika* (New York: Macmillan, 1977; London: Collier Macmillan,

1977); no. 15 as *Prisoners of Power*, ibid. (1977); no. 20 as *Definitely Maybe*, ibid. (1978); no. 21, ibid. (1980).

The first cycle or phase of the Strugatskys is the interplanetary trilogy numbers 1, 3 and 5 with the same group of protagonists, and the cognate short stories collected in numbers 2, 3 and 4, all published 1959 to 1962. Except for a few early stories, this phase constitutes a 'future history' system formally similar to the model of a number of American SF writers (for example, Heinlein and Asimov). It is a not quite systematic series of novels and stories with interlocking characters and locations progressing from the end of the twentieth to the twenty-second century, realistically conveying life on a predominantly communist (classless) Earth and human relations in explorations on and between the planets of the solar system and some nearer stars. Yefremov's monolithic leaders and huge exploits were here supplanted by young explorers and scientists finding romance in their everyday pioneering tasks. Retaining the utopian sense of absolute ethical involvement and personal honour, even the Strugatskys' early protagonists – at times moody or vain, tired or capricious – were much more lifelike than the usual cardboard or marble figures in most Soviet SF. Together with the vividly depicted and variegated surroundings, the sure touch for detail and the adventure-packed action leading to some ethical choice, this immediately brought the young authors to the forefront of Soviet SF. But from good juvenile-adventure SF, they quickly passed to a richer form in which the adventure level serves as a vehicle for socio-philosophical exploration and understanding.

This first Strugatsky cycle is still fairly idyllic. Except for the occasional egotistic and capitalist survivals, conflicts take place – as they formulated it – 'between the good and the better' (i.e., within absolute and generally accepted ethics). Thus the only fundamental conflict left is the epic adventure of man faced with and conquering nature as a 'collective Robinson Crusoe' (Kagarlitsky). Yet at the end of the cycle – in *The Apprentices* and some stories such as 'Wanderers and Travellers', 'The Puzzle of the Hind Foot' and 'The Rendez-Vous' – an element of open-ended doubt and of darkness enters into these somewhat aseptically bright horizons. Some protagonists die or retire, and some 'come home' from cosmic jaunts to Earth and its problems. Though the future is still envisaged as a golden arrested moment of 'noon', historical time with its puzzles, pain and potentialities of regress begins to seep in as shadows of post-meridian experience lengthen. This adventure model is interlarded with quotations from neo-Romantic poets such as R. L. Stevenson and Bagritsky. In the second phase, an adult exploration of a more complex and painful world concentrates, as one of its novels has it, on the 'predatory things of our times', a title appropriately enough taken from Russia's major poetic exploration of relationships in such a world by Voznesensky's *Oza*.

The dialectics of innocence and experience, of utopian ethics and historical obstacles on the way to their enthronement provides henceforth the main tension and pathos of the Strugatskys' opus. In their second phase, consisting of the novels or long stories numbers 6 to 9 – all published between 1962 and 1965 – they were working out the proper form for such dialectics. The black horizon of a history where slavery and high technology go together appears in *An Attempted Escape*, though only as an exception (a backward planet) within the utopian universe of the first phase. In this work the Strugatskys are still defensive about their new tack. Even stylistically, it is halfway between the careful realism of the extrapolative-utopian cycle and a new parable form, so that it reads as a first sketch for *Hard To Be a God*. The protagonist – an escapee from Nazi concentration camps – and the paradoxical society are even less motivated than Mark Twain's Yankee in Camelot. None the less, this story introduces the first fully fledged conflict of utopian innocence and twentieth-century experience using the highly effective device of a protagonist caught in a blind alley of history.

The first two masterpieces of the Strugatskys are the long story 'Far Rainbow' and the novel *Hard To Be a God*. In both of them extrapolation gives way to a clearly focused analogic or parabolic model of mature SF. In both, utopian ethics are put to the test of anti-utopian darkness, of an inhuman and apparently irresistible wave of destruction. On the small planet Far Rainbow this is presented as a physical Black Wave destroying the whole joyous community of experimenting creators. Almost all remaining heroes of the first cycle die here; only the children (and the mysterious deathless man-robot Kamill, personifying perhaps a Cassandra-like lonely and powerless Reason) are saved to carry on the unquenchable human hope and thirst for knowledge. The elemental force let loose by the cheerful seekers and destroying them from behind is valid as a story in its own right, and also a clear parable for the price of historical knowledge and progress.

The conflict of militant philistinism, stupidity and socio-psychological entropy with the utopian idea of the Commune is faced without 'cosmic' disguises, directly within history – and therefore with richer and subtler consequences – in *Hard To Be a God* by way of a very successful domestication of the Scott–Dumas-type historical novel. The hero is one of a handful of emissaries from classless Earth's Institute of Experimental History on a feudal planet. He is perfectly disguised as a native nobleman, under strict instructions to observe without interfering, and trained to adapt himself to the existing way of life – a mixture of medieval Europe and Japan – in all details, from language to hygiene, except in his views. However, the Institute's futurological Basic Theory of Feudalism, which projects a slow linear progress for the planet, turns out to be wrong. The opposition between ethics and history explodes when the protagonist is faced with a regress into organized obscurantism, leading to death and destruction for all poets, scientists, doctors, and other bearers of human values and intelligence in the Arkanar kingdom, and culminating in the slaying of his girlfriend. As in 'Far Rainbow', the problem of meeting an unforeseen, calamitous twist of history is posed, rendered verisimilar (here by vividly recreating the customs, legends and ways of life in Arkanar, as well as the psychology of the troubled hero), and then left realistically open-ended.

Hard To Be a God amounts to an 'educational novel' where the reader learns together with the protagonist the nature of painful conflict between utopian human values – always the fixed Polar Star for the Strugatskys – and the terrible empirical pressures of mass egotism, slavery to petty passions, and conformism. Under such pressures the great majority of the people turn to religious fanaticism, mass murder or apathy. The resulting situation is reminiscent of the worst traits of Stalinism (a 'doctors' plot', stage-managed confessions, recasting of history to exalt the present ruler) and Nazism (storm-troopers and pogroms, the 'Night of the Long Knives'). The spirit of revolt – as in the rebel leader Arata – is undying, but it has to deal with omnipresent historical inertia. Outside interference cannot liberate a people without introducing a new benevolent dictatorship: the Earthling 'gods' are both ethically obliged and historically powerless to act. The true enemy is within each man: slavery and reason, narrowminded class psychology and the axiological reality of a classless future, are still fighting it out in a variant of Dostoevsky's Grand Inquisitor confrontation. The Strugatskys' mature opus retains the utopian abhorrence of 'the terrible ghosts of the past' and belief in the necessity of a humanized future, but it is also intensely aware of the defeats humanity has suffered since the heyday of utopianism in the early 1920s. Thus, from this time on their work takes its place with the insights of the best SF – from Wells and London, to Dick, Disch and Le Guin – into the dangers of social devolution. It is a warning without pat answers, a bearing of witness, and 'an angry pamphlet against tyranny, violence, indifference, against the philistinism that gives rise to dictatorships' (as the Soviet critic Revich well said). Even further, it is a significant rendering of tragic utopian activism, akin in many ways to the ethico-historiosophical visions of the best Hemingway and of poets like Brecht (the protagonist's dilemma in this novel is not too dissimilar from that in *The Measures Taken*), Okudzhava, or Voznesensky. It is no wonder this novel has become the most popular SF work in the USSR.

Predatory Things of Our Times returns to the anticipatory universe of the first cycle, with which it shares the protagonist, a Soviet cosmonaut turned UN Secret Service agent. His task is to flush out an evil new influence in the Country of the Fools, a wealthy, demilitarized capitalist state in a world dominated by socialism; this turns out to be addictive stimulation of pleasure centres, born of social demoralization and feeding into it. The story is a half-hearted try at a more precise Earthly localization of the concern with historical blind alleys, but its focus is blurred. The Country of the Fools is midway between an updated America of Hemingway, Raymond Chandler or gangster movies, and a folktale-like Never-never Land. Though vigorous and swift-paced, it is neither sufficiently concrete for precise socio-political criticisms – as some Soviet critics were quick to point out – nor sufficiently generalized for a parabolic model of a mass welfare state. *Hard To Be a God* remains thus, in its clear and historically vivid yet sufficiently estranged localization, in its fusion of medieval and twentieth to twenty-first-century, public and private concerns (evident even in the epigraphs from Abélard and Hemingway), the Strugatskys' best achievement until 1965.

Since explicit criticism of situations nearer home than its 'thousand years and thousand parsecs from Earth' would have (among other sociological consequences) meant abandoning the SF genre and their readers, the Strugatskys opted for the second possible way – a folktale-like parable form with increasingly satirical overtones. As different from their work so far, marked by growing precision and width of reference of a single model, their third phase, consisting of the looser and more grotesque long tales numbers 10–14, is characterized by a variety of probings, formal manoeuvrings and reading publics – from the juvenile to the most sophisticated intellectual one.

A sign of formal mastery, joined to a certain socio-political bewilderment, can be seen in the changing Strugatsky protagonist. By this phase he has turned into the privileged point of view. As a rule he is, like Voltaire's Candide, a naive glance at the increasingly estranged and disharmonious world, but burdened by the additional twentieth-century problem of how to make sense of the events in a mass society with monopolized information channels. This makes for anxiety as in *The Snail on the Slope*, or activist response, as in *The Inhabited Island*, or a fusion of both, as in *The Tale of Troika* ('troika' meaning here a triumvirate). In *The Second Martian Invasion*, however, the protagonist, ignorant as Candide, is also happy in his conformist ignorance. This Martian invasion does not need to use Wellsian heat-rays and gases to poison a nation, merely local traitors, economic corruption and misinformation. As befits the one-dimensional age, the calamity is muted, and thus more convincing and horrible. The whole story is a *tour de force* of identifying petty bourgeois language and horizons, the almost unnoticeable nuances which lead down the slope of Quislingism. It is 'a grotesque which does not reside in the style but in the point of view' (Britikov). The ironic incongruity between the protagonist's self-serving phraseology and the ideological judgements on it conveyed to the reader is in the great Russian tradition of the 'skaz' form (for example, Zoshchenko). Stylistically, it is on a par with *Hard To Be a God* and the 'Kandid' part of *The Snail on the Slope* as the Strugatskys' most homogeneous achievement.

If *The Second Martian Invasion* was in the same vein as Voltaire or Swift, the anxiety of the two protagonists in *The Snail on the Slope* (one of them named Kandid) is rather Kafkian. The visionary universe of this novel, reduced to a fantastic swampy forest, will be discussed more fully in the second part of this essay.

Perhaps a central place in the Strugatskys' third phase is due to the 'Privalov cycle' – the novels *Monday Begins on Saturday* and *The Tale of the Troika*. In an updated folktale garb, they embody the underlying atmosphere of this phase – a total invasion of human relationships by a lack of linear logic and sense. Modern sciences and modern social relationships in their strangeness for and alienation from the uninitiated majority are equivalent to white and black magic. Conversely, the forms of the magical folktale can be taken as forerunners of, and freely mixed with, contemporary 'quantum alchemy'. Indeed, the old characters – a penny-pinching Baba Yaga, a sclerotic Talking Cat, a parochial Pike Who Grants Three Desires – are small fry, good only for some mild fun, incidental critique and atmosphere-setting in comparison to the estranged horrors of scientific charlatanism and bureaucratic power.

Monday Begins on Saturday deals primarily with the use and charlatanic abuse of science. This is sketched in the career of Janus Nevstruev, director of the Scientific Institute for Magic, which studies the problems of human happiness and in whose folktale-lands both books take place: Nevstruev has split into S-Janus the scientist, and A-Janus the administrator who lives backward in time. But charlatanism is personified in Amvroz Ambruazovich Vybegallo, a semi-literate careerist planning the creation of a happy Universal Consumer, who talks in a mixture of bad French and demagogic bureaucratese. His homunculus, the Model of Full Contentedness, has to be destroyed just short of consuming the whole universe. The novel ranges from such a Goyaesque vision of A Dream of Reason Giving Birth to Monsters to an affectionate return to the roots of Russian and other folktales (the Institute is located with great felicity in the legendary Russian North). The loose picaresque form – the 'ideational adventures' of the candid protagonist – can be used for hitting out at anything that fits the authors' bill. Thus one section, in which Privalov tests out a machine for travelling through 'ideal times', is a spoof of SF from the utopias and *The Time Machine*, through technological anticipations and Soviet cosmic SF (with considerable self-parody), to western SF behind an 'Iron Wall' dividing the Universe of Humanistic Imagination from the Universe of Fearing the Future, where violent warfare with robots, aliens, viruses, etc., reigns supreme.

The Tale of the Triumvirate (or *Troika*) is blacker, concentrating on a bureaucratic triumvirate – originally a commission for checking the plumbing system – that has usurped power in a country of unexplained social and natural phenomena, which it proceeds to 'rationalize' by misusing or explaining them away. Their scientific consultant is Professor Vybegallo, and their main power is the Great Round Seal. A brilliantly detailed picture emerges of their prejudices, militaristic mannerisms and internecine in-fighting – in short, of a despotic approach turning 'scientifico-administrative'. Its semi-literate jargon and fossilized pseudo-democratic slogans, its totally incompetent quid pro quo's and malapropisms are portrayed with a wildly hilarious black humour, which makes this the funniest work of SF I know. It is unfortunate that it has so far not appeared in book form in the USSR, for – as the episode of the Alien most clearly shows – this critique of a degenerated power-situation is applicable to all of present-day mankind, psychologically unprepared for contact with an utopian future. In fact, I know of no more sympathetic insight into the true necessities that bring about the elite power than the Troika chairman's speech (under the influence of an apparatus that induces the surfacing of innermost motives) at the Alien's trial. Though somewhat uneven, this is perhaps the weightiest experiment of the Strugatskys.

The works first published between 1968 and 1980 (numbers 15 *et seq.* in my initial list) will be discussed here more briefly in order to concentrate on *The Snail on the Slope* as their representative. They can be thought of as a further Strugatsky phase, more sombre and uneven, combining such disparate elements as juvenile heroics with increasing alienation and desperation. *Prisoners of Power* is a reduction of the mature Strugatsky model to a 'new maps of hell' adventure-plot. It is still a very good novel at that level: the candid utopian and juvenile protagonist is marooned on an isolated planet, a closed and violent world (so that the original title of *Inhabited Island* would have been more appropriate than the vague sensationalism of the translation title) where high technology, especially in new persuasion media, serves a military dictatorship. To fight it, our hero must undergo this world's ignorance and cruelty, losing some of his innocence. The cumulative unrolling of environment and atmosphere, the brisk plot passing with the protagonist through various social strata of a people bereft of history, all show a masterly touch. But also, the insights into both the Oligarchy and Underground politics and into the genuine fanaticism of the rank and file do not quite blend with the *deus ex machina* happy ending. *The Ugly Swans* was published abroad in an edition repudiated by the authors, but for purposes of this overview I have to assume it as substantially correct. In a Shchedrinian satiric city, persistent rainfall signifies the end of a morally corrupt society

and generation whose children seem to be evolving to higher
intelligence and justice with the help of mutant 'Wetters'. Some
have seen the Wetters as an analogy to Jews, but it seems more
encompassing to see these leprous harbingers of the future as any
midwives of the New, any utopian intellectuals. As in *The Snail*,
boundaries blur, contradictions and metamorphoses between the
known (quarrelling police factions, fascist movements, social
corruption) and the unknown abound. The setting is a despotic
capitalism but the capital seems to be Moscow, and an unrelenting
fog blankets all. The puzzles of the New are again left unsolved: all
we can infer from the childrens' final exodus from the corrupt
present – as well as from the whole story told through an ambiguous
protagonist, a politically suspect writer, and through a hardboiled
vernacular – is that our species of 'ugly swans' is doomed. The novel
presents, thus, an inversion of Andersen's Ugly Duckling as well as
of the Pied Piper tale. It has important failures of focusing; yet it is
also one of the weightiest and most courageous confrontations in
world fiction with the youth movement of the 1960s.

Of the short novels or long stories *Hotel 'To the Lost Climber'*, *Kid
from Hell* and *Space Mowgli*,[3] the first is frankly an entertaining
lightweight, a detective mystery with an SF twist: it turns out that all
the puzzles were due to alien robots with strange powers; a
genological hybrid that rarely succeeds. In the second, human
interference in a grotesque war between two corrupt societies
picks out a trained killer from one and fails to change him even after
exposing him to prolonged intellectual and emotional contact with the
utopian values. This suggests that at least some people can be
irreversibly alienated. The third is a 'wolfchild' tale, except that a
human infant was raised by incomprehensible aliens, and his
location raises false hopes of bridging the gulf between known and
unknown. This is heightened in the conflict of *Beetle in the Anthill*
between ethics and survival, since a returning space explorer is
suspected (on good grounds) of being, unbeknownst to him,
programmed by the aliens, possibly to destroy the human race. The
racy detection puzzle is told by Maxim, the hero of *Prisoners of Power*,
now a middle-aged Terran security officer; at its end, the security
chief, ex-space-hero, murders the suspect – just in case. Another,
and possibly the most chillingly exasperated invasion of darkness
into utopia is *Definitely Maybe*, a tale halfway between supernatural
fantasy and a very black parable. An unknown force disrupts the
lives, work and happiness of the world's leading scientists and

seekers after the New. Their groping hypotheses about it include a malevolent super-civilization or the laws of nature asserting themselves to control destiny. Amid increasingly intimate frustration, the tough-minded clarity and a glimmer of utopian resistance persist.

Perhaps the most consistent work of this phase is *Roadside Picnic*, simultaneously a folktale-like utopian quest and psychological novel with a rich array of standpoints and vernaculars, in which meaning is sought for the strange and dangerous leavings of unknown aliens. The protagonist, Red, is one of the smugglers who penetrates the alien Zone to steal artefacts and, perhaps, to find knowledge which is salvation. The alien influence is a catalyst showing up humans as greedy and courageous, ignorant and ingenious. The story has since been strongly reworked, and to my mind impoverished, in a sequence of the Strugatskys' scenarios for Tarkovsky's Christian-existentialist movie *Stalker*.

To conclude, the Strugatskys' work has been at the heart of Soviet SF. It was a permanent polemic – in their first phase against narrow technological-adventure SF of the Soviet 1950s, in the second against Yefremovian monolithism, in the third against linear progressivism – and it thus acted as an icebreaker clearing aesthetic navigation for the whole Soviet flotilla. More importantly, their first three phases have built up the most coherent series of models in Soviet SF. From static utopian brightness it moved, through a return to the complex dynamics of history, to a final model where the static norm is felt as immorally anti-utopian. Concomitantly, the protagonist grew from a boy in a golden collective, through the pioneering subject of a painful cognitive education, to a solitary hero as final repository of utopian ethics who decides to fight back at inhumanity. The time horizons also evolved from extrapolated future, through a clash of past and future in analogic worlds, to a strongly estranged arrested time (for example, blending a folktale past with futuristic science) where the future values find refuge in ethics as opposed to backward politics and incomprehensible ontology.

There are deficiencies in the Strugatskys' vision. The junction of ethics with either politics or philosophy has remained unclear; the localization of events has oscillated somewhat erratically, the socio-philosophical criticism has sometimes fitted only loosely into the SF framework. Such limitations cannot be glossed over, since they grew in importance in the 1970s, but they may to a great extent be due to the authors' wish to keep in contact with the readers. None the less, half a dozen of the Strugatskys' works approach major, cognitive literature. The predatory bestiary into which people without cognitive ethics are transmuted, the strange countries and monsters becoming increasingly horrible as the authors and readers discover that *de nobis fabula narratur* – all such aspects certify to their final source in the greatest SF paradigm, *Gulliver's Travels*.

Perhaps most pertinent within the Russian tradition is the fact that the best of the later Strugatsky work reads like an updating of Shchedrin's fables (for example, *The Bear Governor*) and his chronicle of Glupovo City and its rulers. However, the hero and ideal reader is no longer Shchedrin's *muzhik*: he is the contemporary scientific and cultural intellectual bridging the 'two cultures' gap, the reader of Voznesensky and Voltaire, Wiener and Wells. Many Strugatsky passages read as a hymn to such young scientists who are also citizen-activists, inner-directed by and toward utopia. In *Monday Begins on Saturday*, for example, they are defined as having 'a different relationship with the world than normal people' and believing that the sense of life resides in 'constant cognition of the unknown'. The central source of the Strugatskys' pathos is an ethics of cognition, sprung from a confluence of utopianism and modern philosophy of science. Such a horizon, of course, transcends Russian borders: it marks the Strugatskys' rightful place in the world SF and, indeed, world literature.

2.   ON 'THE SNAIL ON THE SLOPE'

All the foregoing can serve as the context for the somewhat puzzling *Snail on the Slope*. It is not my intention to explore all the puzzles with which this text abounds, in the best SF tradition – let that be left to the reader as a part of his pleasure. Furthermore, I think some of these puzzles are deliberately ambiguous and cannot be deciphered in any univocal or simplistic way. I simply want to indicate a possible first approach.

The novel is divided into two stories, those of Pepper and Kandid.[4] Their plots appear to be only very loosely connected, but the compositional interlocking (chapters 1, 3, 5, 6, 9 and 10 deal with

Pepper, and 2, 4, 7, 8 and 11 with Kandid) expresses in fact a deeper interplay of their fortunes and attitudes. Pepper and Kandid have many similarities: both are intellectuals, tolerated or even condescendingly liked, yet thrown as outsiders into nightmarish power situations beyond their control; for both, thinking – i.e. an understanding of what is happening in the light of their humanistic ethical and historiosophical principles – is not 'a pastime, it's a duty' (chapter 1). In fact, in an untranslatable Russian idiom beautifully fashioned by the Strugatskys on the model of 'homesickness', they are both sick for understanding, they have the 'yearning for understanding' or 'know-sickness' (chapter 6). Thus the world view of both Kandid and Pepper can be called 'emotional materialism' (chapter 3): as scientists they are materialists, but the painful informational opacity of their environments has caused them to fall back on personally felt ethics in lieu of a dialectical overview. Thus, besides understanding, they both yearn for a minimum of humanist decency: 'just people would do for a start – clean, shaved, considerate, hospitable. No high-flown ideas necessary, no blazing talents' (chapter 9).

Yet, as we gradually find out during the novel, Pepper and Kandid have just as significant dissimilarities. Not only is Kandid directly faced with the central novelty and strange experience of this text, the Forest, while Pepper faces it indirectly, through the Forest Study and Exploitation Authority (or Directorate); but, more importantly, their reactions too – during much of the novel largely identical – eventually diverge so radically that they result in diametrically opposed behaviour. In relation to the other human agents as well as to the overriding and unmanageable presences of the Forest and the Directorate, Pepper and Kandid finally come to stand for the two horns of the dilemma facing modern intellectuals (as the text sees it): *accommodation* or *refusal*.

In relation to other people – perhaps, as opposed to the solitary intellectual protagonists, one could just as well say in relation to *the* people – Pepper has almost from the very beginning a much stronger gut revulsion, which subsumes sex under human animalism (at the end he regrets that he cannot have driver Acey, the obnoxious voice of the people, castrated). Ironically, Pepper is the one who finally succumbs to the seduction of the self-perpetuating power-stucture, symbolized by the Tannhauser–Venus inkpot, in spite of the lugubrious warning in fluorescent colours of 'No Exit' (chapter 5). On the contrary, Kandid – though equally, if not more, helpless and intellectually isolated – lives among his more primitive villagers as a strange and eccentric member of their community, at the outset condescended to as 'Dummy', but at the end revered as the slightly mad 'holy fool' and unparalleled disposer of the 'deadlings'. Though his marriage to Nava, who is frequently called a 'girl' in the sense of a rather young person, is possibly only symbolic, and though it does not last, even such an ambiguous marriage and name are precise symbols for Kandid's precarious partaking of the village community. And for all its rural inertia – so beautifully rendered by the Strugatskys' language in the Kandid part, with its archaic folk-images and idioms, infuriatingly repetitive and monotonous as the life whose flavour it conveys – there is to my mind a clear sense of the moral superiority of this primitive folk community in relation to the egotistic urbanized conformism of the Directorate employees.

This may *explain* Pepper's revulsion, but in a book so fraught with ethical judgements it does not *justify* it. In fact, it is a logical stage on the way to Pepper's fall into power, ironically marked by his eradication of the Eradicators supervised by the chief eradicator. Kandid's irritation and even fury at the 'dozey . . . vegetable way of life' (chapter 9) in the Village is paralleled by his adaptation to the heavy and sometimes oppressive but also astonishingly fertile vegetable imagery; Pepper's revulsion from the Directorate apparatus carries a subtle implication of a hysterical splitting of its members into animals on the one hand and machines on the other. In fact, I would read the 'machine episode' of chapter 9 as a parable on intellectuals stream-lined or reified into serving the military–industrial complex: frustrated by it, destroyed when they attempt to evade it, they are internally subverted by it into scientific or aesthetic acquiescence ('Winnie the Pooh' and the Gardener), militarist aggressivity (the Tank), hysteria (the Doll), etc. If something like this reading is acceptable, this seemingly gratuitous episode would fit well into the Pepper story.

Kandid, on the other hand, after being ejected from his helicopter is faced only with biocybernetic, if you wish 'organic', novelties, not with inorganic machines. The matriarchal or Amazon civilization of the Maidens (another almost untranslatable Russian term: literally something like Women Companions or She-Friends) with its Swampings and Harrowings is, of course, no less ruthless than the patriarchal Exploitation Authority, but Kandid's fellow-yokels have, for all their bumbling, preserved more human dignity than the Directorate's employees. They sin against the 'yearning for knowledge' rather than against other people. And even that sin is overwhelmingly conveyed as being in large part due to the dearth of information and the almost physiological impossibility of generalizing on the part of a social group bereft of history and art (indeed, even of a myth of origin) and subject to unknown destructive forces. No such excuses prevail for the Authority employees, at least as much sinning as sinned against: no Anger-Martyrs amongst them. Though oppressed by the power, they share in it; the villagers do not.

However, what of the two huge and stifling collective entities, the Forest and the Directorate? The Directorate is a simpler case: a Kafkian bureaucracy whose facelessness is horrible because it is composed of Everyman, so to speak – it works in, through, and by means of its victims such as Pepper; it is a 'vector [with] its base in the depths of time' (chapter 10), aptly symbolized by Acey's tattoos: 'What destroys us' and 'Ever onward'. It is 'capable of any extreme' – faith, disbelief, neglect – only not of understanding (chapter 10); thus, it is the moral antipode of the intellectual protagonists. It exists only because of the Forest, but also only for its eradication and exploitation; furthermore, it is dismally failing to deal not only with the Forest but even with the relatively powerless villagers ('Native Population'). Besides the ineffective biostation, breeding ground of careers, pettiness, 'salary and bonuses' rather than of understanding, the Directorate impinges on the Forest only through the new 'luxurious four-hole latrine' (chapter 10), a drastically clear image. Its Kafkian murk – most of the Pepper story happens in total or semi-obscurity – is in the Director's anterooms joined by Carrollian nonsense, while the 'decoding' of the telephone speech rejoins the savager Swiftian satire at Tribnia. The Philistine pseudo-utopia of affluence and leisure – reminding one of the feeblest Wells or other optimistic forecasting, not excluding Philistine pseudo-Marxists: 'stadia, swimming-pools, aerial parks, crystal bars and cafes. Stairways to the sky! Slender, swaying women with dark supple skin! [. . .] Cars, gliders, airships . . . Debates, hypnopaedia, stereocinema' (chapter 5) – only deepens the gloom. It is rendered practically impenetrable when Alevtina's thesis of the historical continuity of bureaucratic authority is confirmed by the evidently sincere impossibility of Pepper's to find what Wells would have called a democratic 'social receiver' for the Directorate: 'Criticize and laugh . . . Yes, they would criticize.

They'd do it at length with warmth and ecstasy since they'd been ordered to do it [. . .] and in between they'd hurry to the latrine overhanging the precipice' (chapter 10).

The Forest is much more complex – in fact, the most multiplex symbol in the novel. As in a story by Le Guin, it is the word for this world. Pepper is too remote from it, and sees far too little; Kandid is too near to it, and sees far too much; such an absence as well as such an overload of information turn the Forest into a blur, a black-and-white cerebral one for Pepper and a technicolour one, replete with noises and smells, for Kandid. But even the latter can, after three years of living within it, penetrate no further than skin-deep into the *meaning* of its half-glimpsed 'unpleasant secrets and terrible puzzles', into the lilac fog of its alien abundance: if Pepper's glance is blocked by the Authority, Kandid's is by the strangeness of the Forest itself, which he does not see for its phenomena.

This unresolved opacity makes it impossible, as I suggested earlier, to 'decode' the Forest as standing allegorically for any one particular entity. Yet clearly, to the protagonists it matters supremely: it is Pepper's romantic dream, and Kandid's realistic existence; Pepper yearns desperately to get into it, Kandid to get out of it. Neither will succeed; but for both, the Forest will remain the central fascination of their existences, a tormenting love/hate (it will only dim for Pepper when he becomes absorbed in the Directorate and follows up his nausea at the alien Forest with the assumption of a bureaucratic responsibility for it which – as his eradication decision gives us to understand – will not lead to significant change). The mysterious Forest stands thus for an encompassing strange truth and value (for intellectuals that is the same) surrounding the modern thinking person. Sociologically, it might stand for society; anthropologically, for the people; politically, for the state; but finally, I think that no such sub-divisions will account for its multiplicity and ambiguity, although at various points in the text they might be applicable to a certain degree. Finally, subsuming all such partial explanations, the Strugatskys' Forest seems to be almost ontologically, life in general, the viscous duration and existence for which the Russian language has the expressive term 'byt''. None the less, it remains true that the forces in the Forest are also in some ways similar to the menacing 'mysticism' (chapter 1) of the Exploitation Authority (even the speech modes of the power-wielders are not too dissimilar). The impressive Newness of the Forest is finally inhuman; whatever the Amazons might have started out like in the past, they are now a parthenogenetic 'higher' species. The authors' final word is given through Kandid's mouth: 'What has their progress to do with me, it's not my progress and I call it progress only because there's no other suitable word' (chapter 11).

It would be disingenuous here not to mention that the black comedy of this novel, and in particular the grotesque satire of the Directorate, have led a few critics to label it simply as an anti-utopian critique of Soviet society. If my argument so far is accepted, that is a reductionist over-simplification. Instead of further discussion, I will quote the Soviet critic Lebedev:

> V. Aleksandrov writes in the *Pravda Buriatii* [a local Siberian newspaper] that 'this work, called an SF story, is nothing but a lampoon against our reality [. . .]'. What is this premise based upon, which characteristic traits allow Aleksandrov to identify the fantastic reality of the Strugatskys with the reality he designates? Here they are: 'The fantastic society shown by A. and B. Strugatsky in the story *Snail on the Slope*,' writes Aleksandrov, 'is a conglomerate of people living in chaos and disorder, engaged in senseless and useless work, carrying out stupid laws and directives. Fear, suspicion, toadyism, and bureaucracy reign there.' – Well now! A truly fantastic aberration: it seems such phenomena and signs are the 'typical' aspects allowing to treat SF with such elements as a kind of 'copy' of our reality? Comrade Aleksandrov seems to have nice ideas about the society around him, it must be confessed. . . .

And Lebedev concludes:

> The affirmation of dreams about the beautiful future, of the romantic impulse forward and higher, finds its necessary complement in the demystification of tendencies which pretend to the historical correctness and the romantic aureole, but are in fact incompatible with the ideal of scientific communism.[5]

No doubt, each reader will wish to conclude for him- or herself, according to his politics, which countries possess bureaucracies, chaos and stupid laws. I personally think this is, unfortunately, not the privilege of any particular country or society. The inertia of monstrous power-structures, the need for intellectuals and, indeed, all people to choose between identifying with them or opting out and opposing them, is a problem of our whole globe and historical epoch. It is therefore regrettable that this novel has in the USSR been published as a whole only in Estonian, and it is hoped that the relevance the English-language reader may well find in it will argue against the Aleksandrovs or similar critics and publishers. For, properly speaking, the Forest is not a political but an ethical and cognitive symbol. As the authors themselves have written: 'The Forest is to be taken as a symbol of the unknown and alien, a symbol of necessity simplified, of all that is at present hidden from mankind because of our incomplete scientific, philosophical and sociological knowledge.'

All this does not mean, of course, that one could not have legitimate doubts, queries or outright disagreements with the novel. The ethics of the Strugatskys' heroes are – as usual – to my mind unexceptionable, utopian socialist ethics. But their protest against the loss of harmony between ends and means, while rightly postulating that unethical politics are self-defeating, does not leave much room at all for intelligent, i.e. ethical, politics. Is not 'drilling the principles of fortification into a future builder of sun cities' (chapter 3) no doubt always unpleasant but perhaps sometimes unavoidable?: for example, when faced with the world symbolized by the contents of the Director's safe in chapter 10 – a pistol, a 'twisted general's epaulette and an iron cross with oak leaves'? Probably in that case, the classical revolutionary and Russian question 'what is to be done?' cannot be solved by pure ethics. The Strugatskys themselves penned what amounts to a credo at the same time as writing this novel. It speaks of SF as

the literature dealing with the ethics and responsibility of the scientist [. . .] with what those, in whose hands lies the realization of the highest achievements of human knowledge, feel and how do they relate to their work [. . .]. Each scientist has to be a revolutionary humanist, otherwise the inertia of history will shunt him into the ranks of irresponsible scoundrels leading the world to its destruction.[6]

From their own point of view, Kandid's final opposition between head and heart – between utopian socialist ethics and an understanding of world and history – may in that case not be a useful answer.

On the contrary, Kandid's final realization that it is necessary to look both at the Authority and the Forest 'from the side' is right on. For this is the classical look of SF as well as of all the scientific estrangement, the wide-eyed 'it ain't necessarily so' look, which is the beginning of all wisdom – a wisdom desperately needed in our world of somewhat different Authorities and Forests. The numerous uses of such a look make of this sombre but unbowed, difficult but rewarding novel one of the most interesting creation of the Strugatsky brothers and of modern SF. Any disagreements that one might have with this or that aspect of their vision is more than compensated for by the humour and relevance of the novel as a whole. It is a legitimate continuation of the Gogol and Shchedrin vein of Russian literature, and of the great Soviet tradition of Ilf–Petrov or Olesha, at the borders of SF and satire as in Mayakovsky's late plays. Fusing this tradition with the stimulus of Swift, Kafka, Lem, and English fantastic literature such as Lewis Carroll, the Strugatskys offer the reader a brilliant work of word-art – a mimicry of bureaucratese and academese, of philistine and fanatic jargon, irony and parody, colloquialisms and neologisms. Thus, they are polemic at the deepest literary level, making untenable what they called the 'fiery banalities' of the genre.

(Originally published in 1974 and 1981)

NOTES

1. See for this breakthrough, and the whole previous tradition of Russian SF, Chapter 11 of *MOSF*, now enlarged in the Spanish and Italian versions (Mexico, 1984; Bologna, 1985), and the discussion of Yefremov in 'Three World Paradigms', with further bibliography in those works. My quotes from the Strugatskys' texts use existing translations but the responsibility is mine; due to their frequent use of the ellipse, only [. . .] designates my own ellipses.
2. Except for book reviews (e.g. by Ursula K. Le Guin in *SFS*, no. 12 (1977) pp. 157–9) and introductions (e.g. by Theodore Sturgeon to most of the Macmillan editions listed at the beginning), the English-language reader could until the latter 1970s use only a first version of this essay and my 'Criticism of the Strugatsky Brothers' Work', *Canadian–American Slavic Studies*, no. 2 (1972) pp. 286–307. Cf. now also Halina Stephan, 'The Changing Protagonist in Soviet Science Fiction', in Henrik Birnbaum and Thomas Eekman (eds), *Fiction and Drama* (Columbus, OH, 1980) pp. 361–78; Vladimir Gakov, *Noon: Twenty-Second Century*, in Frank N.

Magill (ed.), *Survey of Science Fiction Literature* (Englewood Cliffs, NJ, 1979) vol. 4, pp. 1548–54, and 'A Test of Humanity', *Soviet Literature*, no. 416 (1982) pp. 154–61; Patrick L. McGuire, 'Future History, Soviet Style', in Tom Staicar (ed.), *Critical Encounters II* (New York, 1982) pp. 104–24; Stanisław Lem, 'About the Strugatskys' *Roadside Picnic'*, *SFS*, 10 (1983) 317–32; and Simonetta Salvestroni, 'The Ambiguous Miracle in Three Novels by the Strugatsky Brothers', *SFS*, 11 (1984) 291–303.

3. The overview of these late novels is indebted to a yet unpublished encyclopedia article on the Strugatskys which I compiled together with Professor Gina Macdonald; I wish to thank here cordially for understanding that in such a collaboration one often forgets whose sentence was 'originally' whose.

4. My analysis of the novel is indebted to discussions with the excellent translator of the Bantam and Gollancz editions, Alan G. Myers, though its merits and demerits can only be mine. I am also grateful to Dr Roger De Garis, Dr Rafail Nudelman and Ante Starčević for help with finding publication data about, and texts by, the Strugatskys.

5. For full data about the critical debate around the Strugatskys, including Lebedev's article, see my 1972 article and 1976 bibliography adduced in notes 2 and 6.

6. Review of Gansovsky: see my *Russian Science Fiction 1956–1974* (Elizabethtown, NY, 1976).

12

Playful Cognizing, or Technical Errors in Harmonyville: The SF of Johanna and Günter Braun

The Brauns, East German (GDR) writers, are a married couple who publish all their works together.[1] Günter Braun, born 1928, son of a railway engineer, served briefly in an anti-aircraft battery in 1945, then worked as drugstore assistant, reporter on provincial newspaper, editor, theatre critic, librarian. Johanna Braun, born 1929, daughter of an optician, worked briefly as farm-hand and in merchandizing, then as typist, secretary and editor. Since 1955 both have been free-lance writers, living in Magdeburg, GDR. They publish their SF books significantly as *Johanna and Günter* Braun. In 1969 they received the international short-story prize of the Colloquium of Arnsberg (West Germany) for their strories.

The Brauns started writing juvenile (often exotic) adventure long-stories blending the Defoe–Cooper tradition with revolutionary themes, such as *Einer sagt nein* ('Somebody Says No') and *José Zorillas Stier* (*The Bull of José Zorilla*', both 1955), *Tsuko und der Medizinmann* ('Tsuko and the Medicine-Man', 1956), and *Herren der Pampa* ('Lords of the Pampa', 1957), *Kurier für sechs Taler* ('Courier for Six Thalers') and *Gauner im Vogelhaus* ('Crooks in the Aviary', both 1958). Working in suggestions from music, the movies and lyrical prose (in an autobiographical sketch in *Junge Schriftsteller* – see note – Johanna Braun notes her preference for Turgenev, Maupassant, Chekhov, Hemingway, McCullers, and in particular for Halldor Laxness's philosophical lyricism) and changing to historical themes of the further or nearer past, they first achieved recognition for their novels *Preussen, Lumpen und Rebellen* ('Prussians, Bums, and Rebels', 1957) and *Mädchen im Dreieck* ('Girl in the Triangle', 1961), and the long-story *Gefangene* ('Prisoners', 1958). They developed through the novels *Krischan und Luise*

172

('Krischan and Louise', 1958), *Menne Kehraus fährt ab* ('Menne Kehraus Departs', 1959), and *Die seltsamen Abenteuer des Brotstudenten Ernst Brav* ('The Strange Adventures of Ernest Upright, Poor Student', a satirical novel, 1959) to the experimental prose in monologues – later a TV play – *Eva und der neue Adam* ('Eve and the New Adam', 1961–2), which also touched on neuralgic problems of contemporary relationships such as equal rights for women (as already in 'Girl in the Triangle', set in Nazi times, and *Ein unberechenbares Mädchen* – 'A Wayward Girl', 1963). This brave and potent combination of new forms to deal with new problems touched off quite a number of critiques and public discussions. At that time, the Brauns also wrote *Gedanken zum kleinen Roman* ('Thoughts on the Short Novel', 1962), and the beginning of the 1960s can be taken as the period in which they entered into full possession of their narrative voice: lightly ironical, lyrically oriented toward socio-ethical characterization rather than toward a surface plot, yet strongly concerned with the integrity of people in the meshes of politics and economics. They also wrote the TV-plays *Dialoge über die Liebe* ('Dialogues on Love', 1965), *Geschichten aus dem letzen Urlaub* ('Stories from the Latest Vacations', 1967), *Dialoge über den Neandertaler* ('Dialogues on the Neanderthal Man', 1968), and *Ein Dach über dem Kopf* ('A Roof Over One's Head', 1968), as well as more long stories such as *Die Campingbäume von M.* ('The Camping Trees of M.', 1968) and the short stories in *Die Nase des Neandertalers* ('The Neanderthal Man's Nose', 1969 – which includes two SF love stories). Interest in this period was stimulated by their novel *Ein objektiver Engel* ('An Objective Angel', 1967), also dealing directly with contemporary GDR. In it, an authoress attempts a literary portrait of a well-known inventor, learning in the process – for herself and for the reader – about the social and personal implications of that natural science and technology toward which the GDR is so strongly oriented. There followed a book of short stories on love, *Fünf Säulen des Eheglücks* ('Five Pillars of Married Bliss', 1976) and possibly their most interesting novel *Bitterfisch* ('Bitterfisch', 1974) which blends mythomorphic fantasy and everyday GDR life around the eponymous worker-protagonist. In spite of some hesitations, this important experiment can be read as a gentler, atheistic counterproject to Bulgakov's *Master and Margarita*, and one can only regret that its brilliant premises have not been explored at full length and brought to a head. The novel had such a great success in the GDR (as a correspondent from there wrote to me) that it has not been republished there since. However, a number of the Brauns' subsequent SF novels have been published by Suhrkamp Verlag in West Germany.

From 1972 to 1980, the Brauns published four books of what could be considered as SF, the first from the East Berlin publishing house of Neues Leben and the latter three from Das Neue Berlin. These are the novels *Der Irrtum des Grossen Zauberers* ('The Great Magician's Error', 1972), *Unheimliche Erscheinungsformen auf Omega XI* ('Uncanny Phenomena on Omega 11', 1974), and *Conviva ludibundus* (1978), and the stories collected as *Der Fehlfaktor* ('The Mistake Factor', 1975). *The Great Magician's Error* is set in a country ruled by a Great Magician whose power is founded on the obligatory daily chewing of a specially cultivated pear. The original, natural pear was (and still is, if accidentally found) an inebriating yet stimulating nourishment. Yet, abused rather than ennobled by the Magician, it induces apathy, routine and a false sense of irrational pleasure and leisure in the population. The ruling class is represented by specially dressed bureaucrats and technocrats, but they too are rapidly dying out, replaced by computers and robots, notoriously more perfect than men. Our young hero, Input Oliver, drawn to joyous and interesting knowledge rather than to the boredom of routine, to pranks rather than obedience, is chosen by the Magician to be his successor. In spite of a passing temptation of political and technological power, he manages to defeat from within the despotic rule; he is helped by the female principle of intelligence and subversion in the form of a snake-like girl. In the new state of affairs, men will know how to use machines properly, both in the sense of general accessibility to and of collective responsibility for them, and presumably society will be helped along by the original tonic effect of the natural pears. The parable oscillates between choosing for its vehicle SF – that is, an empirically believable surface – or a Hoffmannesque or Andersenian fairy tale, opting at the end for the latter. Nonetheless, this tale is a large step away from naturalistic juvenile adventure and it has a very interesting tenor, which I would interpret as directly applicable to Stalinism and the 'warm current' against it within socialism.

The Brauns started publishing SF stories for the periodical *Magazin* before their first novel was published. The eight stories collected in *The Mistake Factor* are largely parallels to – and in all probability finger-exercises for – both that SF novel and the following one, yet they are also well worth an independent analysis

– indeed, several among them I would insert into any anthology of the best European SF. Their basic conflict is as a rule some variant of the opposition between a critical, socialist humanism and a technocratic-cum-philistine self-satisfaction. In the story 'Das System R' ('System R'), the SF gimmick of reversible time is used for an almost plotless delineation of the rise and fall of a careerist without scruples who can only operate within strict limits of opinion and imagination and breaks down when faced with the truly new. In 'Raumfahrerauswahl' ('Choosing Astronauts'), such a psychological discussion is conducted much better, from the converse side of two positive examples (the two astronauts of the Brauns' second novel). The convincing earthy and quirky independence of Merkur and Elektra as well as of their examiners, is revealed in an amusing series of mutual tests, amounting to an exemplum not only for the fitness of astronauts but of people in general to cohabit, to be not simply humans but 'human to each other' ('irgendwie Mensch sein' *vs.* 'irgendwie *zueinander* Mensch sein'). Two stories present a philistine 'total harmony' which in the nature of things cannot avoid breaking down: in 'Der grosse Kalos-Prozess' ('The Great Kalos Trial'), the breakdown of that harmony is simply a biological accident, and the story is saved only by an intricate and very well conducted collage of shifting viewpoints by trial witnesses and reporters, revealing as much about themselves as about the case in hand; in the slighter 'Kunstfehler in Harmonopolis' ('Technical Mistakes in Harmonyville'), written in detective-mystery form, the motivation is, much more interestingly, a philistine insistence on subservient art (the story's title is itself a pun on both technical mistake and artistic erroneousness, 'fehlerhafte Kunst').

Three further stories can be discussed in terms of collision between a techno-bureaucratic behaviour or frame of mind and an approach fusing new productivity with beauty and tradition (thus looking forward to their third novel). 'Jonatans Rückkehr' ('Jonathan's Return') develops this in guise of a semi-humorous variation on the US 'tough guy' crime story; in a computerized future, an old-fashioned safe-cracker hankering after romantic personal involvement à la *Threepenny Opera* can only satisfy it by opening a quarter of fictitious crime for tourists. The short story 'Cäsars Kuhglockengeläut' ('The Jingling of Caesar's Cowbells') is much more significant. It is excellently told by an involved narrator changing her opinion about the protagonists as she comes to

Positions in SF Practice

understand that, despite his lack of sentimentality, he stands for the dialectical sublation or incorporation of aesthetics into new productivity. It is a *tour de force* of economic clarity, set in a down-to-earth near future and successfully blending the serious theme of a socialist realist 'production tale' with understated sexiness and graceful wit in order to create a deceptively simple SF story. But the masterpiece of this vein and the whole collection is the title story, 'The Mistake Factor', set in a utopian future; in it, the protagonist is sent to find the reasons for the malfunctioning of a computer made of 'ideum' conductors and directing the whole economy. The vivid settings of a national park comprise the Bertolt Brecht Lake, whose rejuvenating qualities are being investigated by a girl-scientist, and the inertia-inducing Computer Centre nearby. The narrator-protagonist finally finds out that a banal malfunctioning was never made public because of the self-satisfied atmosphere induced by the humming apparatus:

> We are fascinated by the perfectness of our grandiose machine. We stare at it as at a fetish. Its noises are music to our ears. Probably people earlier stared in this way at the statues of the idols which they had created for themselves. . . . Our critical thinking has withered away. . . . Believe me, first comes the intoxication, and then the pacification. I have lived through it myself. But if we now get in there with the awareness that there is a mistake factor, that the humming is in no way perfect, then we are stronger than this machine. For we are men.

The allegorical aspects of this tale – opposing the rejuvenation connected with a critical non-pacifying, anti-bureaucratic Marxism of Brecht's stripe (which has to be drunk at the source) to the suppression of critical examination in a huge but tired technocracy – are obvious. None the less, it can also be enjoyed as a scientific puzzle or as a psychological story of a hero divided between the enclosed and sterile apparatus and the female principle of inquisitive and erotic life in the open. In short, this parable or exemplum has both a consistent tenor and a consistent – that is, empirically believable – surface or vehicle. Its final resolution, where the evicted computer crew comes to its senses after one week away from the machine's power, is certainly utopian – in a sense which will vary from positive to contemptuous according to the reader. But the 'conflict in good faith', where both sides share finally the same values, seems to me a quite acceptable form not only in socialist utopianism but in any SF taking the basic *ethos* of science seriously.

The only not quite satisfactory story of this collection is to my mind 'Homo Pipogenus erectus', where a Faustian pact between a lazy humanity and its badly programmed creative powers results in the formation of an intelligent, bird-derived, pseudo-humanity, in the vein of Čapek's Salamanders or indeed of Frankenstein's Creature. The Shelleyan dilemma of an unpleasant yet rightly autonomous creation remains here not only unresolved but also unclear and in fact narratively unconcluded. But the eight stories contain to my mind three small masterpieces ('Choosing', 'Caesar', and 'Mistake Factor'), four good and amusing stories, and one dud – on balance, an extremely respectable showing. They amount to a system which not only has a common conflictual denominator – one could call it, from the wittily ironical title of one story, 'Technical Errors in Harmonyville' – but also a common stock of characters and devices, in particular a precise and beautifully flexible control of the narrative voice. Most important, at the heart of the stories there can be found the feminine principle associated with sexual emotion, productive self-management, and critical intelligence, while the male principle is (in an amusing subversion of patriarchal chauvinism) associated with instinct and/or domestic practicality.

The Brauns' second novel, *Uncanny Phenomena on Omega 11* (the English word 'Phenomena' does not quite render the witty possibilities, exploited at several places, of what would literally be 'Forms of Appearing') has the two astronauts met in the 'Choosing' story investigating a call for help from a colony of Terran refugees on the planet Omega 11. Their apt names, Merkur Erdenson and Elektra Eulenn, suggest, while never directly allegorizing, their complementary tempers: in the first case, a mercurial intellectual and bodily agility of the novel's disrespectful narrator, representative of the best Earth (*Erde*) has at that moment to offer; and in the second case an owl-like (*Eule*) fundamental knowledge and wisdom as well as partial blindness, the somewhat literal-minded naivety of a prize-winning scientist (with a hint at Teutonic bureaucratic precision, and possibly at the great mathematician Euler), which is finally redeemed by the capacity of adapting to new situations. The erotic and cognitive interplay between the playful Merkur and the serious Elektra (according with the inversion of gender roles mentioned in the foregoing paragraph apropos of the Brauns' stories, and with the Graeco-Roman names they often use), are treated with delicate verisimilitude and provide one main strand of the plot: from their grudging acceptance of each other, through connubial bliss on the trip, to estrangement on the planet because of Elektra's initial credulity toward the orderly-appearing help-seekers who turn out to be evil plotters, and then to smooth team-work in solving the political problem found, and their final growing apart during the return trip. The mirror image of that strand is the adventure-puzzle, which besides the treacherous Lumes (an exploiting elite who had fled utopian Earth in 'the grey prehistory' and have by now degenerated) gradually reveals the presence of two more races, originally created by the Lumes through genetic manipulation and now controlled through cunning use of inbuilt physiological addictions – that is, incessant labour for the working and incessant thinking for the intellectual race or class. Our heroes circumvent all this by brain rather than brawn – no arms nor even fistfights are resorted to – and leave a planet of liberated and slowly intermingling races (including the Lumes, who are tolerantly pensioned off). The lightly ironic and playful touch is reaffirmed at the end: Elektra evades Merkur's desire to take back with them Ludana, a girl from the intellectuals' race, and back on Earth Merkur returns to his repairman's job: 'I mean, we can develop as far as you wish, there'll always be something to repair', are the final words of the novel. I would venture to read the ending as delicately suggesting that the time for the 'ludic' spirit of playfulness has not arrived yet in the refreshingly imperfect future utopia of the novel, whose own future yet remains open, reparable. This would be of a piece with the emphasis placed in the course of the whole story on the necessity of fusing play with physical or intellectual work: it is this insight that enables Merkur and the Earth values to overcome at key junctures the extreme, almost Wellsian, class isolation and specialization on Omega 11. This is also the message of the book to the readers, who are in a Brechtian term called 'the ancestors' – read: the potential ancestors of a life as productive play.

The last novel of the 1970s, *Conviva ludibundus*, develops exactly this theme, and begins almost exactly at the point where the former novel left off. Toward its close, Merkur and Elektra were protesting at a statue of them being erected on Omega 11 – a clear 'violation of personality', forbidden on the enlightened Earth. This hidden pun on 'cult of personality' opens the narration of Professor Philemon, chief seabed gardener, concerning the strange adventures around the intelligent 'bio-electronic life-form' in the sea:

Philemon is dreading the 'cult rituals' he is threatened with for his approaching 90th birthday. The Conviva, probably created by accident, and whose Latin name translates approximately as 'playful boon-companion', is the indispensable symbiotic link in the production of the famed 'Green Medallion' mussels which contain all the vitamins, enzymes and trace-elements necessary for the humanity of the third millennium; and only its discoverer Philemon has a tacit, gardener-like understanding of the Conviva's needs and nature. In the plot of the novel, Philemon's scientific successor, Professor Dr H. H. Mittelzwerck (the 'speaking name' could translate roughly as 'ridiculous mediocre pygmy'), intervenes to rationalize the cultivation of mussels by erecting 'necessary' enclosures. The resulting disappearance of the mussel is to be made good by equipping a Verne-like super-technological super-vehicle, designed to navigate in all elements, to seek for it. Both Philemon and the popular performer Friederike, called Kutz, are invited to participate in the expedition of this Ship of State which is also a Ship of Fools. The leader is, of course, Mittelzwerck, a typically dour, unimaginative, hardworking, upwardly mobile, conscientious, vain and pompous 'assiduoaspiringascendentity' (*Fleiss-strebeaufstiegswesen*). The expedition develops following the hallowed folk-tale scheme of the temporary triumph and final downfall of the scientific villain, who manages – by misusing some scraps of Philemon's knowledge – to turn the Convivas into unstoppable producers of gigantic, watery, tasteless mussels as well as information-gatherers about the fate of every grain of sand on the seabed. This finally reduces him to a drooling idiot, and catastrophe for the vessel and the world is only averted by Kutz. Unwittingly, teaching the Convivas playful 'attractions' or 'numbers', she deprograms them from sterile production of things and data. This scene – which is prefigured in Kutz's 'dress-tease' number and her song about 'The grey waters of boredom' earlier on in the novel – with its mobile aquatic bio-constructions (the Convivas are large one-celled beings which can come together into changing multi-celled shapes) and multi-dimensional ballets, is the *pièce de résistance* of the novel, not too far from the description of mimoids in Lem's *Solaris*. Parabolically: an ever dynamic beauty, organized by art, is the only antidote to elitist and self-perpetuating power – with some nasty hints of possible ubiquitous psychological and ideological supervision by authorities – which leads to technocratic catastrophe.

This latest SF novel by the Brauns in the 1970s seems to me darker and weightier, perhaps even more bitter, than the earlier ones. True, it ends well, but all is not well with it. For the first time the sympathetic and right narrator remains more or less passive: conversely, the antagonist has grown more powerful and menacing. Thus the happy ending seems more in the nature of a Pascalian bet than a result of the right side's strength. To put it into Schiller's terms, the 'naïve' optimism of most of the earlier works is giving way to a 'sentimental' – though probably no less believable – approach. This also sets the Brauns' pendulum between SF and folktale again going somewhat toward the folktale side (for example, the mumbo-jumbo with Philemon's pocket-calculator), though this novel is still clearly to be considered as parabolic SF.

On the whole, chances are that this is a critical point in the Brauns' evolution. The horizon of utopian ethics remains constant throughout their development, but by 1978 the road to it leads through increasingly heavy obstacles. This evolution reminds one in some ways of the Strugatskys', except that the Brauns have on the one hand not concentrated on writing SF (or near-SF) and on the other hand have not succumbed to the Russians' frequent temptation to symbolistic abstraction, presenting societal effects without a clear causal chain. Be that as it may, it is heartening to note that the shift from light irony to more sombre satire has remained accompanied by comedy and wit, flowing out of their central orientation toward disrespectful and funny inversion of received authority – power structures as well as opinions – in favour of continual playful cognizing. In that sense the Brauns are in the best German tradition of exempla, parables or witty *contes philosophiques* tempering Teutonic earnestness with productive play, which runs – to cite some great names – from Brandt and Lessing through some Romantics such as Jean Paul or Tieck to Brecht (whom they not infrequently allude to). Their tough-minded gentleness is able to treat serious power-struggles without slam-bang violence, using – as *The Caucasian Chalk Circle* has it – pencils instead of pistols. They do not like fathers, but only – as discussed apropos of *Omega 11* – the forefathers of the playfully radical novum. In that sense, their whole characterization and tone places them at the strategic pivot in GDR writing between the SF of Branstner or Ziergiebel and the 'high lit.', of Anna Seghers and especially of Christa Wolf (both of whom – significantly – have also written SF) or Irmtraud Morgner.

To complete my account with a brief overview of the 1980s, the Brauns have, while keeping to their constant horizons, become more embattled faced with what they perceive as a stronger bureaucratic current in the GDR (among other things, they left the official Union of Writers). This attitude, and the attendant pragmatic pressures on them as freelance writers, has resulted in a genre diversification of their writings. Outside of SF this has led to some brilliant works of travelogue, Hoffmannesque fantasy, essays, a fictional biography of Socrates as parable on the difficulties of an independent and disrespectful thinker, and even a book of witty culinary recipes crossbred with erotics. In SF, this has resulted in a number of short stories published in various East and West German anthologies, and in the books *Der Utofant* ('The Utofant: A Periodical from the Third Millennium Found in the Future', 1981), *Das Kugeltranszendentale Vorhaben* ('The Spherico-Transcendental Design', 1983), *Die unhörbaren Töne* ('The Inaudible Sounds', 1984) and *Der x-mal vervielfachte Held* ('The X-times Multiplied Hero', 6 stories, 1985) – the three latter, just as the Socrates book, published only in West Germany. These are more fragmentary and as a rule briefer then their earlier writings, but just as elegant and ironical. Thus, increasingly dark and forlorn, the Brauns' playful cognizing yet remains part of the 'warm current' in socialism, colliding with the cold one.

Possibly the best way to conclude this account, which has so often led to mention of the Brauns' artful manipulation of narrative voices, is to say that they have managed to attain a distinct narrative voice of their own. This is not a small success. If one compared them only with other writers from the Warsaw Pact countries (to some of whom they are paradoxically more comparable than to a West German writer such as Herbert Franke – though they sometimes remind me also of Ursula Le Guin), one would immediately have to raise the question: who has a characteristic narrative voice there, among the surely nearly 200 writers of SF? The strongest one is, of course, Lem's voice: quite distinct are those of the Strugatskys and of Shefner, the late Ivan Yefremov and Ilya Varshavski each had a habitus of his own, perhaps half a dozen other Soviet writers might also be found to have one, so do or did perhaps four or five more such voices in Bucharest and Budapest, and there was one in Prague. And from the 1970s, there are the Brauns in Magdeburg: a place, a voice, on the SF map of Europe. Denying the division into 'high' and 'low' fictional genres (the very terms proclaim its elitism and mindlessness), this also means: on the literary map of our times.

(Originally published in 1981)

NOTE

1. This essay could not have been written without the friendly help in supplying literature by Verlag Das Neue Berlin and its chief editor, Mr Günther Claus, by Dr Franz Rottensteiner, and by the Brauns themselves, as well as by Mr Luc De Vos and Dr Vladimir Gakov – to all of whom my warm thanks. None the less, I was able to find only a few works by the Brauns apart from the titles discussed at length. My information on those not seen comes from 11 items of secondary literature listed after my essay in *SFS*, no. 23 (1981) 78. I am retaining 6 of them in chronological order and adding two: Wolfgang Paulick (ed.), *Junge Schriftsteller der Deutschen Demokratischen Republik in Selbstdarstellungen* (Leipzig, 1965) pp. 50–62, 190; Paul Behla, 'Was ist das – Wissenschaftliche Phantastik?', *Potsdamer Forschungen*, Reihe A, no. 15 (1975) 65–74; Gustav Schröder, 'Zur Geschichte der utopischen Literatur in der DDR', *Potsdamer Forschungen*, Reihe A, no. 16 (1975) 31–47; Heinz Entner, 'Mauserung einer Gattung: Utopische Literatur eines Jahrzehnts, *Neue Deutsche Literatur*, no. 12 (1976) 137–153; Adolph Sckerl, *Wissenschaftlich-phantastische Literatur* (Berlin, DDR, 1976); Hors Heidtmann, 'A Survey of Science Fiction in the German Democratic Republic', *SFS*, no. 17 (1979) 95–6; Hors Heidtmann, *Utopisch-phantastische Literatur in der DDR* (Munich, 1982); William B. Fischer, *The Empire Strikes Out* (Bowling Green, OH, 1984) pp. 290–8.

Conclusion

Conclusion

13

SF as Metaphor, Parable and Chronotope (with the Bad Conscience of Reaganism)

0. In this study, I wish to explore the depth presuppositions for analysing SF as a specific kind of narrative. So, to begin with, what is a narrative text? Assuming that any text unfolds a thematic-cum-attitudinal field, and that fiction does so by presenting relationships between fictional agents (primarily by means of events in spacetime)[1] – how does, within the domain of fiction, a narrative text differ from a metaphoric text? All of these theoretical questions have been, quite properly, subjects of entire book-shelves, to which I hope to be contributing in the near future. To supply a first answer pertinent to understanding SF, I shall first discuss metaphor and larger 'metaphorical texts', touch upon the central analytic categories of model, paradigm and possible world, and then focus on the connecting link between a metaphoric and a narrative text, the parable. My hypothesis is that all fictional texts are – by way of their paradigm or model – based on metaphoricity, but that the narrative texts add to this a defined presentation in space and time, the *chronotope*. I shall conclude by applying this hypothesis to SF as a specific type of story and by analysing an SF story by Cordwainer Smith, in order to test how much illumination the hypothesis may provide.

1. ON METAPHOR

1.0. In one of the most recent and most illuminating syntheses of metaphor analysis, Umberto Eco notes that the incomplete 1971 *bibliographie raisonnée* by Shibles registers *c.* 3000 titles, and yet that these thousands of pages contain only few which add anything fundamental to the two or three basic concepts introduced by

Aristotle (Eco, 1980, p. 191). I shall therefore in my first part, dealing with some basic properties of metaphor, focus only on those key aspects which are indispensable for my argument, without at all pretending to a complete survey, much less a new theory of metaphor. I simply wish to derive from the discussions of metaphor which I found most useful – Aristotle (1968); Beardsley (1958); Bellert (1980–81); Black (1962 and 1977); Eco (1980); Henry (1971); Lewis (1970); Richards (1936); Ricoeur (1978 and 1980); Shelley (1975); Whalley (1972) – the basic orientations necessary for envisaging similarities and differences between metaphor and narrative.

1.1. This domain, as all of its students know, is both a 'somewhat boundless field' (Ricoeur, 1980, p. 141) and a minefield. I am trying to leapfrog most of it by adopting a probably incomplete working definition of metaphor as *a unitary meaning arising out of the (verbal) interaction of disparate conceptual units from different universes of discourse or semantic domains*. It should be added that metaphor presents a complex cognition not by literal or analytic statement but by sudden confrontation: it is a language deviance that results in the perception of a possible relationship which could establish a new norm of its own.

It follows that it is not necessary to think of metaphor, romantically, as either peculiarly imagistic or peculiarly emotional (cf. Shklovskii, 1929; Richards, 1936), though the metaphor often contains a visualizable image and always embodies a value-judgment correlative to an integral, that is, also emotional, involvement.

1.2. If 'connotation' is taken to mean the difference between an ideal dictionary entry and an ideal encyclopedic entry about the same term, that is, any meaning of a term which is 'normally' thought of as secondary (Eco, 1980, pp. 206–8 *et passim*), then metaphor 'create[s] new contextual meaning by bringing to life new connotations' (Beardsley, 1958, p. 43). Its synthesis does not obliterate discordances, but in order to have any unity at all, its two terms have to share some connotations. In the example 'This man is a lion', the meaning of the lexeme 'man' and the lexeme 'lion', which are the metaphor's two terms, gets to be extended by the context or intratext of the metaphor as a whole. From literal dictionary meaning current in a given culture and sociolect, the meaning modulates into some selection from the encyclopedia of cultural commonplaces, presuppositions and categories (cf. also Eco, 1979, *passim*). This is usually an imaginary encyclopedic entry current in a given sociolect and ideology, but it can also be a new entry, invented *ad hoc* by the metaphor's author and enforced by its context.

The sum of all the cultural *topoi* and categories implied and presupposed by a text constitutes the ideological system of its social addressee. The maxims of this system encompass the connotation chosen in a metaphor. In 'This man is a wolf', the 'normal' connotation of a wolf in our epoch would probably be *cruelty*, a connotation encompassed by the ideological maxim of Social Darwinism where man is necessarily wolf to man. On the contrary, under the maxim of a tribal society, where wolves may be totemic ancestors or reincarnations of people, the above metaphor will work in a totally different, axiologically quite opposed way. The two semantic domains and cultural categories of 'wolf' and 'man' which in a metaphor act as lenses and filters for seeing each other, will be very different; *a fortiori*, so will be their interaction, which in a feedback spiral uses the movement between these domains to emphasize some and suppress other traits potentially present in 'wolfness' (lupineity) and 'manness' (humanity). 'The wolf-metaphor . . . *organizes* our view of man' (Black, 1962, p. 41) and vice versa: when wolf and man are projected upon each other, a new whole emerges (cf. Richards, 1936; Black 1962, pp. 38–42 and 236–7; Eco, 1980).

The two semantic domains interacting in any metaphor *can* work upon each other because the connotations of their representative terms within the metaphor have a common ground. Aristotle (1968, ch. xxi, 1457b) defines metaphor in two main ways, the strongest way being 'transference by analogy':

> . . . for example, to scatter seed is to sow, but the scattering of the sun's rays has no name [in Greek]. But the act of sowing in regard to grain bears an analogous relation to the sun's dispersing of its rays, and so we have the phrase 'sowing the god-created fire'.

In modern language, Aristotle has here picked out the single semantic property or seme of scattering and used it as the common ground between the relation sowing/grain and the relation sun's beaming/light rays. All other semes are neglected in order to establish this common ground; however, while suppressed, they continue to function subterraneously as qualifying dissimilarities: in this case such is, for example, the action of the hand in throwing grain, which also implies a person sowing, the corpuscular nature of the material being scattered, etc. (cf. Henry, 1971, pp. 65–7).

1.3. The discussions of 1.2. hold fully only for what is variously called the high-grade, full (-fledged) or true metaphor (Whalley, 1972, pp. 491, 494; Black, 1962, *passim*; Lewis, 1970, pp. 140–1ff.) – a unique presentation of previously non-existent meaning. On the other end of the metaphor spectrum is the low-grade metaphor, which transposes pre-existent meaning. In the 'full-fledged' metaphor new meaning, accessible to us in no other way, is being formed and thus explored. We have no other ways at hand for thinking through the relationship such a metaphor refers to; if it fossilizes or dies by lexicalization into a 'literal' lexeme, we shall for the time being cease thinking about that relationship (cf. also Köller, 1975, p. 40). For an example from cultural-cum-ideological history, *animales* comes in classical Latin from *anima* = breath; when this is later lexicalized into the dead metaphor of 'soul', the dead-end quandary of medieval theology, whether animals have souls, could arise (and SF has to go back to Greek for its lay naming of beings with souls or conscious intelligences – *psychozoa*). To the contrary, if a low-grade metaphor – such as the late Latin word for and root of 'arrive', *adripare*, whose literal meaning is 'come to a shore' – dies, no great harm is done since we have other ways of thinking about the relationship of bodily translation in space up to a final point. I shall have occasion to return in section 3.5. to the parallel between this polarization of high *vs.* low-grade metaphor and my opposition of true *vs.* fake novum. Here I would just like to note that the low-grade, or indeed fake, metaphor can be recognized, first, by the lack of textual preparation and sustainment of the metaphoric confrontation; and second, by the fact that inserting a copula such as 'to be' or 'to seem' will destroy the metaphoric confrontation or fusion and reveal the emptiness of that metaphor. Using Whalley's example, 'When the play ended, they resumed / Reality's topcoat' (1972, p. 494), if we put 'Reality is (or: seems) a topcoat' (or vice versa), it becomes apparent that the resumption of a topcoat upon leaving theatre is already a re-entry into extra-ludic reality of which any topcoat is a part. Thus, the supposed modifying term is contained in the first term, and we do not enter upon a synthesis of discordant semantic domains. Instead, we are faced with what is in relation to the full metaphor only a formal mimicry.

Therefore, the full-fledged, 'interaction' or transformational metaphors cannot be paraphrased without a significant loss of cognitive yield (Black, 1962, pp. 45–6); while the low-grade, 'substitution or comparison' metaphors *can* be exhausted by paraphrase into commonplaces – for example, 'on leaving the theatre, spectators pick up coats and re-enter reality'.

1.4. If we do not confine cognition to analytical discourse only but assume, in a more realistic vein, that it can equally (and in all probability necessarily) be based on imagination, then *metaphor is not an ornamental excrescence but a specific cognitive organon*. Its specificity of reference is still poorly understood, but metaphor seems to be directed toward and necessary for an insight into continuously variable processes when these are being handled by language, which is composed of discrete signs (Hesse, 1966; Ortony, 1975). If metaphor is such a dialectical corrective of all analytical language, it necessarily refers, among other things, to what a given culture and ideology consider as reality. This means that some conclusions educible from any metaphor – for example, 'people are cruel', 'wolves are conscious' – are pertinent to or culturally 'true' of given understandings of relationships in practice. The metaphor can affirm such an understanding or (in the case of full-fledged metaphors) develop 'the before unapprehended relations of things' in ways at that moment not formulatable except by way of metaphor (Shelley, 1975, p. 357; cf. Shklovskii, 1923, p. 115; and 1929, p. 12). Exploding literal semantic and referential pertinence, turning heretofore marginal connotations into new denotations, it proposes a new, imaginative pertinence by rearranging the categories that shape our experience. Metaphor sketches in, thus, lineaments of 'another world that corresponds to other possibilities of existence, to possibilities that would be most deeply our own . . .' (Ricoeur, 1978, p. 229). In so doing, it redescribes the known world and opens up new possibilities of intervening into it.

In more analytical language, the sum of all literal statements which can be educed from a full-fledged metaphor will be both too restricted and too abundant. *Too restricted*, not exhaustive: people are perhaps cruel like wolves, but how should one formulate the hesitation between 'people are instinctive' and 'wolves are conscious' – connotations or implications simultaneously also present within the over-determination of this, as of any metaphor – in sense-making literal propositions? *Too abundant*: for 'the implications, previously left for a suitable reader to educe for himself, with a nice feeling for their relative priorities and degrees of importance, [will be] now presented explicitly as though having equal weight' (Black, 1962, p. 46). Thus, literal statements are both frozen into connotative univalency and ponderated into cognitive equivalency; in order to acquire analytical functionality, such propositions are left with a binary choice between the 1 of true and the 0 of false rather than with a spectrum of possibilities. To the contrary, cognition through a full metaphor, reorganizing the logical space of our conceptual frameworks, increases understanding of 'the dynamic processes of reality' (Eco, 1980, p. 212). It is, thus, not necessary to think of any such imaginative cognition as a mystical insight or magical transfer but rather as a hypothetic proposition with specifiable yields and limitations. Parallel to other forms of cognition – say, analytic conceptual systems, plastic representation, music or mathematics – metaphoric cognition can be partly or wholly accepted or rejected by feedback from historical experience, verbal and extra-verbal. However, its potentially cognitive function is not an extrinsic but a central quality of metaphor (cf. ibid., p. 209ff.; and Ricoeur, 1978, *passim*). Technically, it is graspable as the distinction between *vehicle* and *tenor* (first introduced, though not fully clarified, by Richards (1936)). Following refinements by students of parable, I propose to call *vehicle* the metaphoric expression as a whole taken literally and *tenor* the meaning it conveys.[2]

1.5. What can, then, be considered to be the basic conditions for a full-fledged metaphor? I think there are three:

(1) it is *coherent* or *congruent*: the connotations admissible in interpretation must have a cultural-cum-ideological common ground;

(2) it is *complex* or *rich*: consonant with (1) above, it uses *all* the connotations that can be brought to bear, 'it means all it can mean' (Beardsley, 1958, p. 144);

(3) it contains or embodies a *novum*: 'it constitutes a set of
conclusions which would not follow from any conventional
combination of words . . .' (Bellert, 1980, p. 34); it is 'not
inferrible from the standard lexicon' (Black, 1977, p. 436); it is
'the emergence of a more radical way of looking at things'
(Ricoeur, 1980, p. 152). This novum is necessarily (at least in
part) historico-referential insofar as it disrupts the synchronic
cognitive system current when it was coined. The criteria for
deciding which metaphors are to be seen as dead, remotivated
or farfetched are all drawn from historical semantics and
pragmatics.

We may call these basic conditions the three axioms of *coherence,
richness and novelty*. Beardsley – who admits only the first two – notes
that such axiomatic conditions may be considered as analogous to
Occam's razor in literal, for example, scientific, texts (1958, p. 145).
While I agree with Bellert not only that among the conditions for
metaphor are consistency and novelty but also that any metaphor
necessarily contains a multiple reference to what in a given sociolect
and ideology is taken for reality, I do not think it is necessary to erect
such a partial 'reference to reality' (Bellert, 1980/81, p. 38) into a
separate condition or axiom, since it is already implied in my second
and third axioms as the norm against which both the richness and
(as I just argued) the novelty are necessarily measured: Occam's
razor again. I shall return to this in 3.5.

1.6. This argument can be opened up in the direction of larger texts
by adopting Bellert's delimitation of a *metaphorical text*. It is 'a text not
supposed to be interpreted literally . . . but assumed to have an
interpretation different from that which would follow merely from
the application of conventional semantic rules to the constituent
expressions and their combinations' (ibid., p. 25). I would point out
that this delimination holds for a text of *any* kind, and there is no
reason to confine it to lyrics or small forms.

Thus, the interpretation of metaphorical texts can, on the one
hand, not even begin unless an intertext of the literal or
conventional senses of its constituent propositions is first assumed.
On the other hand, the metaphor is defined by violating at least one
semantic, syntactic or pragmatic conventional rule in a meaningful
way, by a 'paradigmatic deviance' (Ricoeur, 1980, p. 144). A
shuttling operation is established between the metaphor's initial

semantic im-pertinence, its *pars destruens,* and (in successful cases) the *pars construens* of its final heightened pertinence.

2.   METAPHORS AND LARGER TEXTS

2.1. Proceeding toward larger metaphorical texts, attention should be drawn to the well-known but curiously neglected fact that in many poems, prominently including longer poems, there appears the *métaphore filée* or drawn-out (sustained) metaphor. This is a syntagmatic series of metaphors conjoined by sense, where each single metaphor presents one particular aspect of the paradigm, which is then an integration of all the textually occurring metaphors. That paradigm is the common tenor of them all – so much so that common usage calls the sum of all the syntagmatic occurences a 'metaphor' in the singular (cf. Henry, 1971, pp. 122–3). In the drawn-out metaphor each syntagmatic occurrence may come from the same semantic domain, which is used as vehicle, but this is secondary to the fact that the *tenor* common to all the single occurrences uses the same semic field. Such drawn-out metaphors are especially abundant and well-known in Baroque and Mannerist poetry, for example, in Marino, Gongora, Théophile de Viau or Donne, as the *concetto* or conceit, but another privileged example could be Hugo, for example, the poem *Dieu* analysed by Henry (1971, pp. 122–3) in terms of heaven as a place of torture.

Just as 'a metaphor is a miniature poem' (Beardsley, 1958, p. 144), so such drawn-out metaphors are an intermediate stage between, on the one hand, a single independent or lyrical metaphor, and on the other hand, a narrative text syntagmatically deploying an overall paradigm that can be taken as the tenor to which all narrative devices centripetally tend. The *métaphore filée* is an intermediate case in which the concentration on *one* common and unmistakably sustained tenor is a basic device for unifying the attention of readers in a longer – even though usually a verse – text. Other things being equal, this device does a better job of unification than the scattershot use of unconnected metaphors employing different tenors, whose compatibility and final unity has then to be established as an extra – i.e., uneconomic – operation by the reader.

An almost indistinguishable intermediary device is found also, *mutatis mutandis,* in many a stretch of prose that demands a comparable reading attention and unification. A good example are the 80 or so pages in Proust's *A l'ombre des jeunes filles en fleur* where the *jeunes filles* are referred to in metaphors of flowers – thus establishing the 'tonal dominant' of those entire three volumes (cf. Henry, 1971, 136–7).

2.2. If the theory of metaphor was a minefield, the no-man's-land between metaphor and narrative which we are now approaching is – to continue this drawn-out metaphor – a desert with shifting quicksand patches and mirages on the horizon. How to fit metaphor, as a rule analysed only in verse or in isolated sentences, into a 'text grammar' or any other approach to textual macro-structures is an almost total *terra incognita*. One crucial signpost is Black's indication that metaphors can (especially in longer works!) be supported by, and draw connotations from, not only the culturally dominant system of commonplaces but also by *new, specially focused* systems of 'implications for the literal uses of key expressions, prior to using them as vehicles for . . . metaphors'. I believe this is, in fact, also implied in every full-fledged metaphor, given that it is a novum. It is only strikingly made explicit as a new anterior context for the functioning of a metaphor when, for example, 'a naturalist who really knows wolves [tells] us so much about them that *his* description of man as a wolf diverges quite markedly from the stock uses of that figure' (both in Black, 1962, p. 43). In other words, in any metaphoric series or system, textual coherence demands that the shifts in meaning implied by each single metaphor gradually produce also shifts in the 'literal' meanings against which each succeeding metaphor of the series is being defined. Barring negative interference by other local, syntagmatic influences, the new context for metaphorization should grow stronger as the series cumulates and it should, in all successful cases, prevail over the context of cultural commonplaces, of current ideological maxims. This prevalence may be marked by the appearance of a single 'encompassing metaphor', approximating closely or indeed identical with the new paradigm and tenor. But the encompassing metaphor may also remain implicit – a case of considerable importance for narrative, and SF in particular.

Thus, we are now entering upon some possibilities of connecting metaphor with narrative, indicated by Vico's description of metaphor – or at least of those fashioned in primitive times by attributing sense and passion to inanimate things – as a 'small story (*picciola favoletta*)' (1974, Book 2:191). This connection may perhaps be most readily established by postulating a *'metaphor theme'* (Hoffman, 1980, p. 405) as a global form of metaphor informing a whole, possibly very long, text by providing a series of metaphoric occurrences, all of which relate to the same paradigm or macro-metaphor used as a system of central presuppositions and ultimate frame of reference for that text (cf. Black, 1962, pp. 239–41). In relation to the imaginary 'possible world' of the text, the metaphor theme acts as its basic cognitive, explanatory or founding hypothesis. I incline to think that it is useful to separate this category from the drawn-out metaphor of 2.1. because it is indispensable as well as central to a large, as a rule prose, text; but it is a nice point whether Donne's 'A Nocturnall Upon S. Lucies Day' or Proust's *A l'ombre* should be envisaged as the former or the latter. The important and pertinent point is perhaps best formulated (except for the intrusion of the wholly redundant concept of 'myth') in Frye's conclusion:

> whatever is constructive in any verbal structure seems to me to be invariably some kind of metaphor or hypothetical identification. . . . The assumed metaphors in their turn become the units of the myth or constructive principle of the argument. While we read, we are aware of an organizing structural pattern or conceptualized myth. (Frye, 1966, p. 353)

2.3. Thus far I have proceeded from a sustained *series of metaphors* by way of a *metaphor theme* ever closer to a global, metaphor-type *paradigm* acting as tenor for a large text which is as a whole its vehicle. The logical next step – much discussed among theoreticians both of metaphor and of science – is the *model*. If one accepts the cognitive status of (full-fledged) metaphor, then both it and the model are *heuristic fictions* or speculative instruments mediating between two semantic domains – say, the atom and the solar system in Bohr's early model of electron orbits, based on Rutherford's identical metaphor. '[M]etaphor is to poetic language as model is to scientific language' (Ricoeur, 1975, p. 85).

Reactualizing the discussion about similarities between metaphors and models, Black claimed that their main difference consisted in the necessity for a model to control a coherent theory (that is, a set of linked and falsifiable concepts) and not merely a system of presuppositions (Black, 1962, p. 221ff., in particular pp. 236, 239–40; cf. Hoffman, 1980, who also gives a valuable survey of many others on pp. 406–23). However, lucid and convincing arguments have been put forward to the effect that criteria of choice between hypotheses are, even in strictest natural science, finally reducible to a preference for one model over another, that in fact the necessary criterion of simplicity assumes nature follows a given *model* of unity or coherence, and that a model is therefore essential to any scientific theory with predictive power (Hesse, 1966, pp. 101–29). Every theoretical explanation is thus *also* a 'metaphoric redescription of the domain of the explanandum' on the lines of an interaction metaphor (ibid., p. 157 *et passim*). As to prediction, which entails falsifiability, its (literally true) meaning of 'saying earlier' (*prae-dictio*) reveals that this was in itself originally a metaphor. Scientists may usually treat it as dead; but it keeps reawakening, thus testifying that all verbal hypotheses are *also*, inescapably, a matter of language, that 'rationality consists just in the continuous adaptation of our language to our continually expanding world, and metaphor is one of the chief means by which this is accomplished' (ibid., pp. 176–7).

Furthermore, one of the most relevant interpretations of Kuhn's scientific (or indeed philosophical, philosophy-of-science) paradigm, that overarches any epistemic epoch and is therefore also to be understood as its overall world model, asserts that any such paradigm 'has also got to be a concrete "way of seeing", . . . a concrete "picture" of something, *A*, which is used analogically to describe a concrete something else, *B*.' Logically, such a paradigm must therefore 'either be, literally, a model; or, literally, a picture; or, literally, an analogy-drawing sequence of word-uses in natural language; or, some combination of these' (Masterman, 1979, pp. 76–7, 79). I think that for the purposes of this essay one can, as I noted in 1.1., rule out the literal picture or image. What remains, therefore, is an argument, even more consistent than Hesse's 'that there is always an analogy or a concrete model at the heart of any mathematics used in science, and . . . that it is this analogy which guides and restricts the theory's articulation, excising and removing, by the need to preserve it [i.e., the analogy, DS], the otherwise excessive possibilities of abstract development inherent in all mathematics' (Masterman, 1979, p. 78; cf. also Gentner, 1982).

At any rate, whether there be a radical difference between metaphor and model (or paradigm) for mathematized scientism, this can scarcely be upheld when we get to non-mathematical description of a model and/or to the *sciences humaines*. In that case, it seems to me the verifiability supposedly proper of the model is not much more than the application of the three axioms for metaphoric texts specified in 1.5.: coherence, richness and novelty. Thus, by the time the term 'model' is applied to a fictional text, say a writer's opus, I can see no useful difference between saying 'Balzac gives us an insightful model of the French society at his time' and saying that his opus is something like a complex and not yet fully understood macro-metaphor. This is what Engels's famous comment that he had learned from *The Human Comedy* more about French society 'than from all the professed historians, economists and statisticians of the period together' (Marx and Engels, 1953, p. 122) is, to my mind, saying.

An example very pertinent to the discussion at hand is used by C. S. Lewis. He argues that Flatlanders – beings living in two dimensions – can be a useful metaphor for understanding the fourth dimension. The analogy would go: as Flatland is to the sphere of our three-dimensional life and understanding, so our three dimensions are to the fourth. Therefore, the Flatland metaphor can make us begin cognizing the fourth dimension, by way of understanding at least some of its implications: for example, we should not be surprised if a four-dimensional being could control our space and time, since this is what *we* could do to the Flatlanders (Lewis, 1970, pp. 139–40). Now, mischievously, Lewis omits to mention that his example is taken from a remarkable SF parable, *Flatland* (1884) by Edwin A. Abbott. This novellette, however, uses geometry for ethico-political tenor, so that the dimensions and limitations in physics signify those in ethics and politics (see *VSF*, pp. 370–3 *et passim*). In this case 'sustained metaphor', 'model', and '(prose) text with metaphor-like paradigm actualized in a metaphoric series' mean the same thing.

3. FROM METAPHOR TO SCIENCE FICTION: THE PARABLE

3.1. The argument thus far, leading up to the discussion of *Flatland*, can serve to introduce the crucial coinciding between SF practice and contemporary semiotics: their simultaneous use of the concept, metaphor or model of *possible worlds*. I mentioned this coincidence in my *MOSF*, but – except for Eco's use of *Flatland* and other unnamed SF works in his *Lector* (1979, pp. 148–54) and the mention in Sparshott (1967: 5) – I know of only one article on this, pioneering but inconclusive (Volli, 1980). To summarize an involved argument very briefly, whatever possible worlds might be in logic, each and every fictional text implies in semiotics a possible world, specifying a state of affairs which differs from the 'normal', and analysable as if based on counterfactual conditionals or 'as if' hypotheses (Eco, 1979, pp. 122–73; and cf. Suvin, 'Performance' (1985) with further bibliography). The difference might be, in a text under the sign of 'realistic' illusion, confined to some wishdream or nightmare elements of the plot, but in texts obeying another verisimilitude it might spread to the 'furnishing' of that whole fictional world. This is obviously the rule in 'estranged' fictional genres such as SF. It is by now a commonplace of SF theory that its *mode* is a hypothetico-conditional one (*MOSF*, p. 52, with further references; and cf. the whole of its chs 1 and 2). As different from the logicians' possible worlds, the fictional ones are not exhaustively posed but are created by the reader on the basis of interaction between the fictional 'counterfactuality' and feedback references to his/her own presupposed factuality. The world of any fictional work is understandable only as the reader's set of cultural and ideological norms, the social addressee's *vraisemblance*, changed in such-and-such ways. The famous SF statement and proposition 'The door dilated', presupposes (see chapter 5) that in this text's universe of discourse and possible world there are intelligent beings (psychozoa) who use sight, locomotion, and constructed edifices; and further, that these edifices incorporate building techniques not used in human history up to the writer's time and that the text's 'otherwise' locus is normal for the implied narrator. Finally, this sentence reassures the reader that the *categories* of visual (or at any rate sensual) observation, locomotion, constructed edifices, building techniques and historical normality are relevant for understanding this universe: the *species* of dilating door may be unfamiliar, but the *genus* of door anchors it again into familiarity. *Per species incognitam sed genus cognitum* seems to be the motto of most SF estrangement.

The syntagm 'possible world' can thus in this case be analysed into the following denotations: 'worlds' refers to space-time communities of psychozoa; 'possible' refers to their not being ruled out by the basic cultural invariants of verisimilitude (for example, the philosophy of science) dominant in the social addressee's ideology. This entails a semantically revised universe of discourse 'within which the usual denotative and connotative properties of sememes are upset – though not at random, but following the rules of a complete semantic structuring' (to adapt Eco, 1977, p. 110, speaking of the cognate estranged literary genre of fairy tales). Of course, this is a generically ideal case: in bad SF, the proportion of random changes rises rapidly, while 'Science Fantasy' juxtaposes incompatible structurings within the same text. None the less, on a theoretical level it should make clear that the SF universe of discourse presents syntagmatically developed possible worlds as models (more precisely as thought-experiments) or as totalizing and thematic metaphors: Eco's above definition is in fact also a definition of metaphor. The main differences between a single metaphor and a fictional text would have to take into account the latter's quite different articulation. The paradigm of a longer fictional (in this case, SF) text must be sufficiently articulated in its syntagmatic development to permit exploration of the underlying key hypothesis – which is also its metaphor – as to its properties, most prominently the relationships between people it implies; in other words, to permit falsification of its thought-experiment. *In any prose tale, it must be possible to verify examined aspects of the central propositions which have by means of coherence, plenitude, and novelty created the narrative universe of that tale.*

3.2. The argument about a continuity between a micro-metaphor and a longer literary text needs, of course, to be supplemented by an argument about their clear *differences*. For given purposes and levels of analysis, such differences might be as important as, or even much more important than, the similarities I have been pointing out so far. My contention is not that a gulf between them does not exist but that it is bridgeable from both sides, and that we can learn of what the bridge consists. From the metaphor side, I have been arguing how any metaphor which goes beyond one sentence begins to organize a narrative argument. From the narrative side, I would argue that the paradigmatic tenor of any fictional and dramatic text is in some important ways a model or macro-metaphor. I propose to look at this with help of a fictional form which is generally acknowledged to be somewhere in between metaphor and story – the parable. It is significant that in this book the parable has been found to be central to the narrative analysis of SF (and, I would claim, of all fiction). For easier comparison to Aristotle's canonic example of full-fledged metaphor, the analogy of sowing quoted earlier, I am choosing the three parables of sowing from Matthew 13. This has also the advantage of allowing me to use insights from witty analyses of that text (Crossan, 1973; Dodd, 1971; Gerhardsson, 1967–8; Jeremias, 1963; Marin, 1971; Ricoeur, 1975, p. 54ff.; and cf. other parable scholars adduced in note 2) while taking a different tack from them.

3.3. The common ground within each of the three parables embedded in Matthew 13:1–43, is – exactly as in Aristotle's classical example of the full analogical metaphor from 1.2. – the seme of implanting or taking root (successful or failed). It arises out of the basic analogy between sowing the good seed and preaching the kingdom of heaven, which is carefully explained in the framing parts of the text. As Ricoeur rightly remarks, '[t]he parable is the conjunction of a *narrative form* and a *metaphorical process*'; he then observes as correctly that the problem of 'how a metaphor may take the mediating form of a narrative' is 'only partially' solved by the contemporary theory of metaphor (Ricoeur, 1975, pp. 30–1). For the classical (lyrical or micro-) metaphor is a local unit of discourse, operating at the level of sentence, whereas the parable is a literary genre (even if a small form) operating at the level of text composition, Aristotle's *taxis* (ibid., pp. 92–3). I submit that the major significant accretion to metaphor (as discussed before) effected in such a parable is that the relationship between sowing/good seed and preaching/kingdom of heaven is actualized through a narrative action leading to *a change of state in a determinate spacetime*. This can be exemplified on the briefest of the three 'sowing' parables, the Parable of the Mustard Seed:

31. . . . The kingdom of heaven is like to a grain of mustard seed, which a man took, and sowed in his field:
32. Which indeed is the least of all seeds: but when it is grown, it is the greatest among herbs, and becometh a tree, so that the birds of the air come and lodge in the branches thereof.

(King James Version)

The vehicle of this parable is a minimal *story* involving precise *space* and *time*, whose characteristic is the deployment of hyperbole and paradox by which the least shall become the greatest, given some preconditions. The space begins with the very small seed, fitting into a man's hand; it is cinematically (both in the sense of moving and of movies) enlarged by way of the connecting 'shot' of sowing to the horizontal dimension of a field (Luke 13:19 speaks of a garden); in it, the mustard seed grows after a lapse of time – tacitly filled in by the hearers from their empirical norm – to a large tree, whose greatness is verified by the last cinematic shot of many birds finding enough place to lodge in it. The spacetime dimensionality unfolds thus from the point-like seed, through the implied hand and the two-dimensional field, to the dimension of vertical development (accommodating both the upward arrow and the arrow of time) and to a final four-dimensional shot of birds flying into and finding protection within the tree (in Mark 4:32, 'under the shadow of it'). As important, the story's spacetime is consubstantial to changes through action: first the sower taking the seed into his hand and sowing it out over the field, second, the growth of the seed into a tree, and third, the arrival and nestling of the birds.

Now whereas in a metaphor like 'The chairman ploughed through the discussion' there is certainly an action (the metaphoric focus is a verb), a micro-metaphor or sentence-metaphor cannot, I would maintain until proof to the contrary, envisage a sequential *change of state*, a succession of events tied to a *mutable chronotope* (cf. Bakhtin, 1981, 84ff.). Though the metaphor compensates for this impossibility by a point-like flash of insight, the cognitive necessity of subjecting aspects and elements of any complex proposition or hypothesis to detailed scrutiny can only be satisfied by a story. It is, therefore, *not action* (by a narrative agent such as the ploughing chairman) which differentiates story from metaphor; it is the development of space and time from seed to field to tree and from sowing through growing time, which add story to metaphor and form the parable – so much richer and more persuasive than an unsupported metaphor would be. The story – the plot – is the organizing backbone of the whole message. Varying Ricoeur, I would say that the kingdom of heaven is not as *who* but as *how* (that is, *what changes have happened when-and-where*); indeed, 'the metaphorical power of the parable proceeds from the plot' (Ricoeur, 1975, p. 125). It is the plot that functions as an analogue model, a developed cognitive metaphor, of the tenor (the kingdom of heaven), and not the mustard seed by itself. Precisely because of this model-like function of the plot, the parable shares in the basic common traits of model and metaphor, those of being 'heuristic fictions' and 'redescriptions of reality' (ibid., pp. 95, 125 *et passim*,) But it adds to the common characteristics of all heuristic fiction a chronotopic, story-telling articulation in which agential and spatial relationships will be unfolded as *choices* (see the above essays on 'Narrative Logic' and on 'Epic Narration'). Any narrative, even a small parable, is an articulated (which means: multiply falsifiable at all the major articulating joints) thought-experiment.

The other two parables of sowing in Matthew 13 are significantly longer. The Parable of the Sower (13:3–8) involves four alternative actions: seeds devoured by the wayside, scorched because of weak roots, choked by thorns, or triumphantly bypassing all these threats and bringing manifold fruit. Its plot, thus, suggests alternative time-streams and possible worlds, based on qualitatively different spaces. Of the alternative chronotopes, the three initial ones traverse the spread of bad agricultural possibilities: 'the whole plot is articulated following an almost land-registry-like topology (*topique*)' (Marin, 1971, p. 59). The chronotopes progress axiologically from the wayside, through the stony or rocky places, to the ground covered with thorns. In other words, the plot traverses the bad ground beginning with the wayside and continuing with the transitional space between wayside and field where rocks and thorns delimit the field: the plot (the story) is plotted upon the plot (the seeding ground), the tenor in time apparently derived from but in fact projected on the metaphoric vehicle of space. These chronotopes are opposed but also lead up to the climax of the one and only perfect possibility – the seeds falling on to the agriculturally good or deep ground (in the Biblical Greek, with an erotic metaphor: the beautiful earth). By the same token, the four locational and axiological chronotopes which make up the plot delineate four alternative possibilities in the zero world of the implied reader. They are *typical*, that is, they are supposed to exhaust the pertinent possibilities of the seed's destiny; so much so that when the parable is explained in 13:18–23, its tenor is four *types* of narrative agents, or four sub-types of 'hearers of the word' (Gerhardsson, 1967–8, p. 175). I do not see how any single metaphor could accommodate four views.

In the final parable of this group, that of the Tares (13:24–30), there is furthermore a violent change of chronotope: the sowing and the (potential) springing up of good seed alone is first supplanted by the addition of tares, which spoilage is then presented as undone at the envisaged future gathering. The plot is here incipiently dramatic, because both the seeming inner contradiction of the Mustard Seed (smallness of seed *vs.* greatness of shrub) and the 'objective' antagonists of the Sower parable (birds, rocks, thorns) have been replaced by the agential conflict between the wheat-sowing Protagonist and the tares-sowing Antagonist: again, the most typical 'good guy' and 'bad guy'. True, the Protagonist does not enter into a face-to-face conflict with the Antagonist, but explains to his Satellites (present servants and future reapers) how the Antagonist will be outsmarted at gathering time; however, this only serves to stress the temporal and substantial depth of the conflict. The mingled didascalic actions and dialogues define an already complex sequence of reversals, leading in a full seasonal sowing-to-reaping cycle from clean through contaminated field to a final cleansing by fire. I do not see how any micro-metaphor, however drawn out, could accommodate more than two agents (that is, more than one action).

3.4. Should the above hypothesis about the constructive elements and factors necessary for a bridge between sentence metaphors and narrative texts prove defensible, it seems intuitively clear that it would be less difficult to pass from a small narrative form such as the parable to any other, larger narrative form, such as the short story and the novel. We may provisionally define a narrative as *a finite and coherent sequence of actions, located in the spacetime of a possible world and proceeding from an initial to a final state of affairs*. Its minimal requirements would be an agent, an initial state changing to a commensurate final state, and a series of changes consubstantial to varying chronotopes (I am spelling out the last element from the seminal discussions of Eco, 1979, pp. 70, 107–8 *et passim*, where it already seems implied). Since all of these elements have been found in the above discussion of parable, there is no generic difference between it and any other narration. As Ricoeur convincingly argues, '[m]etaphoricity is a trait not only of *lexis* but of *muthos* [story or plot] itself' (Ricoeur, 1978, p. 244). It should be therefore possible – if not necessarily always useful – to read any longer narration as an enlarged and otherwise modified parable, and in a final reduction as a metaphor.

3.5. Restricting the focus again to direct correspondences, I may perhaps refer to my argument that not only is 'each and every poetic metaphor . . . a novum' but that this also holds for all SF narrations (*MOSF*, p. 64 *et passim*). Superadded to the always necessary fictional properties of coherence and richness, this indicates that the analogies between a metaphorical and a narrative text will be especially strong and clearly visible on the textual surface itself in SF. The three axioms that metaphorical and SF texts have in common make for what I have called an ontolytic effect: the social addressee's empirical norms are being challenged by the estrangement inherent in the oscillation the text sets up between them and a new normative system, between the addressee's 'zero world' and the possible world of the SF text. Such analogies or parallels extend even to the vexed discriminations between what *is* and what *is not* SF, as well as what is *good* and *bad* SF. Just as in 1.3. 'reality's topcoat' was found to be only a mimicry of metaphor, falsifiable simply by putting its two terms into a relation of identity or synecdoche (topcoat = [part of] reality), so is any such SF tale that can be translated into another literary genre simply by changing surface *realia* (for example, the ray guns and aliens into the Indians and six-shooters of the Western) by that token a fake mimicry of SF. Further, even when we agree that something should count as a genuine metaphor or SF, we need criteria for distinguishing run-of-the-mill from optimal SF just as we do for low grade *vs*. full-fledged and successful metaphor. I suggest that these criteria are quite analogous, given the difference between brief and long writings. Thus, I have argued how the existence of various aspects of a true – that is, not pre-existent and not fully paraphrasable – novum is the touchstone for distinguishing SF from non-SF (*MOSF*, pp. 80–2). The other two axioms found in the discussion of metaphor, coherence and richness, allow us to distinguish the level or quality of an SF text.

As important as any other aspect is that both the fictional and the metaphoric novum always refer and are relevant to a common human history. Every text of fiction in the wider sense (including epic, lyric and dramatic writings, to put it in a familiar way), from the micro-text of a metaphor to the macro-text of, say, Shakespeare's late romances or the *Comédie humaine*, implies a possible world whose tenor is some different possibility of human relationships. This necessarily accompanies the cognitive status of metaphors and other texts: as Frege saw, every predication presupposes a 'striving for truth', which 'drives us always to advance from the sense to the reference' (quoted in Ricoeur, 1978, p. 218; and cf. his whole ch. 7). And furthermore, any 'second-level reference [that is, one which suspends literal description in favour of what I here call the novum] . . . is properly the metaphorical reference' (ibid., p. 221). Since freedom is 'the possibility of making it different' (Bloch, 1976, p. 143), aesthetic quality is in SF, as in any other metaphoric text, correlative to its ethico-political, liberating qualities.

4. SF AS PARABLE – CHRONOTOPE AND VEHICLE: THE AMERICAN SHIP OF THE STATE-SOUL AND THE BRIDEGROOM

4.1. In order to engage in the interpretation of an SF text, I need one more piece of theoretical equipment. That is Angenot's hypothesis of the 'absent paradigm' as a necessary characteristic of SF, to my mind the most important theoretical contribution to the study of this genre in the last years. To condense it exceedingly, it argues that to read SF according to the proper contract implied in the genre necessarily means a constant shifting back and forth from syntagmatic flow to an implicit semiotic paradigm. Very significantly, the paradigm hinges on the narrative agents (and I would add on the narrative chronotopes). A reading of 'mimetic' or 'naturalistic' fiction (cf. *MOSF*, pp. 18–21 *et passim*) couples the referential *topoi* directly with the text being read: the norms of adultery are the presuppositions for Madame Bovary's adultery. On the contrary, a reading of estranged fiction such as SF proceeds from the syntagmatic events first of all to the rules of authentication that form a narratively coherent possible world (which, I have argued, is also a macro-metaphor). For example, the events in P. J. Farmer's *Strange Relations* are not referred directly to the social addressee's sexual mores but first of all to the tenor and model suggested by each story, the new norm of sexuality. It is only in a second series of operations, fully completed only toward the end of the plot, that the SF reader can relate the fictional given as a whole – the tenor of the story – to his empirico-referential norms.

This proceeding, paralleling the one in a full-fledged metaphor or metaphorical text, means that SF will – in proportion to its quality – establish an *optimal* distance between the reader's initial 'normal' paradigm and the new, not fully existent but sufficiently clearly suggested paradigm of the SF story. The optimal distance should be neither so great as to render the narration incomprehensible, nor so small as to mechanically transpose culturally 'normal' paradigms – for example, the detective story or the Western, as argued earlier. Angenot concludes that the basic verisimilitude of SF is 'strongly related to the metaphorical . . . and other transformations from the empirical cognitive systems to the paradigms of the story' (Angenot, 'Absent Paradigm' (1979), p. 17). Of course, it should also be added that the 'switching device' routing the reader from meaning to meaning is neither – as Butor remarked of *Finnegans Wake* – each word (Butor, 1972, p. 12) nor – as in a metaphorical text – each metaphor, but that this device is in an SF work each 'world-creating' proposition, each narreme or narrative device for suggesting paradigm through syntagm. Most notably, such are agents with their actions and chronotopes. Finally, while in a metaphorical series or metaphorical text the principal term or encompassing metaphor may or may not appear (cf. 2.3.), in an SF story the paradigm necessarily must remain partly implicit, since a fully explicit stipulation of a possible world is impossible in narrative.

4.2. I would like, finally, to undertake a short analysis of an SF text in this perspective. As is very often the case in SF, its plot is that of a journey. Retracing on a more concrete level the trajectory of my argumentation so far, I shall – for reasons to become clear soon – start from the nautical metaphor of the 'boat of the mind' unfurling the sails for some great, communally significant venture. This *topos* is most memorably deployed into a sustained metaphor toward the beginning of Dante's *Paradiso* (ll. 1–15; cf. Curtius, 1963, pp. 128–30):

> O voi che siete in piccioletta barca
> Desiderosi d'ascoltar, seguiti
> Dietro al mio legno, che cantando varca,
> Tornate a riveder li vostri liti:
> Non vi mettete in pelago, chè, forse,
> Perdendo me rimarreste smarriti.

> L'acqua ch'io prendo già mai non si corse:
>   Minerva spira, e conducemi Apollo,
>   E nove Muse mi dimostran l'Orse.
> Voi altri pochi che drizzaste il collo
>   Per tempo al pan de li angeli, del quale
>   Vivesi qui ma non sen vien satollo,
> Metter potete ben per l'alto sale
>   Vostro naviglio, servando mio solco
>   Dinanzi a l'acqua che ritorna equale.

> [O you who in a fragile bark thus long,
>   Eager to harken, have followed close behind
>   My masted ship, that singing sails along,
> Turn back to view again your safer coast:
>   Do not put out to sea, lest ere long
>   By chance you lose me and may yourselves be lost.
> Never traversed was the sea where my craft fares:
>   Minerva inspires, Apollo steers my fate
>   And Muses nine point out to me the Bears.
> You other few, who craned up not too late
>   Your necks for bread of angels, on which here
>   The souls are fed but never satiate,
> You may now launch upon the salty deep,
>   And glide within my wake, ahead of where
>   The waters again an equal level keep.]
>   (modified from the translation by J. B. Fletcher)

Dante here contrasts those readers who are sailing in a small boat, fit only for hugging the shore, with those who, having oriented themselves in time toward angelic, permanently sustaining nourishment, are now able to follow his (Dante's) singing ship even in high-sea navigations through waters never traversed before and accessible only by help of gods and Muses. His metaphor is a continuation of the oppositional typifying we encountered already in Matthew's Parable of the Sower. I suggest it is not too foolhardy a leap from this tradition – whose later avatars I shall return to – to an unduly neglected SF writer, Cordwainer Smith, and in particular to his 1960 short story 'The Lady Who Sailed *The Soul*', written with Genevieve Linebarger (Smith, 1975, pp. 40–66). Already the title makes its pedigree perfectly clear.

However, as different from Dante's age, when rules of rhetorics and poetics were complex but clear, so that it was possible for interpretation to claim univocal status, at the latest since the Romantics metaphors and *topoi* are 'purposefully endowed with vague meanings, . . . which cannot be anchored in a pre-established code' (Eco, 1982, p. 37). Though I shall argue that (paradoxically) Smith's powerfully anchored ideology makes interpretation of his texts as nearly univocal as this is possible in a modern writer, there is no doubt that this great admirer of the French Symbolists shares the privatization happening in that type of poetics and rhetorics in the midst of its desperate attempts to harken back to earlier (for example, religious) certainties. The very effort to concoct a stable ideology from a recombination of various ideologemes is a privatized effort, however it may then be secondarily rendered public. There is little doubt in my mind that it was precisely this intimate ideological, and therefore also stylistic, kinship to the Symbolists and their own ascendants which made of Smith an inveterate borrower and refashioner (to say no more) from older literatures. Except for Chinese texts, this seems primarily to apply to Romance ones, from Dante to at least Rimbaud (cf., for example, his stories 'A Planet Named Shayol' and 'Drunkboat'). In Eco's terms, Smith's texts are halfway between symbol and allegory: from the outside, to the uninitiated, they function on the level of a supposedly futuristic adventure story. However, as in all significant SF, they are under more or less precise inside or esoteric control (ibid., p. 41). As I argued in my book, and as Angenot's approach powerfully confirms, 'any significant SF text is always to be read as an analogy [to the writer's present], somewhere between a vague symbol and a precisely aimed parable' (*MOSF*, p. 76). In the best cases SF, just as parable and metaphor, relates to a significant problem of the social addressee in indirect ways, through estrangement into a seemingly unrelated concrete and possible set of situations. The possible world (intensionally speaking) or the plot (extensionally speaking) as vehicle creates the novum as tenor. The relationships in outer space and/or farther time, the strange new chronotopes, *always* signify human relationships in the writer's here and now.

Worthwhile SF texts therefore always leave in an attentive reader the feeling that more is going on under the surface than a story about starships or mutants, and in Smith's case this feeling is overpowering. His story takes the *topos* and metaphor of the bark of the mind by way of its Symbolistic variant, the *navire de l'âme*. This 'ship of the soul' recurs especially in Baudelaire (for example, in the poems 'La Chevelure', 'Le Serpent qui danse', 'La Musique', 'Les sept Vieillards', 'Un Voyage à Cythère', 'Le Voyage') as well as in Rimbaud, the poets of soul navigation away from the bourgeoisie. However ideologically transmogrified, this is the direct ascendancy of Smith's religious SF concoction, the photon-ship of the soul. Thus, my hypothesis about 'The Lady Who Sailed *The Soul*' (how much more parabolic or indeed allegorical can one get?) is that there are different readings for its vehicle and for its tenor, and that the richest reading is the one which takes in both synoptically. The literal vehicle can be mildly enjoyed as a somewhat grotesque love-cum-adventure story as well as a referential puzzle on its own. It is composed of two strands which might be called the '*Spieltier*' strand and the 'Helen America' strand, and I believe that the grotesque in both arises precisely out of a not wholly controlled and comfortable discrepancy between the text's vehicle and tenor. On the literal level, for example, the interstellar ship captained by Helen is propelled by the photon wind from the stars; however, the story's paradigm and tenor is a divine intercession, imitation, and nourishment for the typical narrative agents who stand for super-individual forces. All of this is, then, squarely in the tradition of the New Testament parable and of the Dantean (of course, not only Dantean) metaphor theme of the ship of the mind or soul, reworked in a watered down, post-Symbolist, privatized fashion. I can here draw only some bold outlines of such an interpretation, which follows.

4.3. In the Linebargers' story, the traditional *bark of the mind* is contaminated in a typically Symbolist fashion with the cognate nautical metaphors of the *ark of Noah* transporting representative agents to a better life and the *ship of state* sailing through perilous waters, thus becoming a (star)ship of the collective as well as individual soul. The inner and major strand, the focal narration, is the legendary love story of Helen America (the supreme model of beauty as an American or indeed as America, that is, the USA) and Mr Gray-no-more. It culminates in a voyage in interstellar space. Or, better, Helen's lonely voyage as ship commander is the culmination of a clearly developed chronotope: that of a painful finding of oneself in the maturity and charity of caring about another (again, first about an individual and then a collective Other). This tale has – in a manner inherited from Christian tradition, for example, the parables of sowing from Matthew – a religious tenor. It can, of course, be read simply on the surface level: literally, its crucial incident or crisis recounts how the sails of the photon-ship *The Soul* slip away from the proper position for the cosmic wind to exert pressure on them, endangering thus the ship with its cargo of 30,000 frozen travellers. The lady-captain, Helen America – the exemplary representative of a seeking and mainly frustrated, but ultimately triumphant, USA – fails in all her attempts to adjust the thousands-of-miles long sails – until the vision of her kind lover appears and enables her to right the ship. Significantly, she does so in a very American fashion, by using a gun to destroy the obstacle; thus she continues sailing on to her destination. It is only for a more detailed explication that one would have to know that Smith-Linebarger was both a High Anglican cum Mason, that is, intensely religious in a very specific bourgeois way that identifies the nation-state with the supreme transcendental value, and an important member and ideologist of the US intelligence establishment during the Cold War. that is, intensely political in a very specific right-wing way that equates flexible piety toward the past with imperial renewal.[3] Basic historical knowledge of Protestantism and the US ideologies of Manifest Destiny in our epoch suffice to read this tenor aright. Clearly, Christ is the Bridegroom and Saviour appearing not simply to the individual but also (somewhat blasphemously, I should think) to the personification of the USA as a nation, in order to supplement her insufficient works (technology) by his loving intercession. *The Soul* which after his intervention gets 'back on her course' (p. 46) is literally the name of the photon sailship but also, in a Symbolist polysemy, Helen the representatively beautiful and unhappy (contaminated by feminism) *individual* as well as America (the USA) the *collective* tenor.

The double position of Helen on the ship is, then, indicative: she is both part of and responsible for a very large collective (the pods with frozen people – shades of *Invasion of the Body Snatchers!* – towed behind the sailship) and utterly alone (the only conscious being, unless one counts the robots and the vision of her beloved, both of which anyway exist in the narration as her helpers). This paradoxical simultaneity of final individualist isolation and yet supreme collective incidence indicates well Smith's sometimes awkward Symbolist oscillation and correspondences between national and individual destiny. Such a salvational anxiety is not only an *imitatio Christi* but also one of the basic 'structures of feeling' in US SF (from, for example, Heinlein through the *Invasion* and later movies to Le Guin's opus).

This kind of interpretation seems the only one which can make sense not only of the key vision on the ship in the central strand but also of the story's composition as a whole, that is, of both this and the *'Spieltier'* tale. In that second strand, happening centuries later, the central tale is 'realistically' an old legend mentioned and discussed between a compassionate mother and her inquiring daughter. But there are more important subterranean connections: at the end, the daughter has grown up and become fed up both with this type of legend and with an endearing but now worn out animal-cum-toy (a cyborg, I suppose), the *Spieltier*. In her youth it was flexible, but it eventually wore out, lost its shape-changing power, and is now frozen into the semblance of a senile blond doll. A common ground as well as tenor must exist between the sailing (place-changing) theme from the inner legend and the shape-changing theme from the mother-and-daughter tale if Smith's story is to stand scrutiny. The common ground is, clearly, what passage of time does to vitality. The common tenor is, in my interpretation, the renewal (shape-change without loss of function and identity) of *the values Smith-Linebarger holds as necessary for the salvation of the USA in this historical epoch.* Smith's was the somewhat anomalous position of a critic of the system very near the centre of the Establishment, a critic very concerned but not at all sure about its durability. A better known and illuminating parallel might be Kipling and the British Empire around 1900 (cf., for example, his 'Recessional'). Smith's frequently recurring theme is Kipling's warning to the Empire against the arrogance of those used to power, 'Lest we forget', and for all their differences they share a kind of right-wing populism and sympathy for the underdog (and therefore a use of animals or 'underpeople' as narrative agents).

Thus, the two strands are related on the surface as the contrary alternatives of ageing with success (Helen) *vs.* without success (the *Spieltier*), but they share the same value-horizon as common tenor for the whole story. The childhood playmate which once inspired affection and security but has grown stiff and bereft of elasticity stands for the danger of the wearing out of some vital aspects of the USA, such as those dominant in the 1940s and 1950s. The danger that central politico-religious creeds and beliefs, perhaps even the whole nation, could become morally outworn and lose the power of going on when faced with the different salvational challenge of communism was constantly present to Smith/Linebarger (who after a youthful fling with communism devoted his professional life to combating it by means of psychological warfare). This framing narrative strand is therefore, among other things, a foregrounding of the parabolic procedure in the whole story: it sets an unmistakably symbolical tonality. The *Spieltier* has to be treated piously both for the sake of the past and because the values it once carried are reaffirmed in a better and clearer way by the central strand. The last word does not, therefore, belong to the cynical young generation in the *Spieltier* strand but to the inner legend. Helen is dying after a happy married life, and Mr Gray-no-more tells her for her viaticum:

> If I came then, my darling, I'll come again, wherever you are. You're my darling, my heart, my own true love. You're my bravest of ladies, MY BOLDEST OF PEOPLE [my capitals, DS]. You're my own. You sailed for me. You're my lady who sailed *The Soul*. (p. 66)

The passage I put into capitals is, I think, not bad grammar but the introduction of a conscious interference between 'people' as individuals and as a collective, between Helen and America (both of which designations constitute, after all, her name). But all such oscillations reconduct the interpretation to analogy, which is itself 'a third way between univocity and equivocity' (Hesse, 1966, p. 141).

4.4. I cannot in this brief account enter into a number of other interesting but perhaps not central aspects – for example, Smith's characteristic motif of the modified sensorium correlative to an SF chronotope. Nonetheless, I strongly suspect Cordwainer Smith would have been extremely content to have his method of writing compared to a New Testament parable, in which – as the Aquinate noted – '*traduntur nobis spiritualia sub metaphoris corporalium*' (spiriritual things are given to us under the metaphors of bodily ones – *Summa theologica*, Iq. Ia. 9: '*Utrum sacra scriptura debeat uti metaphoris*'). I only want to add two points. First, that even the characteristic weaknesses of Smith – the ideological contriving, sentimentality and melodrama – flow out or constitute the obverse of his strengths, or more precisely of an improper balance between the individual and the collective, the vehicle and the tenor, the supposedly extrapolative realism and the underlying, centrally important parabolic intention. And second, that in spite of such undoubted weaknesses, Smith was one of the first writers (at least in the USA – Čapek's splendid novel *Krakatit* comes to mind as one of the earlier European examples) who successfully proved that and how SF can be used as itself a vehicle for the most important of present-day tenors: *politics as salvation*.

Now ever since Gene Debs's and Jack London's defeats, this realization has shone stronger on the American Right than on its Left. But this is a historical accident, supremely important for us living here and now but on a wider view fugitive. Whatever our ideologies as readers, therefore – or to say it more clearly: despite Smith's huge ideological limitations and perversions, so evident now that a debased version of them rules the USA – the importance of understanding what such sacramental politics really signify in the flesh of people (particularly of underpeople), what their structure of feeling may be, is enormous; if only to be able to supersede this particular version of it. But in that case supersession would have to be also a dialectical sublation, an incorporation of its positive or 'utopian' aspects. For all significant stories, from Matthew to Linebarger, exist in a tension between utopianism and ideology; and in many ways we can today, retroactively, see the latter as the bad ethical conscience of Reaganism. I shall therefore conclude this essay with the words of the great dialectical utopologist Bloch on fabulation or narrativity in general:

> Yarns of this kind are not only paid out, one also counts what has struck in them or one pricks up one's ears: what went on here. From events there comes here a marking (*das Merke*), which would otherwise not be here; or a marking which is already here takes up little happenings as traces and examples. They signify a less or a more, which is to be thought through by narrating, and again narrated while being thought through; that in the stories things are not right because we are and all is not right.   (1967, p. 15, transl. DS)

And, conversely, that in the stories things sometimes turn out right because we might and all might still be right. Even though this righting would have to happen in a way radically different from – indeed, diametrically opposed to – the way Smith's Heavenly Bridegroom indicates to America.

(Originally published in 1984)

NOTES

1. See for a longer discussion of agents my essay 'Per una teoria dell'analisi agenziale', *Versus*, 30 (1981) 87–109, forthcoming in a much expanded English version in Cary Nelson (ed.), *Marxism and the Interpretation of Culture* (University of Illinois Press), and of space in my 'On Topoanalysis . . .', forthcoming in *Poetics Today* (1987). All references will be keyed to the Bibliography to Conclusion and entered in the body of the essay by last name with page. Without Dr Denis Terrel-Fauconnier's inviting me to a conference at the Université de Nice, where a first version of this paper was presented, it might not have been written in this shape; I have also profited from discussions with my MA student Mr John Detre.

2. A confusion of central importance is unfortunately present, from Richards on, between 'tenor (or topic) *vs.* vehicle' employed in the meaning 'Subject *vs.* Modifier' (used by psycholinguists such as Hoffman and Ortony and also by Ricoeur) as against the meaning 'metaphor focus *vs.* the metaphor's semantic referent' (used by most students of biblical parable, cf. Bultmann, Crossan, Dithmar, Funk, Jeremias, Jones, Linnemann, Via). I am in favour of the latter use, though I acknowledge the whole question still awaits clarification. I shall for present purposes eschew the probably indispensable semiotic formalization of this approach, which would have to speak about semic fields, isotopies, Porphyry's trees, or meaning quadrangles if not hexagons – cf. Eco, 1977 and 1980; Henry, 1971.

3. The Linebargers' story is cited from Cordwainer Smith [pseud. of P. M. A. Linebarger], *The Best of Cordwainer Smith* (New York: Ballantine, 1975). The secondary literature is too scanty. As usual, it is best to begin with the reliable entry by John Clute: 'Smith, Cordwainer', in Peter Nicholls (ed.), *The Encyclopedia of Science Fiction* (London, 1979). Cf. also John Bangsund (ed.), *Exploring Cordwainer Smith* (New York, 1975); John J. Pierce, 'Cordwainer Smith', in the Ballantine edition cited above, pp. viii–xix; Gary K. Wolfe, 'Mythic Structures in Cordwainer Smith's "The Game of Rats and Dragons"', *SFS*, no. 12 (1977) 144–50; Alan C. Elms, 'The Creation of Cordwainer Smith', *SFS*, no. 34 (1984) 264–83 and Anthony R. Lewis, *Concordance to Cordwainer Smith* (Cambridge, MA, 1984). For a different interpretive frame, which I had not seen but which also concludes that this story involves 'the quest for national dreams as well as personal fulfilment – particularly the American dream', see Gary K. Wolfe and Carol T. Williams, 'The Majesty of Kindness', in Thomas D. Clareson and Thomas L. Wymer (eds), *Voices for the Future*, vol. 3 (Bowling Green, OH, 1984) pp. 52–74. For a diachronic context, cf. Sacran Bercovitch, *The American Jeremiad* (Madison, WI, 1978).

Bibliography

Only titles referred to in this book have been included, by short title and in the most accessible edition. References for the chapters of Part Three on individual SF writers, written before the spate of secondary literature which today exists on them and which is under accessible bibliographic control, will be found in their notes.

BIBLIOGRAPHY TO PART ONE

See further works in Angenot (1975) and in his 'A Select Bibliography of the Sociology of Literature', *SFS*, no. 13 (1977), to which I am deeply indebted, as well as in Birnbaum (1960), Langenbucher (1964), Lowenthal (1967), Shaw (1974), and a number of other entries below.

Adorno, Theodor W., *Aesthetische Theorie* (Frankfurt, 1973).
——, *Einleitung in die Musiksoziologie* (Frankfurt, 1981).
——, *Soziologische Schriften. Gesammelte Schriften VIII–IX* (Frankfurt, 1962–5).
Angenot, Marc, *Le Roman populaire* (Montreal, 1975).
——, and Darko Suvin, 'Thèses sur la "sociologie" de la littérature', *Littérature*, no. 44 (1981) 117–27.
Auerbach, Erich, *Das französische Publikum des 17. Jahrhunderts* (Munich, 1933).
——, *Mimesis* (Garden City, NY, 1957).
Bakhtin, M. M., *The Dialogic Imagination*, ed. Michael Holquist (Austin, TX, 1981).
——, *Rabelais and His World* (Cambridge, MA, 1968).
Barthes, Roland, *Mythologies* (Paris, 1970).
Benjamin, Walter, *Gesammelte Schriften*, 5 vols (Frankfurt, 1980–2).
——, *Charles Baudelaire* (London, 1973).
——, *Illuminations* (New York, 1969).
Birchall, Ian, 'The Total Marx and the Marxist Theory of Literature', in Paul Walton and Stuart Hall (eds), *Situating Marx* (London, 1972).
Birnbaum, Norman, *The Sociological Study of Ideology* (Oxford, 1960).
Bloch, Ernst, *Das Prinzip Hoffnung*, 2 vols (Frankfurt, 1959).
Brecht, Bertolt, *Gesammelte Werke*, vols xv–xx (Frankfurt, 1973). See partial translation in English in Bibliography to Part Two.
Bürger, Christa, *Textanalyse als Ideologiekritik* (Frankfurt, 1973).
Burke, Kenneth, *The Philosophy of Literary Form* (Berkeley, CA, 1973).
Cawelti, John G., *Adventure, Mystery and Romance* (Chicago, IL, 1976).
Ciccotti, G. et al., *L'Araignée et le tisserand* (Paris, 1979).
Cros, Edmond, *Théorie et pratique sociocritiques* (Paris, 1983).
Dröge, Franz, *Wissen ohne Bewusstsein* (Frankfurt, 1972).
Eagleton, Terry, *Literary Theory* (Minneapolis, MN, 1983).
Eco, Umberto, *Apocalittici e integrati* (Milan, 1964).
——, *Il superuomo di massa* (Milan, 1978).

Enzensberger, Hans Magnus, *The Consciousness Industry* (New York, 1974).
Escarpit, Robert, *Sociology of Literature* (London, 1971).
—— (ed.), *Le Littéraire et le social* (Paris, 1970).
Flaker, Aleksandar, and Viktor Žmegač (eds), *Formalismus, Strukturalismus und Geschichte* (Kronberg, 1974).
Frye, Northrop, *The Secular Scripture* (Cambridge, MA, 1978).
Goldmann, Lucien, *Cultural Creation* (Oxford, 1977).
——, *The Hidden God* (London, 1964).
——, *Structures mentales et création culturelle* (Paris, 1974).
——, *Towards a Sociology of the Novel* (London, 1975).
Gramsci, Antonio, *Letteratura e vita nazionale* (Turin, 1966). For partial English translations see Bibliography to Part Two.
Hall, Stuart, 'Notes on Deconstructing "the Popular"', in Raphael Samuel (ed.), *People's History and Socialist Theory* (London, 1981) pp. 227–40.
——, 'Some Paradigms in Cultural Studies', *Annali dell'Istituto orientale*, 21, no. 3 (1978).
Hart, James D., *The Popular Book* (Berkeley, CA, 1963).
Hauser, Arnold, *The Social History of Art*, 4 vols (New York, 1962).
Hirsch, E. D., *Validity in Interpretation* (New Haven, CT, 1971).
Hoggart, Richard, *The Uses of Literacy* (London, 1957).
Holz, H. H., *Vom Kunstwerk zur Ware* (Neuwied, 1972).
Jakobson, Roman, 'Closing Statement: Linguistics and Poetics', in Thomas A. Sebeok (ed.), *Style in Language* (Cambridge, MA, 1960).
James, Louis, *Fiction for the Working Man, 1830–1950* (London, 1963).
Jameson, Fredric, *Marxism and Form* (Princeton, NJ, 1971).
Langenbucher, Wolfgang R., *Der aktuelle Unterhaltungsroman* (Bonn, 1964).
Laurenson, Diana, and Alan Swingewood, *The Sociology of Literature* (London, 1972).
Lem, Stanisław, *Phantastik und Futurologie*, 2 vols (Frankfurt, 1984).
Lenin, V. I., *Tolstoy and his Time* (New York, 1952).
Lifshitz, Mikhail, *The Philosophy of Art of Karl Marx* (New York, 1977).
Lowenthal, Leo, 'Literature and Sociology', in J. Thorpe (ed.), *The Relations of Literary Study* (New York, 1967).
——, *Literature, Popular Culture and Society* (Palo Alto, CA, 1961).
Lukács, Georg, *Entwicklungsgeschichte des modernen Dramas: Werke XV* (Neuwied, 1981).
——, *Essays über Realismus: Werke IV* (Neuwied, 1971); partly as *The Meaning of Contemporary Realism* (London, 1963) and partly as *Realism in Our Time* (New York, 1971).
——, *The Historical Novel* (Harmondsworth, Mddx, 1969).
——, *History and Class Consciousness* (Cambridge, MA, 1971).
——, *Schriften zur Literatursoziologie*, ed. Peter Ludz (Neuwied, 1968).
Macherey, Pierre, *A Theory of Literary Production* (London, 1978).
Marcuse, Herbert, *Counter-Revolution and Revolt* (Boston, MA, 1972).
——, *One-dimensional Man* (Boston, MA, 1966).
Marx, Karl, *Grundrisse* (London, 1973).
——, and Friedrich Engels, *Werke* (Berlin, DDR, 1956–68).
——, *Selected Works in One Volume* (New York, 1968).

——, *The German Ideology* (Moscow, 1976).

——, *The Holy Family* (London, 1957).

——, *The Marx–Engels Reader*, ed. Robert Tucker (New York, 1972).

Medvedev, Pavel (pseud. of M. M. Bakhtin), *The Formal Method in Literary Scholarship* (Baltimore, MD, 1978).

Meszaros, Istvan, *Marx's Theory of Alienation* (London, 1970).

Mukařovský, Jan, *Aesthetic Function, Norm and Value as Social Facts* (Ann Arbor, MI, 1970).

Nagl, Manfred, *Science Fiction* (Tübingen, 1981).

Neuburg, Victor E., *Popular Literature* (Harmondsworth, Mddx, 1977).

Nutz, Walter, *Der Trivialroman, seine Formen und seine Hersteller* (Cologne, 1962).

Nye, Russell B., *The Unembarrassed Muse* (New York, 1970).

Orwell, George, *A Collection of Essays* (Garden City, NY, 1957).

Poe, Edgar Allan, *The Works of Edgar Allan Poe in Eight Volumes* (Philadelphia, PA, 1906).

Rosenberg, Bernard, and David Manning White (eds), *Mass Culture* (New York, 1963).

——, *Mass Culture Revisited* (New York, 1971).

Rossi-Landi, Ferruccio, *Language as Work and Exchange* (The Hague, 1975).

Sánchez Vázquez, Adolfo, *Art and Society* (New York, 1973).

Sartre, Jean-Paul, *What Is Literature?* (New York, 1949).

Schenda, Rudolf, *Volk ohne Buch* (Frankfurt, 1970).

Schulte-Sasse, Jochen, *Die Kritik an der Trivialliteratur seit der Aufklärung* (Munich, 1971).

——, *Literarische Wertung* (Stuttgart, 1971).

Seesslen, Georg, and Bernt Kling, *Romantik und Gewalt*, 2 vols (Munich, 1973).

Shaw, Martin, *Marxism Versus Sociology* (London, 1974).

Sohn-Rethel, Alfred, *Warenform und Denkform* (Frankfurt, 1971).

Suvin, Darko, 'Le Discours de la fiction comme nouveauté et marchandise', *Sociologie et sociétés*, 17, no. 2 (1985) 85–91.

——, 'Some Introductory Reflections on Sociological Approaches to Literature and Paraliterature', *Culture & Context*, no. 1 (1980) 33–55.

——, 'Two Holy Commodities' *Sociocriticism*, no. 2 (1985) 31–47.

Tocqueville, Alexis de, *Democracy in America*, 2 vols (New York & London, 1900).

Trotsky, Leon, *Literature and Revolution* (Ann Arbor, MI, 1971).

Vološinov, V. N. (pseud. of M. M. Bakhtin), *Marxism and the Philosophy of Language* (New York, 1973).

Watt, Ian, *The Rise of the Novel* (Berkeley, CA, 1974).

Widmann, Hans, *Geschichte des Buchhandels vom Altertum bis zur Gegenwart*, enlarged edn by Ernst Kuhnert (Wiesbaden, 1952).

Williams, Raymond, *Communications* (Harmondsworth, Mddx, 1970).

——, *Culture* (London, 1981).

——, *Culture and Society, 1780–1950* (New York, 1966).

——, *Keywords* (London, 1983).

——, *The Long Revolution* (Harmondsworth, Mddx, 1971).

——, *Marxism and Literature* (Oxford, 1977).

Winkler, Lutz, *Kulturwarenproduktion* (Frankfurt, 1973).
Ziermann, Klaus, *Romane vom Fliessband* (Berlin, DDR, 1969).
Žmegač Viktor, *Književno stvaralaštvo i povijest društva* (Zagreb, 1976).

BIBLIOGRAPHY TO PART TWO

NB: for Angenot (1975), Barthes (1970), Benjamin (1973), Bloch (1959), Eco (1964 and 1978), Jameson (1971), Marcuse (1966 and 1972), Marx–Engels (1957), Sohn-Rethel (1971), Suvin ('Commodities', 1985, and 'Discours', 1985), Vološinov (1973), and Williams (1977), see Bibliography to Part One.

Altick, Richard, *Victorian People and Ideas* (New York, 1973).
Amis, Kingsley, *New Maps of Hell* (New York, 1975).
Angenot, Marc, 'The Absent Paradigm', *SFS*, 6 (1979) 9–19.
——, *Glossaire pratique de la critique contemporaine* (Montreal, 1979).
——, 'Intertextualité, interdiscursivité, discours social', *Texte*, no. 2 (1983) 101–12.
——, 'Présupposé – topos – idéologème', *Etudes françaises*, no. 1–2 (1977) 12–34 (now in his *La Parole pamphlétaire* (Paris, 1982) pp. 169–89).
——, 'La science fiction: genre et statut institutionnel', *Revue de l'Institut de sociologie* (Bruxelles), no. 3–4 (1980) 651–60.
——, 'Science Fiction in France before Verne', *SFS*, 5 (1978) 58–66.
——, and Darko Suvin, 'L'implicite du manifeste', *Etudes françaises*, no. 3–4 (1980) 43–67.
Aristotle, *Poetics*, ed. Leon Golden and O. B. Hardison, Jr (Englewood Cliffs, NJ, 1968).
Barthes, Roland, *Sade, Fourier, Loyola* (New York, 1976).
——, *S/Z* (Paris, 1976).
Bellert, Irena, *On the Logico-Semantic Structure of Utterances* (Wrocław, 1972).
Bloch, Ernst, 'Entfremdung, Verfremdung: Alienation, Estrangement', in Erika Munk (ed.), *Brecht* (New York, 1972).
——, *Karl Marx* (New York, 1971).
——, *Man on his Own* (New York, 1970).
——, *A Philosophy of the Future* (New York, 1970).
Brecht, Bertolt, *Collected Plays* (New York, 1971–).
——, *The Messingkauf Dialogues* (London, 1965).
——, *Brecht on Theatre*, ed. John Willett (New York, 1966).
Communications, no. 16 (1970).
Culler, Jonathan, 'Presupposition and Intertextuality', in his *The Pursuit of Signs* (London, 1981) 100–18.
Dijk, Teun A. van (ed.), *Pragmatics of Language and Literature* (Amsterdam, 1976).
Ducrot, Oswald, *Dire et ne pas dire* (Paris, 1972).
Eco, Umberto, *Opera aperta* (Milan, 1967).
Eliot, T. S., *Selected Essays* (London, 1951).
Elkins, Charles, 'Science Fiction Versus Futurology', *SFS*, 6 (1979) 20–31.

Engels, Friedrich, 'Socialism: Utopian and Scientific', in *Marx and Engels: Basic Writings*, ed. L. Feuer (Garden City, NY, 1965).

Faye, Jean Pierre, *Théorie du récit* (Paris, 1972).

Frye, Northrop, *Anatomy of Criticism* (New York, 1966).

Gramsci, Antonio, *The Modern Prince and Other Writings* (London, 1957).

——, *Prison Notebooks* (London, 1970).

Groupe Mu, *Rhétorique générale* (Paris, 1970).

Jameson, Fredric, *Fables of Aggression* (Berkeley, CA, 1979).

——, 'Generic Discontinuities in SF', in R. D. Mullen and Darko Suvin (eds), (see below), pp. 28–39.

——, *The Political Unconscious* (Ithaca, NY, 1981).

Jenny, Laurent (ed.), *Poétique*, no. 27 (1976).

Kristeva, Julia, *Sémèiotikè* (Paris, 1966).

Lawrence, D. H., 'Study of Thomas Hardy', in his *Phoenix*, ed. Edward D. McDonald (New York, 1936) pp. 398–516.

Lotman, Jurij M., *Aufsätze zur Theorie und Methodologie der Literatur und Kultur* (Kronberg, 1974).

——,*The Structure of the Artistic Text* (Ann Arbor, MI, 1977).

Lukács, Georg, *The Theory of the Novel* (London, 1971).

Mullen, R. D., and Darko Suvin (eds), *Science-Fiction Studies . . . 1973–1975* (Boston, MA, 1976).

Nudelman, Rafail, 'An Approach to the Structure of Le Guin's SF', in Mullen and Suvin (eds), (see above) pp. 240–50.

——, 'On SF and Futurology', *SFS*, 6 (1979) 241–2.

Parrinder, Patrick, *Science Fiction: Its Criticism and Teaching* (London, 1980).

Petöfi, J. S., and D. Franck (eds), *Präsuppositionen in Philosophie und Linguistik* (Frankfurt, 1973).

Poulantzas, Nikos, *Political Power and Social Classes* (London, 1973).

Prieto, Luis J., *Pertinence et pratique* (Paris, 1975).

Propp, V., *Fol'klor i deistvitel'nost'* (Moscow, 1976).

——, *Russkii geroicheskii epos* (Moscow, 1958).

Russ, Joanna, 'SF and Technology as Mystification', *SFS*, no. 16 (1978) 250–60.

Sartre, Jean-Paul, *Search for a Method* (New York, 1968).

Segre, Cesare, *Le strutture e il tempo* (Turin, 1974).

Shklovskii, Viktor, *O teorii prozy* (Moscow, 1929).

Solomon, Maynard (ed.), *Marxism and Art* (New York, 1974).

Somay, Bülent, 'Towards an Open-Ended Utopia', *SFS*, no. 32 (1984) 25–38.

Stalnaker, R. C., 'Pragmatic Presuppositions', in M. K. Munitz and P. Unger (eds), *Semantics and Philosophy* (New York, 1974).

Suvin, Darko, *Metamorphoses of Science Fiction* (New Haven, CT, & London, 1979); abbreviated as *MOSF*.

——, 'On What Is and What Is Not an SF Narration', *SFS*, 5 (1978) 45–52 (now in *VSF*, pp. 86–95).

——, *To Brecht and Beyond* (Brighton, Sussex, 1984).

——, *Victorian Science Fiction in the UK* (Boston, MA, 1983); abbreviated as *VSF*.

Wellek, René, and Austin Warren, *Theory of Literature* (New York, 1970).

[Wells, H. G.], *H. G. Wells's Literary Criticism*, ed. Patrick Parrinder and Robert M. Philmus (Brighton, Sussex, 1980).
Williams, Raymond, *Problems in Materialism and Culture* (London, 1980).
Wilson, D. M., *Presupposition and Non-Truth-Conditional Semantics* (New York, 1975).

NB: for references for Part Three see note at the beginning of the Bibliography.

BIBLIOGRAPHY TO CONCLUSION

NB: for Bakhtin (1981) see Bibliography to Part One; for Angenot's 'Absent Paradigm' (1979), Aristotle (1968), Frye (1966), Shklovskii (1929), and my *MOSF* and *VSF*, see Bibliography to Part Two.

Beardsley, Monroe, *Aesthetics* (New York, 1958).
Bellert, Irena, 'Sherlock Holmes' Interpretation of Metaphorical Texts', *Poetics Today*, 2 (Winter 1980/81) 25–44.
Black, Max, *Models and Metaphors* (Ithaca, NY, 1962).
——, 'More about Metaphor', *Dialectica*, 31 (1977) 431–57.
Bloch, Ernst, *Experimentum Mundi* (Frankfurt, 1976).
——, *Spuren* (Frankfurt, 1967).
Blumenberg, Hans, 'Paradigmen zu einer Metaphorologie', *Archiv für Begriffsgeschichte*, 6 (1960) 7–142.
Bultmann, Rudolf, *The History of the Synoptic Tradition* (New York, 1968).
Butor, Michel, *Introduction aux fragments de Finnegans Wake* (Paris, 1972).
Crossan, John Dominic, *In Parables* (New York, 1973).
Culler, Jonathan, 'The Turns of Metaphor', in his *The Pursuit of Signs* (London, 1981) pp. 188–209.
Curtius, Ernst Robert, *European Literature and Latin Middle Ages* (New York, 1963).
de Man, Paul, 'The Epistemology of Metaphor', in Sheldon Sacks (ed.), *On Metaphor* (Chicago, IL, 1980) pp. 11–28.
Dithmar, Reinhard (ed.), *Fabeln, Parabeln und Gleichnisse* (Munich, 1972).
Dodd, C. H., *The Parables of the Kingdom* (Brooklyn, NY, 1971).
Eco, Umberto, *Lector in Fabula* (Milan, 1979).
——, 'Metafora', in *Enciclopedia Einaudi*, vol. IX (Turin, 1980) pp. 191–236.
——, 'On Symbol', *Semiotic Inquiry*, 2 (1982) 15–44.
——, *A Theory of Semiotics* (London, 1977).
Funk, Robert W., *Language, Hermeneutic, and Word of God* (New York, 1966).
Gentner, Dedre, 'Are Scientific Analogies Metaphors?', in David S. Miall (ed.), *Metaphor: Problems and Perspectives* (Brighton, Sussex, 1982) pp. 106–32.
Gerhardsson, Birger, 'The Parable of the Sower and Its Interpretation', *New Testament Studies*, 14 (1967–8) 165–93.
Henry, Albert, *Métonymie et métaphore* (Paris, 1971).

Hesse, Mary B., *Models and Analogies in Science* (Notre Dame, IN, 1966).

Hoffman, Robert R., 'Metaphor in Science', in Richard P. Honeck and Robert R. Hoffman (eds), *Cognition and Figurative Language* (Hillsdale, NJ, 1980) 393–423.

Jeremias, Joachim, *The Parables of Jesus* (New York, 1963).

Jones, Geraint, *The Art and Truth of the Parables* (London, 1964).

Köller, Wilhelm, *Semiotik und Metapher* (Stuttgart, 1975).

Kuhn, Thomas S., *The Structure of Scientific Revolutions* (Chicago, IL, 1970).

Lewis, C. S., 'Bluspels and Flalansferes', in his *Rehabilitations* (Folcroft, PA, 1970).

Linnemann, Eta, *Parables of Jesus* (London, 1966).

Marin, Louis, 'Essai d'analyse structurale d'un récit-parabole: Matthieu 13/1–23', *Etudes théologiques et religieuses*, 46 (1971) 35–74.

Marx, Karl, and Friedrich Engels, *Ueber Kunst und Literatur*, ed. Michail Lifschitz (Berlin, DDR, 1953).

Masterman, Margaret, 'The Nature of a Paradigm', in Imre Lakatos and Alan Musgrave (eds), *Criticism and the Growth of Knowledge* (Cambridge, 1979) pp. 58–89.

Ortony, Andrew, 'Why Metaphors Are Necessary and Not Just Nice', *Educational Theory*, 25 (1975) 45–53.

Reverdy, Pierre, *Le Gant de crin* (Paris, 1926).

Richards, I. A., *Philosophy of Rhetoric* (New York, 1936).

Ricoeur, Paul, 'Biblical Hermeneutics', *Semeia*, no. 4 (1975) 27–148.

——, 'The Metaphorical Process as Cognition, Imagination, and Feeling', in Sacks (ed.) (see under de Man), pp. 141–57.

——, *The Rule of Metaphor* (Toronto, 1978).

Shelley, Percy Bysshe, *A Defence of Poetry*, in Charles Kaplan (ed.), *Criticism: The Major Statements* (New York, 1975).

Shibles, Warren A., *Metaphor: An Annotated Bibliography and History* (Whitewater, WI, 1971).

Shklovskii, Viktor, *Khod' konia* (Moskva-Berlin, 1923).

Sparshott, Francis E., 'Truth in Fiction', *The Journal of Aesthetics and Art Criticism*, 26 (1967) 3–7.

Suvin, Darko, 'The Performance Text as Audience-Stage Dialog Inducing a Possible World', *Versus*, no. 42 (1985) 3–20.

Via, Dan Otto, Jr, *The Parables* (Philadelphia, PA, 1967).

Vico, Giambattista, *La scienza nuova*. . . . (Bari, 1974).

Volli, Ugo, 'Gli universi paralleli della semiotica e della fantascienza', in Luigi Russo (ed.), *La fantascienza e la critica* (Milan, 1980) pp. 113–24.

W[halley], G[eorge], 'Metaphor', in *Princeton Encyclopedia of Poetry and Poetics*, ed. Alex Preminger *et al.* (Princeton, NJ, 1972) pp. 490–4.

Index